ELIZABETH
WOODVILLE

Four things come not back:

The spoken word;
The sped arrow;
Times past;
The neglected opportunity

Old Saying

ELIZABETH WOODVILLE

MOTHER *of the* PRINCES IN THE TOWER

DAVID BALDWIN

SUTTON PUBLISHING

This book was first published in 2002 by
Sutton Publishing Limited · Phoenix Mill
Thrupp · Stroud · Gloucestershire · GL5 2BU

This paperback edition first published in 2004

British Library Cataloguing in Publication Data.
A catalogue record for this book is available from the British
Library.

ISBN 0 7509 3886 2

Typeset in 10.5/12pt Galliard.
Typesetting and origination by
Sutton Publishing Limited.
Printed and bound in Great Britain by
J.H. Haynes & Co. Ltd, Sparkford.

Contents

Picture Acknowledgements

The author and publisher would like to thank the following for supplying photographs and allowing them to be reproduced here: Geoffrey Wheeler (Plates 1, 2, 3, 4, 5, 6, 7, 9, 10, 11, 12, 13, 14, 15, 16, 17, 18, 19, 22, 25, 26), John Gallimore (20, 21), Joseph Sargeant (23, 24), and the Dean and Chapter of Liverpool Cathedral (8). We are grateful to the Worshipful Company of Skinners for permission to reproduce their portrait of Elizabeth (no. 7) and the Society of Antiquaries of London for allowing us reproduce their portrait of Richard III (no. 16).

Genealogical Tables

1: YORK AND LANCASTER

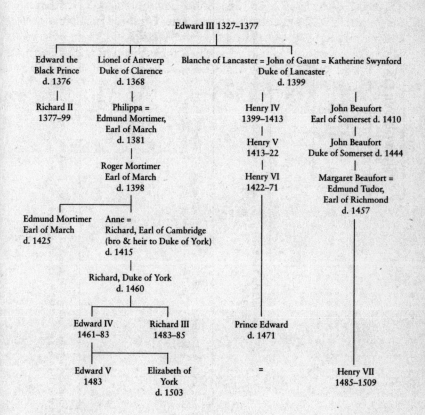

Edward III 1327–1377

Edward the Black Prince d. 1376

Richard II 1377–99

Lionel of Antwerp Duke of Clarence d. 1368

Philippa = Edmund Mortimer, Earl of March d. 1381

Roger Mortimer Earl of March d. 1398

Edmund Mortimer Earl of March d. 1425

Anne = Richard, Earl of Cambridge (bro & heir to Duke of York) d. 1415

Richard, Duke of York d. 1460

Edward IV 1461–83

Richard III 1483–85

Edward V 1483

Elizabeth of York d. 1503

Blanche of Lancaster = John of Gaunt = Katherine Swynford Duke of Lancaster d. 1399

Henry IV 1399–1413

Henry V 1413–22

Henry VI 1422–71

John Beaufort Earl of Somerset d. 1410

John Beaufort Duke of Somerset d. 1444

Margaret Beaufort = Edmund Tudor, Earl of Richmond d. 1457

Prince Edward d. 1471

=

Henry VII 1485–1509

2: THE WOODVILLES

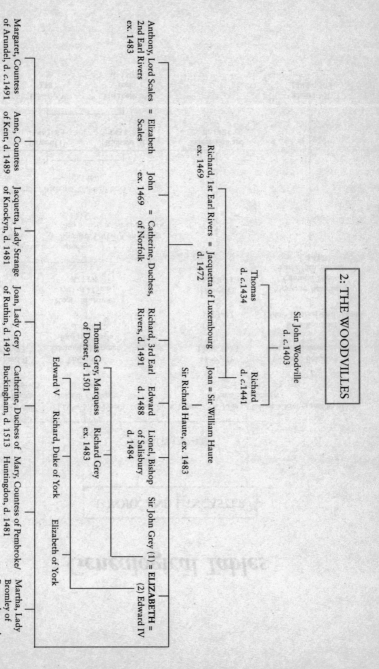

Sir John Woodville d. c.1403

— Thomas d. c.1434

— Richard d. c.1441

Richard, 1st Earl Rivers = Jacquetta of Luxembourg
ex. 1469   d. 1472

Joan = Sir William Haute

Sir Richard Haute, ex. 1483

Anthony, Lord Scales = Elizabeth
2nd Earl Rivers   Scales
ex. 1483

John = Catherine, Duchess,
ex. 1469   of Norfolk

Richard, 3rd Earl   Edward   Lionel, Bishop   Sir John Grey (1) = ELIZABETH =
Rivers, d. 1491   d. 1488   of Salisbury   ex. 1483   (2) Edward IV
                     of Dorset, d. 1501   d. 1484

Thomas Grey, Marquess
of Dorset, d. 1501

Edward V   Richard, Duke of York   Elizabeth of York

Richard Grey
ex. 1483

Catherine, Duchess of   Mary, Countess of Pembroke/   Martha, Lady
Buckingham, d. 1513   Huntingdon, d. 1481   Bromley of
                                                      Bartomley and
                                                      Hextall

Margaret, Countess   Anne, Countess   Jacquetta, Lady Strange   Joan, Lady Grey
of Arundel, d. c.1491 of Kent, d. 1489 of Knockyn, d. 1481   of Ruthin, d. 1491

3: THE CHILDREN OF ELIZABETH WOODVILLE

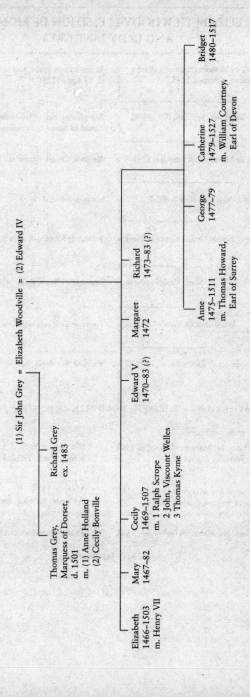

(1) Sir John Grey = Elizabeth Woodville = (2) Edward IV

(1) Sir John Grey:

Thomas Grey,
Marquess of Dorset,
d. 1501
m. (1) Anne Holland
(2) Cecily Bonville

Richard Grey
ex. 1483

(2) Edward IV:

Elizabeth
1466–1503
m. Henry VII

Mary
1467–82

Cecily
1469–1507
m. 1 Ralph Scrope
2 John, Viscount Welles
3 Thomas Kyme

Edward V
1470–83 (?)

Margaret
1472

Richard
1473–83 (?)

George
1477–79

Catherine
1479–1527
m. William Courtney,
Earl of Devon

Bridget
1480–1517

Anne
1475–1511
m. Thomas Howard,
Earl of Surrey

4: ELIZABETH WOODVILLE, SIMON DE MONTFORT AND LADY JANE GREY

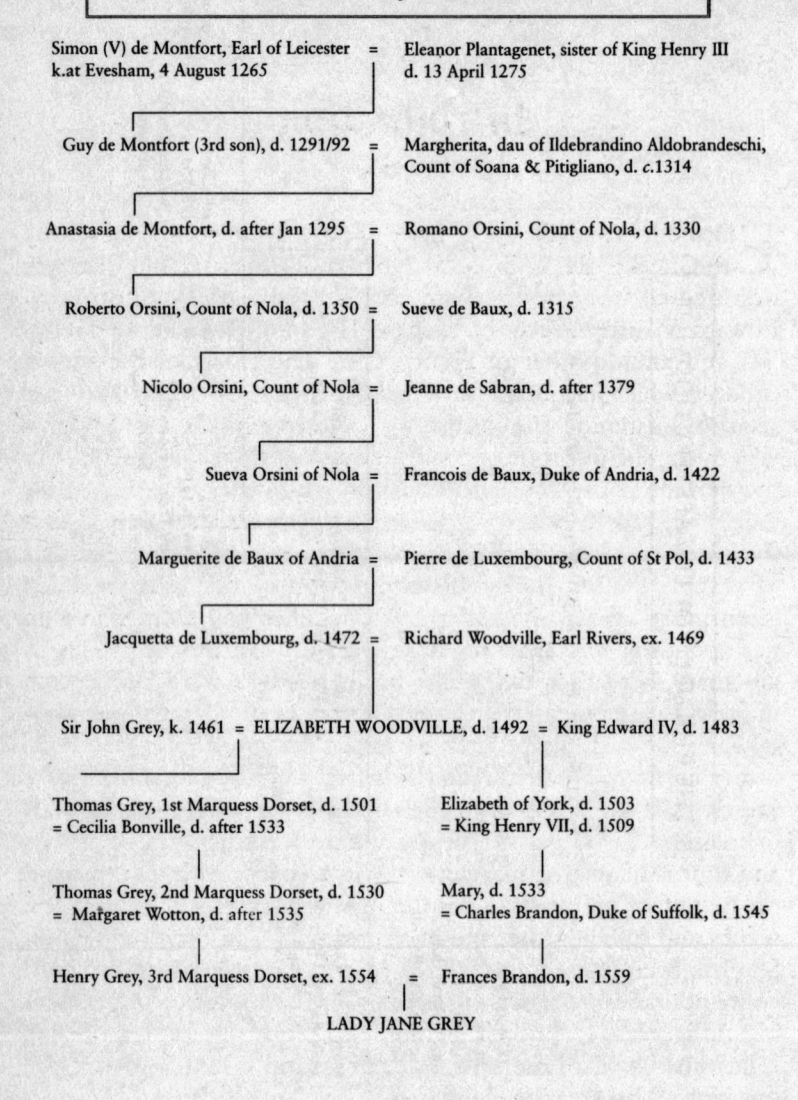

Simon (V) de Montfort, Earl of Leicester = Eleanor Plantagenet, sister of King Henry III
k.at Evesham, 4 August 1265   d. 13 April 1275

Guy de Montfort (3rd son), d. 1291/92 = Margherita, dau of Ildebrandino Aldobrandeschi,
                                        Count of Soana & Pitigliano, d. c.1314

Anastasia de Montfort, d. after Jan 1295 = Romano Orsini, Count of Nola, d. 1330

Roberto Orsini, Count of Nola, d. 1350 = Sueve de Baux, d. 1315

Nicolo Orsini, Count of Nola = Jeanne de Sabran, d. after 1379

Sueva Orsini of Nola = Francois de Baux, Duke of Andria, d. 1422

Marguerite de Baux of Andria = Pierre de Luxembourg, Count of St Pol, d. 1433

Jacquetta de Luxembourg, d. 1472 = Richard Woodville, Earl Rivers, ex. 1469

Sir John Grey, k. 1461 = ELIZABETH WOODVILLE, d. 1492 = King Edward IV, d. 1483

Thomas Grey, 1st Marquess Dorset, d. 1501   Elizabeth of York, d. 1503
= Cecilia Bonville, d. after 1533   = King Henry VII, d. 1509

Thomas Grey, 2nd Marquess Dorset, d. 1530   Mary, d. 1533
= Margaret Wotton, d. after 1535   = Charles Brandon, Duke of Suffolk, d. 1545

Henry Grey, 3rd Marquess Dorset, ex. 1554 = Frances Brandon, d. 1559

LADY JANE GREY

Introduction

Elizabeth Woodville spent her earliest years in relative obscurity at Grafton Regis in rural Northamptonshire, but she was destined to become the wife of King Edward IV, mother of Edward V, sister-in-law of Richard III, mother-in-law of Henry VII and grandmother of Henry VIII. The eldest of the twelve children which Jacquetta, dowager Duchess of Bedford bore her second husband, the middling county knight Sir Richard Woodville, she was to experience more vicissitudes of fortune than the heroine of any novel or television soap opera. Her legendary meeting with Edward IV beneath the oak tree at Grafton and their secret marriage baffled contemporaries and led to allegations of witchcraft; her husband's promotion of her relatives bred resentment among the older noble families and contributed to her spending two fearful phases of the Wars of the Roses in sanctuary; her father, two of her brothers, and a son from her first marriage were executed and the 'Princes in the Tower', her sons by King Edward, disappeared mysteriously; and the last five years of her life were spent in religious seclusion after a plot to depose Henry VII misfired. But her reign as queen was not all tribulations. There were royal progresses, great state occasions and tournaments, the satisfaction of interceding with her husband on behalf of plaintiffs, of influencing his policies behind the scenes and fulfilling the role of a 'great lady' on her own estates. She has been praised and vilified (more often the latter) by both contemporaries and later writers, but few have tried to understand her difficulties, to probe her mind (to plumb her unfathomable relationship with Richard III, for example), or answer the question 'What was she really like?'.

Some prospective biographers may have been dissuaded from studying Elizabeth by a vague, and possibly erroneous, notion that it would be difficult to bring their work to a satisfactory conclusion. It is sometimes said that it is all but impossible to write 'the life of' a medieval man or woman because the detailed, personal information needed to understand their motives and actions is not available. Only seldom are there memoirs by contemporaries who knew their subject, and almost never a substantial body of correspondence between friends or family. The dry mass of chronicles and administrative records may tell us what a person did or received or suffered but not what he or she thought or hoped for; and there has been a tendency to produce books which describe themselves as the 'Life and Times' of the subject (with much space and emphasis given to the 'Times') or alternatively, to resort to an unacceptable amount of speculation in order to create a real, thinking individual. Informed guesswork is probably essential, but when overused can result in caricature bearing only passing resemblance to the person concerned.

These difficulties apply to Elizabeth as much as they apply to her contemporaries, but the lack of some evidence and of absolute certainty does not render a conventional biography impossible. Much material has survived, and if it does not always tell us all that we would like to know it still provides the basis for a reasoned assessment. I have tried to tell the story of her life as accurately as possible, resorting to conjecture only when her involvement is distinctly likely: few kings, or chroniclers writing on their behalf, would openly declare they acted upon their wife's suggestion or recommendation, although there must have been many occasions on which queens obtained favours or directly influenced policy.

My intention has been to provide enough background information to make Elizabeth's career intelligible to readers who have little or no previous knowledge of the late fifteenth century, but not to make her an excuse for another general book on the Wars of the Roses. Accordingly, the events of the reign of Edward IV, her second husband, are discussed only insofar as she influenced or was affected by them. I have tried to let contemporary documents tell their own story, wherever possible, rather than interpret them to conform to a preconceived view of her character, and have found little to substantiate the conventional portrait of the haughty queen and her grasping family. Certainly her relatives were ambitious, but Warwick, Hastings, Clarence and Gloucester – the men with whom they clashed so bitterly – never themselves refused a grant or declined an opportunity, and the modern view of them is essentially that created by Warwick's propaganda in 1469 and Gloucester's of 1483.

Elizabeth is a fascinating but neglected character – there have been three biographies of her Lancastrian rival, Margaret of Anjou, in English since the Second World War – and much new material has come to light since the publication of David MacGibbon's 'Life' in 1938. Historians will continue to argue about some of the episodes of Elizabeth's career – for example, her part in the Simnel conspiracy – but she was, I believe, one of the most politically aware, and, at the same time, judicious, Queen Consorts, who fulfilled her difficult role as competently as anyone before or since. My over-riding concern has been 'would Elizabeth Woodville recognise herself in these pages'? I hope – and I think – that she would.

On a practical note I have tried to distinguish carefully between the several John Pastons, the various Margarets, and Elizabeth's two sons named Richard (to give but three examples) and to refer to noblemen principally by their titles rather than by their lesser-known personal names. The footnotes are designed primarily to acknowledge quotations and sources of evidence and to enlarge upon and justify interpretations; I have not, generally speaking, given references for facts which are accepted and uncontroversial and have only provided such information where, as it seemed to me, a question might arise from the main text.

I am grateful to those who have given permission for the use of copyright material, to Peter and Carolyn Hammond of the Richard III Society for much advice and the loan of books from the Barton Library, to Susan Blake, John Gallimore, Charles Reece and Joseph and Mary Sargeant at Grafton Regis, and to Geoffrey Wheeler for supplying many of the illustrations and other items from his collections. Special thanks are due to Geoffrey Wheeler and Joanna Laynesmith for reading my typescript and suggesting improvements; and to my wife Joyce for patiently living with Elizabeth Woodville while this book was in preparation and for all her help and encouragement over the years.

David Baldwin
February 2002

1

Elizabeth's Early Life

Elizabeth Woodville, the eldest child of Sir Richard Woodville and Jacquetta, daughter of Pierre de Luxembourg, Count of St Pol (Artois), was probably born at Grafton in Northamptonshire in 1437.[1] Sir Richard's family home was at the Mote, near Maidstone (Kent), but he may have lived at Grafton manor from shortly after the death of his father's elder brother, Thomas, in 1435, and perhaps brought his new bride there towards the end of 1436.[2] Richard had earlier joined his father, another Richard, in the service of John, Duke of Bedford as he struggled first to extend, and then to retain, his brother Henry V's French conquests, and probably met the teenage Jacquetta in 1433 when Bedford wed her to secure his alliance with Burgundy. She soon came to admire the handsome young knight whose prowess and gaiety contrasted strikingly with the cares which burdened her middle-aged husband; and their relationship developed rapidly after Bedford died on 15 September 1435. They wished to marry, but were obliged to recognise that a widow who had been England's second lady and who could trace her ancestry back to Simon de Montfort[3] and the Emperor Charlemagne, was all but inaccessible to so humble a suitor. She was part of an aristocratic society which set great store by social precedence, and a liaison with a subordinate, even a member of a dependable knightly family well-known to her, was unthinkable. The Woodvilles had been settled at Grafton since the thirteenth century[4] and had served regularly as Commissioners of the Peace, Sheriffs, and Members of Parliament for Northamptonshire; but neither this nor the good service rendered by the elder Richard (he had been an Esquire of the Body to Henry V and had risen to become Bedford's chamberlain) could justify a union with a member of the royal family. Jacquetta, now twenty, was granted her dower on 6 February 1436 on the understanding that she did not remarry without royal permission; but within a year she was obliged to ask King Henry to pardon her for marrying Richard in contravention of this undertaking (for which, she said, they had already suffered 'right grate streitnesse'[5]) and to beg him to set the fine her action warranted at a reasonable level. The result was that she was ordered to pay the Crown £1,000 on 23 March 1437, the money being found by the wealthy Cardinal Beaufort, the King's half great-uncle, in exchange for some of her west country manors.[6]

The Woodvilles' disgrace was short-lived, however. They were pardoned on 24 October that year (perhaps at about the time their eldest daughter was born, or shortly afterwards) and Sir Richard was soon back with the English armies in France. He took part in the Duke of Somerset's attempt to relieve Meaux in September 1439, competed in the lists with Pedro Vasque de Saavedra, the Duke of Burgundy's chamberlain, when he visited London in 1440 (clear evidence of his burgeoning military reputation), and was again in France, in the Duke of York's company, when the Duke relieved Pontoise in 1441. He became a knight banneret on 25 September 1442, and new opportunities for advancement opened when Henry VI's councillors arranged for the King to marry the French princess, Margaret of Anjou.

Sir Richard and his wife were among those chosen to escort the royal bride to England in 1444, and it was only natural that Jacquetta, whose sister, Isabel, was married to Margaret's uncle, Charles, Comte du Maine, would find favour with the new Queen. These factors probably combined to secure Richard's elevation to the peerage as Baron Rivers on 8 May 1448, although his choice of title is puzzling. Dugdale thought that he borrowed the name from the old family of Redvers, or De Ripariis, Earls of Devon, since he added an escutcheon bearing a griffin segreant which had formed part of Redvers's device to his own arms; but a casual reference to his son as Lord Anthony Angre (in a letter of 1475) may indicate a connection with the barony of Rivers or De Ripariis of Aungre (Ongar), which had been in abeyance for some time. His value to the government was again demonstrated when he played a prominent part in the suppression of Jack Cade's rebellion in June 1450; and he was admitted to the Order of the Garter on 4 August the same year.[7]

Elizabeth's earliest years were spent in the nursery at Grafton, where she was joined by a growing number of siblings: her brothers Anthony, born about 1440, John, and Margaret, the sister nearest to her in age. Grafton (the word is a combination of 'grove' and 'tun') was, in the mid-fifteenth century, a substantial village straddling the main road between Northampton and London. The church and the manor house, the two largest buildings, stood well back from the eastern side of the thoroughfare, while the hermitage, once the cell of a solitary monk and by now, in all probability, the Woodvilles' private chapel, lay just to the west. There were two 'parks' (enclosed areas of wood and lawn [open spaces] in which deer were retained and protected), a cluster of cottages and, beyond, the great open fields (already displaying unmistakable signs of enclosure) and the forest. It was a rural, almost idyllic, setting, sometimes enlivened by the arrival of travelling players and musicians or when great men and their ladies riding between the capital and the provinces were invited to break their journey and enjoy the family's hospitality. Elizabeth would have eagerly anticipated the two great festivals of the year: Christmas, when the boar's head was carried to the high table and the 'Lord of Misrule' ushered in twelve days of feasting and entertainments, and Easter when the 'wrythe', a garland of branches, was ceremoniously brought into the manor house, and women 'hocked' men (and men hocked women), binding them with ropes until they had paid a forfeit to obtain their release.

The evidence of Elizabeth's later years suggests that she was a bright, intelligent child who was close to her parents, although convention, and their frequent absences on great matters, allowed them to play only a limited part in her upbringing. Nurses and servants, and then perhaps a master or mistress, would have been responsible for her early care and education, until, at some time after her seventh birthday, she was sent to join another landed household. The purpose of this custom was to allow children to make social contacts which would ultimately benefit their family while at the same time encouraging self-reliance; and although there is no clear evidence of where Elizabeth was boarded it was probably with Sir Edward Grey and his wife Elizabeth, Lady Ferrers, at Groby in Leicestershire. The relative nearness of Grafton would have allowed her to return home periodically; the status of the family – a knight married to a higher-born wife – perhaps appealed to the Woodvilles; and part of the arrangement was that she would marry John, the Greys' eldest son.[8]

Her day began with mass in the family chapel, followed by breakfast (at six or seven according to the season) and then formal lessons, reading, writing (in English, with some French and Latin) and a grounding in the law and mathematics which she would find useful in managing an estate and keeping accounts in her future husband's absence. Dinner would be taken at perhaps ten or eleven, and later, if the weather was good, there might be outdoor activities, hunting and hawking, or perhaps sewing and embroidery in the company of the other ladies of the household. Supper followed at between three and four, and then there would be time to linger in the garden or alternatively play games (cards, chess and backgammon were popular), dance and listen to music. Her 'polite accomplishments', good manners and breeding complemented by her growing physical beauty, made her an ideal partner for the young heir to the family's wealth and title, but there is no evidence to support Thomas More's story that they gained her a place in the household of Queen Margaret. More was probably confusing her with Lady Isabella Grey, David MacGibbon's candidate, a married woman who had accompanied Margaret to England (when Elizabeth Woodville was only eight), or perhaps with another Elizabeth Grey who served the Queen but who is known to have been a widow and mother in 1445.[9]

Jacquetta's dower – a third share of Bedford's manors and annuities in England, worth over £4,000 a year, and the same proportion of his considerable interests in France – meant that Elizabeth was born into the lap of luxury, but as she reached her teens the family's finances became more straitened. The French lands were lost as the Hundred Years' War drew to a close in the 1440s and early 1450s, and Henry VI's government became increasingly unable to meet the claims of those who, like Jacquetta, were entitled to regular payments from the Exchequer. This, and the fact that the dower was for life only (Jacquetta's rights would have reverted to the Crown if she had died as a consequence of one of her many pregnancies), ought to have persuaded the Woodvilles to seek an opportunity to exchange their temporary wealth for something more permanent. They could have used the income from the dower to buy land (and particularly to buy out the co-holders of those manors in which they already had a third share), and could have asked the King to convert their own temporary interest into a full title in return for surrendering some of the annuities. But little progress seems to have been made in this direction – grants made from the Bedford estates to others often *included* the reversion of Jacquetta's dower interest – and Baron Rivers and the dowager Duchess of Bedford owned only eight scattered manors in England in 1461.[10]

There is no record of precisely when Elizabeth and John Grey were married, and contemporary references to the age of their eldest son, Thomas, are not very helpful. He may have been born in 1455 if the statement that he was '37 and more' (that is between 37 and 38) in 1492 is accurate, but we cannot discount the possibility that he was '13 and more' in 1464 and had entered the world in 1451.[11] It is, perhaps, unlikely that Elizabeth was married at thirteen and a mother at fourteen; but the Lady Margaret Beaufort gave birth to the future Henry VII when she was only thirteen and this may be another instance of a family's desire to seal an agreement as quickly as possible taking precedence over the well-being of the bride.[12] The young couple probably resided at the Greys' second principal manor house at Astley (Warwickshire), and a second son, Richard, was born to them later in the 1450s.

This decade in Elizabeth's life is all but lost to us, although we can assume that its pattern, and her daily responsibilities, would have been similar to those of other ladies of gentle and knightly status. Her domestic round doubtless included supervising servants, overseeing the work of the brewhouse, bakehouse and dairy, making clothes, preserving and storing provisions, and, most importantly, planning ahead to ensure that everything was available when needed. While the household tried to be as self-sufficient as possible, there were still many things which had to be bought in, not least scarcer commodities such as exotic fruits and spices which could only be obtained from the larger towns. There must have been many occasions when Sir John rode to Leicester, Coventry or London on business carrying in his pocket a 'shopping list' prepared by Elizabeth detailing not only what she wanted but how much she expected to pay. It was during her husband's absences that she became his partner in a very real sense, negotiating with farmers and neighbours, arranging leases and parrying lawsuits, and taking his place in any and every matter which affected their interests. There is no evidence that she was ever obliged to hazard her person (as was her contemporary Margaret Paston, for example),[13] but there can be little doubt that, like Margaret, she wrote regularly to her husband to acquaint him with developments and reassure him that everything was satisfactory. Their personal relationship must remain conjectural, but there is every likelihood that genuine affection grew out of the original 'arrangement' and they became firm friends.

These years spent in the Warwickshire countryside with her young family were the most settled and perhaps among the happiest Elizabeth experienced; but from time to time she would have shared her husband's anxiety as defeats in France and the loss of virtually all of Henry V's conquests led to increasingly bitter divisions among the English nobility. Henry VI was a weak ruler who proved unable to hold the ring between the jealousies and conflicting ambitions of the great lords and their retinues and fell increasingly under the influence of the faction headed by Queen Margaret and the Dukes of Somerset and Suffolk. Their rivals, the Duke of York, his brother-in-law the Earl of Salisbury, and Salisbury's son the Earl of Warwick, found themselves progressively excluded from the King's counsels, and this threatened both York's ability to recover the money he had spent trying to bolster the English position in France in the 1440s and their collective access to the royal patronage – the large number of offices and annuities which the Crown had at its disposal and which they could crucially secure for both themselves and their followers if they enjoyed the king's ear. Throughout the conflicts of the 1450s York maintained that his only aim was to rescue Henry (and himself) from this situation, and his decision to claim the crown after his victory at Northampton in July 1460 surprised everyone. It was true that his maternal great-great-grandfather, Lionel of Antwerp, Duke of Clarence (Edward III's third son) was older than John of Gaunt, Duke of Lancaster, Henry's paternal great-grandfather and King Edward's fourth son; but primogeniture was only one factor (and not necessarily the determining one) in the succession, and Henry VI, his grandfather's usurpation notwithstanding, was an anointed king. There had been four occasions between the Conquest and the end of the twelfth century – in 1087, 1100, 1135 and 1199 – when a deceased ruler had been succeeded by a claimant other than his nearest blood relative; and although the precedent that a reigning king should be succeeded by his eldest son (or, alternatively, his eldest grandson) had been established by 1400, it was still unclear what should happen if the king died childless. It is one of the ironies of the situation that if the revolution of 1399 had not taken place and Richard II had died from natural causes after reigning a year or two longer, the peers would almost certainly have turned to Gaunt's son, Henry of Derby, who was in his mid-thirties and enjoyed a reputation as a man of action, rather than York's then youthful uncle, Edmund Mortimer. A child who was nearest in blood to the late king could not expect to prevail against the claims of a more distant but potentially more able candidate, and York's argument that Edmund's right (and, by extension, his own) had been violated owed more to wishful thinking than to the realities of the situation. Henry VI's father had been king before him and his son, Prince Edward of Lancaster (born 1453), was entitled to be king after him; and the compromise agreed after York claimed the Crown – that Henry should continue to reign until his death whereupon York and his heirs would succeed him – was as devoid of legality as it was unacceptable to Queen Margaret. York was slain at the Battle of Wakefield fought on 30 December 1460 (Salisbury was executed afterwards), and Warwick was defeated at the second Battle of St Albans the following February. These were devastating blows for the Yorkist party, not least because Queen Margaret regained possession of her hapless husband at St Albans (Henry had been captured by the Yorkists at Northampton) and prevented Warwick from claiming that he was acting with royal approval. Warwick, in what were now desperate circumstances, crowned York's son, Edward, Earl of March, as his own rival monarch, and the future husband of Elizabeth Woodville was acclaimed by his supporters as Edward IV.

The first phase of this conflict, known to later generations as the Wars of the Roses, did not seriously affect the Woodville and Grey families. Lord Rivers became one of the Duke of Somerset's lieutenants at Calais in the early 1450s, an appointment which prevented him from fighting for King Henry at the first Battle of St Albans (22 May 1455), and there is no evidence that Sir Edward and John Grey, if they were present, came to any harm. The defeat of the Lancastrians, and Somerset's death, resulted in the Earl of Warwick becoming the new, Yorkist, captain of Calais; and it was to Calais that Warwick, his father Salisbury and Edward, Earl of March retired after their reversal at Ludford Bridge on 12–13 October 1459. King Henry's government ordered Lord Rivers and his eldest son Sir Anthony to muster forces at Sandwich against them, but on the night of 15 January 1460 the Yorkists attacked unexpectedly and the two Woodvilles were captured. 'They were brought to Calais' wrote William Paston, 'before the lords with eight score torches, and there my Lord of Salisbury rated him (Rivers), calling him knave's son, that he should be so rude to call him and these other lords traitors, for they shall be found the king's true liegemen when he should be found a traitor &c. And my Lord of Warwick rated him and said that his father was but a squire and brought up with King Henry V, and sithen himself made by marriage, and also made lord, and that it was not his part to have such language of lords, being of the king's blood. And my Lord of March rated him in like wise. And Sir Anthony was rated for his language of all three lords in like wise.'[14]

The Woodvilles were not physically harmed and were released after the Yorkist victory at Northampton, but the memory of this verbal dressing-down would have lingered, particularly when 'my Lord of March' married Elizabeth and became Rivers's son-in-law and Sir Anthony's brother-in-law four years later. It would be fascinating to know if they ever reminded one another of this occasion when they met socially, and, if they did, whether they laughed about it or whether the scorn poured on Rivers still rankled. But perhaps he had the last laugh when the young man who had so berated him made him an earl!

The news of these events inevitably caused concern in the households at Grafton, Groby and Astley, but worse was to follow. The newly knighted Sir John Grey was killed fighting for the Lancastrians at the second Battle of St Albans, leaving Elizabeth a widow of twenty-three or twenty-four with two young children; and her father and brother were captured at Towton (Yorkshire) on 29 March 1461, still vigorously resisting the recently proclaimed King Edward. Elizabeth returned to Grafton to be with her mother, and Cora Scofield suggests that this may have led to her first, chance, meeting with her future husband. Edward spent some time establishing his authority in the north after the battle and then made his way by easy stages towards London. He spent two days at Stony Stratford in June, and before he left sent word to the Chancellor that 'of our grace especial' he had 'pardoned and remitted and forgiven unto Richard Woodville, knight, Lord Rivers, all manner offences and trespasses of him done against us' and had also granted him the enjoyment of all his goods and chattels. It seems likely that the King had summoned the staunchly Lancastrian Woodvilles to Stony Stratford, or had perhaps stopped at nearby Grafton when he was out riding, and that mutual assurances had been exchanged between them. Miss Scofield's suggestion 'that a pair of bright eyes which Edward IV had just seen, probably for the first time, the eyes of Elizabeth Woodville, had pleaded for a father's pardon', may not be entirely without foundation, but the King would have been conscious that his own success depended in some measure on his ability to win over the more able and influential supporters of the former government. Lord Rivers's pardon passed the great seal on 12 July, and Sir Anthony, now Baron Scales in right of his wife, received his later the same month.[15]

These measures sealed the reconciliation between the Woodville family and the new ruling dynasty, but Elizabeth's troubles were by no means over. In 1456, the year before he died, Sir Edward Grey and his wife had conveyed three manors, Newbottle and Brington in Northamptonshire and Woodham Ferrers in Essex, to a group of feoffees (trustees) to provide an annual income of 100 marks for their son John, his wife and heirs; and although Elizabeth quite reasonably expected to continue to receive the revenues after Sir John's death, her mother-in-law and her new husband Sir John Bourchier (a son of the Earl of Essex and King Edward's aunt, Isabel) tried to recover them. Both parties petitioned the Chancellor asking him to require the three surviving trustees, Robert Isham, William Boldon and William Fielding, to 'make astate' of the properties to them; and Elizabeth's father further protested that although he had long since paid Sir Edward 200 marks in full settlement of his daughter's marriage portion he had not troubled to obtain a receipt or discharge and now Lady Ferrers was dunning him for 125 marks which she claimed was still due! Elizabeth was fortunate that two of the trustees confirmed that the enfeoffment had been arranged to provide an income 'for the saide John Grey and Elizabeth his wife, and to the heires of the saide John's body' (the third, William Fielding, was non-committal, saying 'that he was uncertain as to the intent of the assignment');[16] but this was unlikely to be the end of the matter. Thomas, Elizabeth's elder son, had become heir to his grandmother's estates and barony when his father fell at St Albans, and she began to fear that the deteriorating relationship between the two families would cause Lady Ferrers to entail the rest of her lands on herself and her new husband in jointure with remainder to their heirs (if they had any) and only a reversion to the offspring of her first marriage. This would have allowed the much younger Bourchier and his successors to enjoy the inheritance indefinitely;[17] and Elizabeth appealed to William, Lord Hastings, King Edward's friend and chamberlain, who was now effectively the Yorkist viceroy of the midland shires. It was agreed that Elizabeth and Hastings would share equally in the rents and profits of any Grey family lands (other than Newbottle, Brington and Woodham Ferrers) which might be secured for Thomas while he was under twelve years of age; and that Thomas, or, in the event of his death, his younger brother Richard, would marry Hastings's as yet unborn daughter, or, failing this, a daughter of Ralph, his brother, or Anne, his sister. Hastings was to pay Elizabeth 500 marks for the marriage, but if Thomas and Richard both died, or if, after 'five or six years' there was no daughter or niece for one of them to marry, she would pay him 250 marks.[18] The formal indenture of covenants (contract) which 'Elysabeth Grey' signed on 13 April 1464 has been described by Professor Lander as a 'very hard bargain',[19] and it is possible that Hastings's readiness to profit from her misfortune turned potential gratitude into resentment. This was her first taste of the harsh world of aristocratic landed society, but the arrangement was effectively cancelled when, only eighteen days later (if we can accept the version of events given by the chroniclers), she married King Edward!

No one knows when or how their deep and personal attachment developed, or when the King decided to marry her. The traditional story is that Elizabeth heard that Edward was hunting in Whittlewood Forest and waited under the tree later known as the 'Queen's Oak' holding her two sons tightly by the hand. When the King rode by she threw herself at his feet begging him to endorse her arrangement with Hastings, and Edward was so struck by her 'mournful beauty' that he at once fell in love with her. He assumed that, like other ladies who had attracted him, she would be content to become his mistress; but she virtuously refused to give herself unless and until he agreed to marry her, 'and so increased his passion by her refusals that he came to realise that he could not live without her'.[20] The story that Elizabeth resisted even when a dagger was put to her throat was long assumed to be a late, peculiarly Italianate, detail invented by Dominic Mancini; but Antonio Cornazzano's reference to a similar incident in his *De mulieribus admirandis*, probably written in the closing months of 1468 (in which

Elizabeth is said to have produced the dagger) shows that it was then circulating in Europe and may indicate how surprised foreign observers received the news.[21] The King stopped at Stony Stratford on 30 April while he was on his way northwards to meet a renewed threat from the Lancastrians, and next morning, Mayday, slipped away from his entourage and rode to Grafton where he secretly wed Elizabeth in the presence of Jacquetta, a priest, perhaps two others and 'a young man who helped the priest sing'.[22] The couple consummated their marriage, and the King then returned to his camp and told his followers that he had been hunting. He found excuses to visit Grafton on several other occasions while he remained in the vicinity (the arrangements were stage-managed by Jacquetta, who secretly brought Elizabeth to him when the house had retired for the night and, if Polydore Vergil may be believed, kept the whole matter from her husband); and this cat-and-mouse game presumably continued until the Council, meeting at Reading in September, pressed him to marry Bona of Savoy, the French King's sister-in-law, when Edward was forced to admit the truth.

The reality may be rather different, however. The idea of a young, handsome king marrying for love on Mayday may have been borrowed from romantic tradition and Edward, who was constantly attended by courtiers and had virtually no privacy, would have found it difficult to meet his bride secretly over a period of almost five months. The fact that Elizabeth was crowned in May 1465 may have added to the confusion, and it is perhaps more likely that they were married when the King again stopped at Stony Stratford on his return journey, or when he was at his manor of Penley, halfway between London and Grafton, in the late summer. But if some of the details of the tradition are speculative, it is clear that there was little time between the proposal and the marriage, and that Elizabeth was surprised by the speed of events. She would not have sought the assistance of Lord Hastings, or for that matter, any other nobleman, if she had expected to marry the King in the near future,[23] and many contemporaries would probably have agreed with Charles Ross that it was 'the impulsive love match of an impetuous young man'.[24]

No contemporary recorded the scene at Reading when Edward made his admission to the assembled noblemen and clerics, but it is not difficult to imagine their reaction. Some probably fell silent, dumbfounded, as they grappled mentally with the consequences for themselves and their country, while others, including, perhaps, Warwick and those who had been negotiating for the hand of the Lady Bona, could barely conceal their anger that their master had not consulted them on such an important matter. They had fully expected him to use his marriage to forge an alliance between the new Yorkist dynasty and one of the great ruling houses of Europe replenishing his depleted treasury with a large dowry in the process, and could hardly believe that he had squandered the opportunity with such apparently scant regard for his public duty.[25] Their anger might have been mollified if he had chosen a maiden who was a member of one of the great (preferably Yorkist) noble families; but the new Queen's father was a former Lancastrian who had only been ennobled comparatively recently while she herself was some five years the King's senior, a widow with two young sons.[26] The Burgundian chronicler, Jean de Waurin, lacked firsthand knowledge of events in England, but there seems no reason to doubt his report that 'they answered that she was not his match, however good and however fair she might be, and he must know well that she was no wife for a prince such as himself; for she was not the daughter of a duke or earl, but her mother, the Duchess of Bedford, had married a simple knight, so that though she was the child of a duchess and the niece of the count of St Pol, still she was no wife for him'.[27]

Elizabeth had been widowed long enough to ensure that she was not carrying her late husband's child, but this was by no means the only difficulty. The Church took the view that a marriage was not entirely dissolved by death (in the sense that the couple could expect to meet again in heaven), and could decline to bless a second union on the grounds that it was motivated principally by a desire for sex.[28] This would scarcely have worried the average peasant, but a greater man, with lands and even a crown to bequeath to his offspring, would be bound to recognise that any suggestion that his marriage was incomplete or partial would be likely to encourage hostile claims to the inheritance after his death. There was also the problem that Elizabeth's large family – which now included five brothers and seven sisters – would have to be provided with such wealth and status as befitted the Queen's kinsfolk; and the danger that as the children of her first marriage grew to maturity, they like Henry III's relatives of the half-blood would form a new and perhaps discordant element in the existing social structure of the court.

But however 'impolitic and unprecedented'[29] Edward's marriage appeared both to contemporaries and to later generations, Elizabeth did have some assets and advantages to bring to her new role. She was beautiful, in an age which personified beauty as goodness and ugliness and deformity as evil; her strength of character and personality were (as we will see) suited to the demands of queenship; and she was able to produce healthy children, a factor which more than any other would be the yardstick of her success. It can also be argued that she was a political asset – Edward could not be accused of favouring one of the great Yorkist families at the expense of the others, and the consequences of the Wars of the Roses, the need to heal old wounds and forge new alliances, gave an English-born queen a distinct advantage over a foreign rival. Elizabeth's links with the House of Lancaster, and particularly with the much-admired John of Bedford, placed her at the centre of the process of reconciliation, and helped to emphasise Yorkist propaganda which associated her husband with Edward, the Black Prince. The Prince, who had sometimes been styled 'Edward IV' before 1461, was a more appropriate role model for his namesake than Richard II for a host of reasons, not least because he too had married an English widow for love. His chosen bride, Joan of Kent, was a member of the royal family (she was a granddaughter of Edward I by his second marriage to Margaret of France) and had been his childhood companion, but at the time of their union in October 1361 she was a twice-married widow with five children. It appears that in about 1340 (when she was only twelve years old) she contracted an informal but valid union with a Lancashire knight, Sir Thomas Holland, both promising themselves to each other in the presence of witnesses. Holland spent the next few years serving abroad and, in 1341, Joan (still only 13) allowed her then guardians, the Earl and Countess of Salisbury, to marry her to their son. Holland did not have the necessary funds or social standing to protest immediately; but in 1347, after capturing two French noblemen at Crecy and becoming one of the first Knights of the Garter, he appealed to the Pope. The Pope, Clement VI, ruled in his favour in November 1349, and Joan (whose union with the Salisburys' son had proved childless) lived with him and bore him five children before he died in 1360. She married the Black Prince only nine months later, when she was thirty-three and he two years younger, and, according to a contemporary, 'still one of the loveliest women in the world'. The parallels between this situation and the union between Edward IV and Elizabeth Woodville are obvious; and however much the decision annoyed Edward III, the Prince's father, there was clearly no question of annulment and the political nation had no alternative but to accept his choice.[30]

The assembled counsellors doubtless discussed these considerations but were obliged to recognise that they, too, were confronted by a *fait accompli*. Edward, their chosen and anointed King, had married without consulting them and there was nothing for it but to make the best of an unhappy situation. Some Venetian merchants reported that 'the greater part of the lords and the people in general seem very much dissatisfied at this [the marriage], and for the sake of finding means to annul it, all the peers are holding great consultations in the town of Reading', but this is disputed by a letter written by Sir John Howard, possibly to Elizabeth's father, in which he assures him that the union had met with popular approval in East Anglia. 'Also my lord I have bene in dyverse plasese wethein Norfolke, Suffolke and Hessex, and have ad komenkasion of thes marygge to fel howe the pepel of the konteryes wer despossed and, in good feythe, they ar despossed in the best wysse and glade ther of. Also I have ben wethe many dyverse astates, to fel theyer hertes, and, [in good feythe] I fowende them al ryte wele despossed, safe on (save one), the wesche I schal henforme yower good lordesche at my next komhenge to yowe be the grase of God, ho have yowe, my ryte spesyal god lord, in his blesed safegard.'[31] This quaintly written missive must have cheered Lord Rivers and his daughter (it is distinctly possible that they had asked Howard to sound out 'grass roots' political opinion and report to them), but the fact that certain great noblemen obviously disliked the new arrangement meant that they were not entirely out of danger. King Edward was still a recently enthroned usurper in the eyes of some of his influential subjects, and in breaking with tradition had denied himself a number of potential advantages: 'the strength of a diplomatic alliance, the opportunity to display his majesty in a public wedding, and the validating role by which a foreign, noble, virgin, queen could make his sovereignty more "whole".'[32] He was acutely aware of this – the extreme secrecy which surrounded the wedding and the ensuing period shows he recognised that Elizabeth did not conform to the conventions of queenship, and that he saw no other way of forcing the Council to accept her as his wife. For Elizabeth, the transition from oppressed widow to Queen of England was literally a fairy tale became reality – but with no guarantee of a happy ending. She was the first English-born consort since the eleventh century and could not have anticipated that her new position was fraught with dangers which went far beyond the criticisms of the moment and derived from the fact that she was one of her husband's subjects. In 1470 Queen Margaret of Anjou could look to her kinsman, Louis XI of France, to help restore her husband, Henry VI, to the throne of England, and Catherine of Aragon's powerful Habsburg connections all but prevented Henry VIII from ending their marriage a generation later; Elizabeth, by contrast, had no recourse but to flee into sanctuary in the two great crises of her queenship (in 1470 and again in 1483), and Henry VIII executed two of his English queens in a manner which would have been unthinkable if they had been closely related to foreign rulers. But however much – or little – Edward and his bride were conscious of the difficulties which might ultimately afflict their union, it is perhaps unlikely that either would have made any other decision in the heady summer of 1464.

Elizabeth was formally introduced to court on Michaelmas Day (29 September), when the Duke of Clarence (the King's brother) and the Earl of Warwick escorted her into the chapel of Reading Abbey. There she was 'openly honoured as queen by all the lords and all the people', although Warwick's close associate, John Lord Wenlock, probably expressed the feelings of many when he wrote 'we must be patient despite ourselves'.[33] The royal couple stayed at Reading for several weeks after the Council disbanded before moving to Windsor in November and then to Eltham for Christmas. There, Edward commanded the treasurer and chamberlains of the Exchequer to pay £466 13s 4d 'to our right entirely well beloved wife, the Queen, for the expenses of her chamber, wardrobe and stable against this feast of Christmas next coming', and shortly afterwards made provision for her permanent establishment by granting her lands worth about £4,500 a year. The gifts of the King's 'manor of Grenewich' and the manor of Sheen (later Richmond) soon followed,[34] and her brothers and sisters began to share in her good fortune. Margaret, her eldest sister, was married to Thomas, Lord Maltravers, son and heir to the Earl of Arundel, in October 1464, and the following January John, her eldest unmarried brother, caused no little scandal when he wed the elderly Catherine Neville, dowager Duchess of Norfolk, the Earl of Warwick's aunt. Marriages between ambitious but impoverished young noblemen and wealthy dowagers were by no means unusual in medieval society, but the age difference in this case (John was probably little more than twenty while his thrice-widowed bride was in her sixties) shocked their contemporaries. Ironically, John was executed in 1469 and Catherine long outlived him: her last recorded appearance was at Richard III's coronation in 1483.

Arrangements for Elizabeth's coronation began as soon as the Christmas festivities were over. In January the King sent envoys to Philip, Duke of Burgundy, inviting him to send an appropriate delegation (and particularly his wife's uncle, Jacques de Luxembourg, Seigneur de Richebourg) to represent him at the ceremony, planned for the Sunday before Pentecost, 26 May 1465. The date was then over four months away, and Edward may have effectively delayed the proceedings to ensure that the most aristocratic of Elizabeth's relatives would be present. The sum of £400 was advanced to the treasurer of the Household to defray the costs of the occasion, and among the more specific disbursements were £27 10s paid to Elyn Langwith, a London silkwoman, who provided materials for the Queen's 'chairs, saddle and pillion', £108 5s 6d to Matthew Philip for a gold cup and basin, £280 to John de Bardi of Florence for two cloths of gold, and £20 to Sir John Howard who supplied 'the plate that the Queen was served with the day of her coronation'.[35] On 14 April Edward wrote to the Mayor of London 'from our manor of Shene' to inform him that 'we have certainly appoynted and concluded the coronacion of our mooste dere and moost entierly beloved wiff the Quene to be at our palois at Westminster upon the Sunday before Witsonday next comyng';[36] and the Mercers and other city companies began to prepare to receive her in an appropriate manner. The Mercers resolved to choose twenty-four:

> lykly parsones, parsonable and good horsemen, to mete and receyve the Quene Elizabeth on horsebak with the Maire and other of the Citie, at her comyng to this Citie to her coronacion, and that the parsones so chosen shalbe redy to ryde whan they be duely monysshed by the Custoses or oon of them or their deputie in that behalf. And if any parsone so chosen and monysshed, by infirmytie or other cause resonable can not com

and so knowen to the Custoses, that than he purvey and ordeyn an other lykly parsone in his stede, in tharay after lymeted, and what parsone dothe the contrarie in the premysses shall paye to the box xls. Also hit is accorded that euery parsone so chosen to ryde shall fett in oure Hall at sent (Saint)Thomas, clothe of murrey sufficiant for a rydyng gowen, whiche coloure is assigned for the Comens of the Citie to ryde in, whiche clothe shalbe paide fore oute of the boxe.[37]

King Edward rode to London on 23 May where, in the Queen's honour, he created thirty-nine new knights of the Bath at the Tower,[38] and the following day (Friday) Elizabeth herself entered the capital to be greeted with the traditional pageantry on London Bridge. The bridge had been 'dressed' with forty-five loads of sand and the drawbridge fumigated; there was music and singing; a tableau, which included angels with wings made from 900 peacock feathers, had been assembled on a specially constructed platform covered with ninety-six ells of 'sultwych' (a coarse cloth); and 'St Paul', 'St Elizabeth' and 'Mary Cleophas' (the latter two played by men, as was customary) made speeches of welcome. Joanna Chamberlayne suggests that St Paul had been chosen to again emphasise Elizabeth's descent from the counts of St Pol, and that St Elizabeth (the Virgin's cousin and mother of John the Baptist) and Mary Cleophas (the Virgin's half sister and, according to medieval tradition, mother of four disciples) were obvious role models for the future mother of the King's children. Contemporary artists often showed the Virgin, St Elizabeth, and Mary Cleophas together, and when the Queen (perhaps wearing her blonde hair loose beneath a jewelled coronet in imitation of stylised portraits of the Virgin) joined the two 'ladies' in the pageant, the symbolism would have been as obvious as the spoken texts.[39] Elizabeth was then conducted by way of more celebrations and entertainments to the Tower, where English queens traditionally spent the penultimate night before their coronations; and the next day the newly created knights of the Bath, wearing blue gowns with white silk hoods, escorted her in an open horse litter through streets lined with liveried guild members to Westminster Palace. She was led into Westminster Hall the following morning by the Bishops of Durham and Salisbury 'clothed in a mantyll of purpull & a coronall upon hir hede' beneath a purple silk canopy carried by four barons of the

Cinque Ports. They were followed by the Abbot of Westminster, the dowager Duchess of Buckingham, who bore Elizabeth's train, two of her sisters-in-law, Elizabeth, Duchess of Suffolk and Margaret, the future Duchess of Burgundy, and her mother Jacquetta, their way being cleared by the Duke of Clarence, who discharged the ceremonial office of Lord High Steward, the Earl of Arundel, hereditary butler and constable for the occasion, and the Duke of Norfolk, hereditary marshal, who rode about the Hall on horses 'rychely in cloth of goulde trapped to the grounde'. Elizabeth held the sceptre of St Edward in her right hand and the sceptre of the Realm in her left, and was brought to the north door of the monastery where she was met by the Archbishop of Canterbury and the assembled clergy. She discarded her shoes 'going barefote upon ray clothe' and was preceded into the Abbey by the three principal officers of state (now dismounted) and 'divers Erlys and Barons and the newe made knyghts nexte before theym'. The ladies following were joined by thirteen duchesses and countesses dressed in red velvet, fourteen baronesses in scarlet and miniver, and the ladies of twelve knights banneret wearing scarlet. The peers included young Henry Stafford, Duke of Buckingham (the late Duke's grandson) 'borne a pon a squyer shouldr', and among the ladies was his new wife, Catherine Woodville, likewise carried, the latest of the Queen's sisters to be married to a member of the higher nobility. The only notable absentees were the Earl of Warwick, who had been sent on a diplomatic mission to Burgundy, partly, perhaps, to avoid any embarrassment or ill-feeling on what was intended to be a joyous and triumphal occasion, and the King, who was excluded by convention (although Henry VII watched his wife's coronation from behind a screen). The procession passed through the choir and the Queen knelt and alternately prostrated herself before the High Altar while the Archbishop conducted the service. She was anointed on her forehead and breast (to the words 'let the anointing of this oil increase your honour and establish you for ever and ever') and then received the regalia, the ring and the crown, the latter with the injunction to treasure 'the gold of wisdom and the pearls of virtue'. She was then led to the throne 'with grete reverence & solempnyte', and the sceptres, which had been entrusted to the Abbot of Westminster and the Earl of Essex during the previous part of the ceremony, were restored to her while she listened to the

Gospel. Mass was then celebrated and Elizabeth joined in the singing of the *Te Deum*.

What were Elizabeth's feelings at this great moment? We can only speculate, but it is likely that foremost among them would have been apprehension, an apprehension stiffened by a determination to fulfil her new role as England's first lady. Perhaps now, for the first time, she sensed the reality, and the enormity, of the task facing her, and the finality of the process which had begun with her simple, private wedding. She was awed (rather than over-awed) by the magnificent solemnity of the Abbey and the ceremony, and was acutely conscious that some of the watchers thought her unsuitable and unworthy. Were they perhaps hoping for some lapse, some indication that she lacked the 'queenliness' of a lady born into the purple, and were they relieved or disappointed when everything ran smoothly? It was an exciting, almost dream-like, experience, but she controlled the emotions which crowded upon her and displayed a calm exterior to the assembled peers.

The procession left the Abbey in the same order with the Duke of Suffolk and the Earl of Essex carrying the sceptres, and Elizabeth was conducted through the Hall to her chamber where she was 'newe revestyd in a surcote of purpull'. The two Bishops then brought her back into the Hall, where she washed, the Earl of Oxford, the hereditary Chamberlain, pouring the water into a basin held by the Duke of Clarence. The presence of the strongly pro-Lancastrian Oxford (who would one day lead Henry Tudor's army to victory at Bosworth) is some indication that the wounds of the past were being healed. The fact that his office entitled him to take the Queen's bed and the basin and towels she used at the ceremony may have been a consideration, but it is more likely that it was her Lancastrian antecedents which allowed him to endorse what he (and others of his persuasion) could regard as a union between the two warring factions.

And the Queene was set in hir astate to mete crownyd the saide lordys kneling ayther syde of hir at the table holding the sayde septours in their handes. And the Countess of Shewsbury the yonger, the Countess of Kent on the lefte hande knelyng helde the vayle before the Queene at all tymes when she toke any repace & knelyd nexte unto thastate. And at any tyme when she so dyd she hirselfe toke of the croune and when she had done she put yt on agayn.[40]

The banquet which followed, with perhaps as many as 3,000 invited guests, was a fitting reminder of the largesse at the King's disposal. The senior members of the nobility were assembled at the highest table with the Archbishop on the Queen's left and the Duchess of Suffolk and Margaret, her sister, on her right. Thirteen bishops and abbots sat at the middle table on the right while Jacquetta and the countesses and baronesses sat opposite them on the left. The judges and other legal officers sat 'beneath' the bishops and abbots and the new knights of the Bath 'beneath' the ladies, while the Mayor of London, and the aldermen and other civic dignitaries, occupied a table on the left side next to the wall and the barons of the Cinque Ports and the Chancery officials sat adjoining the wall on the right. The first course consisted of seventeen dishes, the second, nineteen, and the third, fifteen, the number offered to each of the respective diners being determined by their social rank. Trumpeters announced the commencement of each stage of the meal, the courses being preceded by the steward, butler and marshal on horseback and by other knights and noblemen on foot. The intervals were occupied by the King's minstrels 'and the minstrals of other lords (more than a hundred in total) playing and piping in their instruments great and small before the Queen full melodiously and in the most solemn wise'. Finally, Elizabeth was formally escorted back to her chamber, and the cup in which the 'wyne of voyde' (the dessert or parting drink) had been served to her was carried through the Hall before the Mayor.

The ceremonial part of the coronation was completed by the tournament, held at Westminster the following day (Monday). Some of the Burgundians who had accompanied Jacques de Luxembourg participated, but the 'winner' was Thomas, Lord Stanley, who received a ruby ring from the Queen as his prize. Elizabeth was now in every sense Queen of England. She who, a year earlier, had seemed destined to become the wife of a Northamptonshire knight or squire, now found her position transformed beyond recognition. Those who regarded her as a parvenu could still grumble in private, but she was now as much their sovereign lady as if she had been the greatest princess in Europe. It was a role she intended to enjoy.

2

Elizabeth's First Years as Queen

The process of marrying Elizabeth's relatives into the greatest noble families which, as we saw, had begun even before her coronation, continued apace thereafter. Her sisters Anne and Joan were joined to William, Viscount Bourchier, eldest son and heir of the Earl of Essex, and Anthony Grey, son and heir of the Earl of Kent, while Jacquetta wed John, Lord Strange of Knockin, probably early in 1466.[1] Their sibling, Mary, was betrothed to William Herbert, son of William, Lord Herbert, in September (they were married on 20 January following), and the next month Elizabeth paid her sister-in-law Anne, Duchess of Exeter, 4,000 marks for the marriage of her eldest son Thomas Grey with the Duchess's daughter and heiress Anne Holland – clear evidence that her agreement with Lord Hastings was dead. Lord Rivers was appointed to the highly lucrative office of Treasurer on 4 March 1466, was created an Earl two months later, and became Constable of England for life (with remainder to his eldest son, Anthony) on 24 August the year following. Anthony, who already had a comfortable income as the son-in-law of the deceased Lord Scales, was given the lordship of the Isle of Wight in November 1466, and arrangements were made for John Woodville to join the royal service and for Lionel, their younger brother, to embark on a potentially lucrative career in the Church.

King Edward's promotion of the Woodvilles has been the subject of much debate in recent years. Some writers suggest that he was acting primarily as a good husband and brother-in-law, that convention and the example of earlier kings obliged him to make suitable provision for his extended family,[2] while others consider that his real purpose was to bind the great aristocratic houses to his dynasty and perhaps build up a 'court' party among the nobility to break the power of Warwick and the Nevilles. The first two ideas are both compatible and likely. Edward could not allow the lowly position of his wife's relatives to diminish his own status, and, as a usurper, would have seized every opportunity to forge links with the great noble families; but there is no evidence that he was beginning to resent Warwick's alleged tutelage or that he endowed the Woodvilles to distance himself from him. He had begun to advance Lord Rivers and Sir Anthony before (as far as we can tell) he decided to marry Elizabeth, and the great rewards given to Warwick and his relatives in the first years of the reign would not suggest that he was trying to limit their authority. The Earl's uncle, William, Lord Fauconberg, was created Earl of Kent in 1461 and endowed with more than fifty-six manors and lordships; John, his younger brother, who had become Lord Montague in 1461, was raised to the earldom of Northumberland three years later although the attainted Percy heir was still living; George, the third brother, became Archbishop of York within a few days of Edward revealing his marriage; and Warwick himself continued to receive grants (including the valuable wardship of Francis Lovel, the heir to five baronies) to add to those he had secured during the recent conflict. Edward's cornering of the noble marriage market on behalf of his wife's family was perhaps 'too rapid and too great for discretion'[3] (to quote J.R. Lander), but even if some noblemen resented the process (mainly because they would have to compete with the newcomers for a share of the limited royal patronage) they could hardly have expected that the Woodvilles (or anyone else in their fortunate position) would not try to benefit from it. It could be argued that the estates and offices which the King granted to William, Lord Hastings, another parvenu raised to the peerage in 1461 because he was Edward's closest friend, and to others such as William, Lord Herbert, exceeded his generosity to Elizabeth's relatives (although by 1464 there were few forfeited lands left to distribute); and it is possible to agree with Professor Lander that Edward 'may well have encouraged the development of diverse factions'[4] (to avoid excessive dependence on any one of them), but had no intention of building up a royal or court party among the peerage which would effectively take the Nevilles' place.

The attitude of some of the older noble families towards the Woodvilles was, as mentioned above, one of apprehension or even dislike, although it is possible that this has been over-exaggerated. Henry Stafford, Duke of Buckingham, may have thought that his union with Catherine, Elizabeth's sister, demeaned him (he was, of course, too young to have influenced the decision one way or the other), and Professor Hicks has argued that it is unlikely that any of the marriages would have been solemnised if Edward had not offered sweeteners, or inducements, to the older, more established, families.[5] But the opportunity to marry a brother or sister of the Queen, to become a member of the royal family with regular, direct access to the King, would surely have appealed to many of these noblemen and women, and it is possible that if Elizabeth had had fewer siblings there would have been little or no objection to them. The late medieval nobility were socially conservative, always fearful that they were about to be swamped by an influx of base-born newcomers who had 'made good' in the world; and although their rapid rates of extinction left them with no alternative but to admit rising families there was always the feeling that the process should be strictly limited. Their attitude towards the Queen's relatives was probably no different to that which they would have adopted towards any sizeable group of parvenus, and any concern or ill-feeling which they felt for these reasons would have diminished with the passing of the years.

But however much the intrusion of the Woodvilles into high places was resented in some quarters, no one, it appears, ever questioned their loyalty or their ability to perform good service. It is the complex personality of Anthony, the Queen's eldest brother, which has perhaps most taxed historians: man of letters, patron of learning, and with an inclination to mortify the flesh by wearing a hair shirt, he was nevertheless regarded as one of the greatest warriors of the age. The story is told of how, in April 1465, when he was visiting Elizabeth at Sheen, he knelt before her and doffed his hat, whereupon 'the fair ladies of the court gathered about him, tied round his thigh a collar of gold and pearls with "a noble flower of souvenance enamelled and in manner of an emprise" and dropped into his bonnett a little roll of parchment tied with a thread of gold'. Anthony realised that he was being challenged to perform a noble deed in order to win the flower of souvenance, and, after thanking his sister and her ladies for the honour they had done him, took the parchment to the King. Edward broke the seal and informed the assembled courtiers that the ladies had requested that Sir Anthony be given licence to compete with a nobleman 'of four lineages and without reproach' at a tournament to be held in London in October.[6] It was decided to invite Anthony, the 'Bastard of Burgundy' (the illegitimate son of Philip, Duke of Burgundy) to come to England for this purpose since he had already written to Anthony Woodville suggesting they 'break lances' together; and although events on the Continent delayed his arrival until the middle of 1467, the result was what Professor Ross has described as 'a calculated use of chivalric pageantry to impress the people and focus attention on the high connections of the Woodville family'.[7] The Bastard was received in London with all due honour, and on 3 June the King granted him a formal audience and invited him to attend the opening of Parliament in the Painted Chamber. The tournament, which began at West Smithfield in Edward's and Elizabeth's presence on Thursday 11 June, was something of an anti-climax. The death of the Bastard's horse in the initial charge ended the first day's proceedings, and although they began to fight on foot with axes on the second day 'that ffygth contynuyd not, ffor afftyr iij or iiij strokis at the moost, the kyng cast doun a warderer (baton) which he held in his hand & commaundid theym to be dysseverid, and soo that day was endid indyfferently of honour'.[8] The King had no wish to see either of the protagonists killed or injured – he was more concerned to build bridges than to risk destroying them – and did not want anything to interfere with his plan to feast them in the Grocers' Hall on the following Sunday. Olivier de la Marche, the Burgundian historian who had accompanied the Bastard and his party to England, commented that the meal was 'great and plentiful' and boasted that they were joined by sixty or eighty ladies 'of such noble estate that the least noble was the daughter of a baron'.[9] It was intended that the tournament should last for another week (with other members of the Burgundian party and the English aristocracy jousting for the public entertainment) and would culminate in a banquet which the Bastard would give in honour of the Queen, her sisters and ladies; but news of the sudden death of Duke Philip led, inevitably, to the curtailment of the programme, and the mourning Burgundians returned home.

It was while the court was waiting for the Bastard to arrive in England that the Queen gave birth to Elizabeth, her first child by the King, on 11 February 1466. The baby was baptised by Archbishop George Neville assisted by other bishops, with all the appropriate ceremony, while the Earl of Warwick and the two grandmothers, Cecily, dowager Duchess of York and Jacquetta, dowager Duchess of Bedford, stood as godparents at the font. The event must have been tinged with disappointment – a son (and successor) would have given the new dynasty a greater sense of permanence – but neither this nor the birth of two more daughters, Mary and Cecily in 1467 and 1469 respectively, had any discernible effect on the royal marriage. Edward seems to have more closely resembled Charles II (who tolerated his barren wife Catherine of Braganza) than his grandson Henry VIII (who disposed of two wives, Catherine of Aragon and Anne Boleyn, in quick succession because no male heir was forthcoming); but perhaps Edward, like Charles (and unlike Henry), had the assurance that his brother would succeed him in the event of his premature death.

The ritual of giving birth began perhaps a month before the child's arrival when the Queen 'took her chamber' and formally withdrew from the public life of the court. She first attended mass, accompanied by lords and ladies, and was then conducted to her great chamber, furnished with a chair of estate, covered in cushions, with a cloth of estate above it and carpets below, where she was served with wines and spices. The party then passed into the inner chamber, which was likewise carefully furnished and decorated according to the prevailing custom. The walls and ceiling were hung with blue cloth of arras covering all but one of the windows, the Queen's bed had down pillows and an ermine-edged scarlet counterpane, and the pallet or day-bed which lay at its foot was surmounted by a crimson satin canopy. The only decorations permitted were golden fleur de lys on the cloth of arras (signifying the Virgin Mary, the ideal mother) with crowns and the Royal Arms on the day-bed canopy because, in the words of a contemporary writer, further elaboration was 'not convenient about wymen in suche cas'.[10] The room also contained two cradles, one 'litille' and the other the 'gret cradille of estat', and an altar on which lay holy relics, including, probably, 'our Lady's girdle and ring'. There were a number of such girdles in England which were thought to have belonged to saintly ladies and to be particularly efficacious in childbirth. Prayers were said in front of the beds in the presence of the whole party and the men were then excluded from the chamber, the Queen passing her last few weeks of waiting in an exclusively female world. The male doctor or doctors who attended her at other times had no part to play in the process, and Elizabeth's well-being was in the hands of ladies such as Marjory

Cobbe, described as an *obsterix*, who was granted a £10 annuity in 1469.[11] Miss Schofield recounts the story of how one Master Dominic, who had foretold that the child would be a boy and who succeeded in gaining access to the outer chamber at the time of the birth, called to the ladies seeking confirmation as soon as he heard the child crying. But one of them informed him that 'whatsoever the Queen's grace hath here within, sure it is a fool standeth there without . . . whereupon Master Dominic departed in confusion without seeing of the King for that time'.[12]

The period of recovery (and of ritual impurity) normally lasted between forty and sixty days and was formally ended by the ceremony of churching, when the court gathered in the great chamber to witness the Queen being gently lifted from a newly installed bed of state by two dukes. A Bohemian gentleman, Gabriel Tetzel, was visiting London with his master, Leo of Rozmital, and others, and was invited to observe the service and the banquet which followed.[13] He writes:

The Queen left her child-bed that morning and went to church in stately order, accompanied by many priests bearing relics and by many scholars singing and carrying lights. There followed a great company of ladies and maidens from the country and from London, who had been summoned. Then came a great company of trumpeters, pipers and players of stringed instruments. The King's choir followed, forty-two of them, who sang excellently. Then came twenty-four heralds and pursuivants, followed by sixty counts and knights. At last came the Queen escorted by two dukes. Above her was a canopy. Behind her were her mother and maidens and ladies to the number of sixty. Then the Queen heard the singing of an Office, and, having left the church, she returned to her palace in procession as before. Then all who had joined the procession remained to eat. They sat down, women and men, ecclesiastical and lay, each according to rank, and filled four great rooms.

Then my lord [Leo of Rozmital] and his retinue and the noblest lords were provided with food apart in the hall and at the tables where the King and his court are accustomed to dine. And one of the King's most powerful earls sat at the head of the King's table on the King's chair in his stead.[14] My lord sat also at the same table only two paces from him. No one else sat at that table. All the honour which is shown to the King, with carvers, buffets and side tables in profusion, was shown to us as if the King himself had been present. Everything was supplied for the Earl, as representing the King, and for my lord in such costly measure that it is unbelievable that it could be provided.

While we were eating, the King's gifts were distributed among his trumpeters, pipers, jesters and heralds, the heralds alone receiving 400 nobles. All those who had received gifts went about the tables crying out what the King had given them. When my lord and the Earl had eaten, the Earl conducted my lord and his honourable attendants to an unbelievably costly apartment where the Queen was preparing to eat. My lord and his gentlemen were placed in an alcove so that my lord could observe the great splendour. The Queen sat alone at table on a costly golden chair. The Queen's mother and the King's sister had to stand some distance away. When the Queen spoke with her mother or the King's sister, they knelt down before her until she had drunk water. Not until the first dish was set before the Queen could the Queen's mother and the King's sister be seated. The ladies and maidens and all who served the Queen at table were all of noble birth and had to kneel so long as the Queen was eating. The meal lasted for three hours. The food which was served to the Queen, the Queen's mother, the King's sister and the others was most costly. Much might be written of it. Everyone was silent and not a word was spoken. My lord and his attendants stood the whole time in the alcove and looked on.

After the banquet they commenced to dance. The Queen remained seated in her chair. Her mother knelt before her, but at times the Queen bade her rise. The King's sister danced a stately dance with two dukes, and this, and the courtly reverence they paid to the Queen, was such as I have never seen elsewhere, nor have I ever seen such exceedingly beautiful maidens. Among them were eight duchesses and thirty countesses and the others were all daughters of influential men. After the dance the King's choristers entered and were ordered to sing. We were present when the King heard mass in his chapel. My lord and his company were let in and I do not think that I have heard finer singing in this world. Then the King let us see his relics and other relics which are to be found in London. Among them to be specially noted are a stone from the Mount of Olives in which one of our Lord's footprints was embedded, and our Lady's girdle and ring and many other relics.[15]

Some commentators have criticised Elizabeth for conducting herself in a haughty, even arrogant, manner at this banquet, pointing particularly to her insistence that the noble ladies who served her remain kneeling as evidence that her sudden elevation had 'gone to her head'. They fail to realise that this, like the unnatural silence which surprised Tetzel, was part of the strict formality of the occasion, and that the Queen could neither insist upon, nor dispense with, an accepted practice. An alternative interpretation would be that Elizabeth used the occasion to show that she had adapted well to her changed circumstances, notwithstanding that nothing in her earlier life had prepared her for her new burden. She was to be accused of many things in the course of her reign, but an unwillingness to bend to, or abide by, the conventions of her new role was never among them, and a fairer judgement would be that on this, as on other occasions, she acquitted herself well.

The same may be said of her patronage of learning, which, although not strictly a royal obligation, had been close to the heart of her predecessor, Queen Margaret. Queens' College, Cambridge, founded by Margaret in 1448, had languished since Henry VI's downfall, but as early as March 1465 King Edward granted the members a licence to hold property to the value of £200 annually. The licence made it clear that the College was now '*de patronatu Elizabeth regine Anglie*' and when a set of statutes regulating the conduct of the institution was issued ten years later she was described as '*vera fundatrix*' ('true foundress') and her arms replaced Margaret's on the College seal. The members, a president and twelve fellows, were encouraged to pray for the King and Queen and their deceased ancestors and to study theology rather than law. This probably reflected concerns that many clerics (including some later medieval popes) lacked a sense of spirituality because they had been trained as lawyers, and Elizabeth was said to be 'specially solicitous concerning those matters whereby the safety of souls and the public good are promoted, and poor scholars, desirous of advancing themselves in the knowledge of letters, are assisted in their need'.[16] She may also have been instrumental in saving Eton College, another Lancastrian foundation, from being closed or at best absorbed into the Yorkist St George's Chapel. Not only were all the grants which Henry VI had made to it revoked in King Edward's first parliament, but the Pope was persuaded to issue a Bull authorising its suppression in

1463 and an order transferring the bells, jewels and furniture to Windsor was made two years later. Building work stopped (the chapel was left roofless) and the school was probably discontinued: but in 1467 the King suddenly relented, restored some of the confiscated properties and petitioned the Pope to cancel the Bull. It is sometimes suggested that Jane Shore, Edward's mistress, interceded with him on behalf of the College. But there is no evidence that Jane enjoyed real, political, influence, and it is more probable that it was Elizabeth, with her Lancastrian antecedents, who persuaded her husband to allow it to continue as a separate institution. The story of Jane's involvement appears to be only as old as the seventeenth century, and, as Professor Ross notes, the portrait of her which hangs at Eton is really of Diane de Poitiers, mistress of King Henry II of France.[17]

Elizabeth's special position meant that petitioners regularly asked her to intercede with the King for them, and although little evidence now survives for these special pleadings, a comparison with the Paston family of Norfolk may provide some parallels. The Pastons, a rising gentry family whose legal practice had gained them a place in county society, found themselves in difficulties when, in November 1459, John Paston, then head of the family, persuaded his client, the wealthy knight Sir John Fastolf, to bequeath him all his estates in Norfolk and Suffolk to the exclusion of those who had expected to inherit them. The result was that the Pastons were plunged into a lengthy legal and sometimes physical battle to maintain their precarious title to Fastolf's properties, and, since their ambitions conflicted with those of the Dukes of both counties, were obliged to seek the assistance of other senior figures who, they believed, had equal or even greater influence at court. In March 1469 Sir John Paston (John's eldest son) informed his younger brother (also called John) that 'at the special request of the Qwen' he had given a sinecure associated with the disputed castle of Caister to John Yotton, one of her chaplains, and was shortly afterwards advised that 'the Quene hath sent a lettre unto my Lady of Norffolk and a nother lettre unto my Lady of Suffolk the elder (Alice Chaucer, the then Duke's mother) desyeryng theym to common (speak) with my lordis (the Dukes) that all such materis as the Kyng wrote unto them fore mabe kept so that no defaute be founden in them, as ye may understand by youre lettre sent frome the Quene'.[18] Sir John for many years toyed with the idea of marrying Anne Haute, one of Elizabeth's kinswomen (Joan, her father's younger sister, had married into the Haute family), but the matter was quietly abandoned after the Duke of Norfolk's death in 1476 finally secured his position as master of Caister when Woodville assistance may no longer have been required.

But however much Elizabeth sought to assist her new subjects (so far as she was decently able to intervene in matters which, strictly speaking, did not concern her), there were, supposedly, other occasions when she used her authority and influence to do them harm. One of her alleged victims was Thomas Fitzgerald, Earl of Desmond, whom King Edward had appointed deputy, or governor, of Ireland under the nominal lieutenancy of the Duke of Clarence. Desmond was initially popular and successful, but a disagreement with the Bishop of Meath in 1464 (when both brought their complaints to England) and other serious disturbances led the King to replace him with the ruthless John Tiptoft, Earl of Worcester, temporarily in 1465 and permanently two years later. Worcester crossed to Ireland and caused Desmond to be attainted in a parliament held at Drogheda; and when the Earl came to answer the charges had him arrested and beheaded on 14 February 1468. Such treatment seemed harsh even by Worcester's uncompromising standards, and it was said that when Desmond had visited England in 1464 he had suggested to Edward that it was still not too late to annul his union with Elizabeth and marry a well-connected foreigner. This roused the Queen's anger against him, and she persuaded her husband to replace him with Worcester (who had agreed to avenge her) and even purloined the King's signet ring to sign his death warrant. The story has little to commend it, however. It appears to be part of a 'family tradition' first mentioned by the Earl's grandson in a memoir delivered to Henry VIII's Privy Council, and which subsequently gained credence from some instructions which Richard III gave to the Bishop of Enachdune (Annaghdown), his ambassador to Desmond's son, authorising him to prosecute any he held responsible for his father's killing. Richard sympathised with the young man, pointing out that he had suffered similar misfortune 'within this Royaulme of England, aswele of his brother the duc of Clarence, as other his nighe kynnesmen and gret frendes'; but he did not mention Elizabeth, and only someone who believed she had helped to bring about Clarence's downfall could assume that this was the point he was trying to make.[19] There is no evidence that Edward was afterwards angry with the Queen or Worcester (he sent the Earl a silver cup when a son was born to him in Ireland), and if Desmond's dismissal had been in any way personal he would not have been re-appointed as deputy when Worcester failed to mount an expedition in 1465. It was the Irishman's defeat in a campaign against Offaly in 1466 which seriously undermined the English position and culminated in his downfall; and if Worcester treated him brutally his sufferings hardly exceeded those of the Southampton rebels whom he ordered to be impaled in 1470, or his request made at his own execution that he should be beheaded with three blows 'in honour of the Trinity'. Professor Ross believes that the story can be dismissed as a later fabrication, and it would be harsh to condemn Elizabeth on the basis of what may be no more than a Tudor myth.[20]

A more substantial allegation, levied against not only Elizabeth but also other members of the Woodville family, was their treatment of a former Mayor of London, Sir Thomas Cook. Cook was apparently approached by John Hawkins, an agent of the exiled Queen Margaret, who reminded him of the many kindnesses she had done him and asked him if he would advance her some funds. Cook was too cautious (or perhaps too hard-headed a businessman) to risk aiding the enemy, and although Hawkins eventually reduced his original request from a thousand marks to a hundred pounds, gave him nothing. But he did not report the matter to the authorities, and was arrested on suspicion of treason when Hawkins was captured and forced to reveal the names of his contacts in June 1468. His London house was seized by Lord Rivers and Sir John Fogge (another of the Woodvilles' Haute relatives who was Treasurer of the King's Household) and ransacked in the search for evidence against him. The chronicler Robert Fabyan, who was then aged seventeen or eighteen and was apprenticed to Cook, says that his wife and servants were turned out, many valuables were stolen, and that the men who Rivers and Fogge assigned to keep the house 'made such havok of such wyne as was lafft . . . that what they mygth not drynk & gyve away they lete runne in the seler'.[21] Rivers and his wife apparently disliked Cook because he had earlier refused to sell her a magnificent arras depicting the siege of Jerusalem, which had cost him £800, 'at hir pleasure and pryce'; but he was not a particularly attractive or popular figure. Fabyan describes him as 'replete & lumpysh', and in fairness to the Woodvilles it must be said that the 'othir sort' who took possession of his country property in Essex no less 'destroyed his dere in his park his conyes & hys ffysh wythowth reson and spoylid his howse w'owth pyte'. He was tried before Sir John Markham, Chief Justice of the King's Bench, and found not guilty of treason but guilty of misprison of treason (being aware that the crime was being committed but not revealing it) and was ordered to be fined at the King's pleasure. His penalty was set at £8,000 less the value of the goods taken by Rivers, Fogge and others,[22] and Queen Elizabeth added to his woes by demanding an additional 800 marks to which she was entitled in such cases according to the ancient right of 'Queen's Gold'. She has been much criticised for what is claimed to be an example of an unpleasantly vindictive streak in her character, but closer examination of the evidence suggests that such a conclusion is again rather doubtful. Elizabeth was certainly entitled to the money – to accuse her of undue harshness on these grounds would be to condemn all previous queens who had exercised the privilege – and Cook does not seem to have been unduly impoverished since Fabyan records that, after he was released from prison, he 'buyldyd & purchacid as he dyd beffore'. Fabyan also implies that there were discussions between his master and some members of Elizabeth's council, that a number of presents were given, and 'by the ffavour of oon mastyr page then solycytour unto the Quene he hadd his ende, how well ther was noon opyn spech of it aftyr'. The precise meaning of this passage is uncertain, but it seems likely that he was not required to pay the whole amount.

King Edward did not, as we have already seen, wish to diminish the Earl of Warwick, still less to alienate him, but there were a number of incidents during these years which may, collectively, have produced this effect. Warwick probably felt that as well as having behaved foolishly, Edward had also made him appear foolish when he secretly married Elizabeth in the midst of negotiations for the hand of the Lady Bona; and several of the subsequent marriages contracted by members of the new Queen's family cannot have been much to his liking. He may have resented the misuse of his aged aunt, the dowager Duchess of Norfolk, and felt cheated by the loss of Anne of Exeter, who was to have been married to George, his nephew; and if he was disappointed in his hopes that the young Duke of Buckingham would one day marry his own eldest daughter, Isabel, he was hardly mollified when the King subsequently refused to sanction Isabel's union with his own brother, George, Duke of Clarence. He must have been equally unhappy with Edward's very public dismissal of his brother George, Archbishop of York, from the chancellorship on 8 June 1467 (Edward and a dozen supporters rode to the Archbishop's lodgings in Charing Cross and physically deprived him of the Great Seal), and was further disconcerted when the new Chancellor, Robert Stillington, Bishop of Bath and Wells, informed Parliament that the King was planning to invade France. Warwick had continued to favour an alliance with the French King, Louis XI, but found that his royal master (probably with Elizabeth's encouragement) leaned increasingly towards Burgundy. The Valois Dukes of Burgundy were legally vassals of the King of France, but in practice were semi-independent princes who dreamed of uniting their southern lands – the Duchy of Burgundy in France and the County of Burgundy in the Empire – with their northern possessions, Brabant, Flanders, Hainault, Luxembourg and other territories, to resurrect the old 'Middle Kingdom' of the Carolingians. Charles 'the Rash' (or 'the Bold'), who succeeded his father, Duke Philip the Good, in 1467 (when the great tournament in London was in progress), had formerly leaned towards the House of Lancaster (John of Gaunt was his mother's great-grandfather); but fear of King Louis, who was actively seeking to bring Burgundy and the other great semi-independent Duchy, Brittany, under his direct authority caused Charles to turn increasingly towards Yorkist England where close relatives of his Luxembourg subjects enjoyed positions of power. The result of these negotiations was that Charles married Margaret, King Edward's sister, who became his third wife in a magnificent ceremony at Damme on 3 July 1468, and Warwick's hopes of a closer relationship between his own country and his good friend King Louis were at an end.

It is likely that some of these events upset Warwick more than others, but none of them appears to have been critical. He may have regarded the Woodvilles as upstarts and disliked the way in which they had cornered the marriage market, but he did not, apparently, object when his nephew, Lord Maltravers, was married to the Queen's sister Margaret, when William, Lord Hastings (another newcomer) married his sister Katherine, or when his aunt, the widowed Duchess of Buckingham, wed Walter Blount,

Lord Mountjoy, who had been ennobled as recently as 1465. Edward's alliance with Burgundy no doubt irked him – the knowledgeable Croyland continuator thought it 'the real cause of dissension between the king and the earl'[23] – but it clearly did not upset the relationship to the extent that Warwick felt unable to escort the Princess Margaret to Margate on her way to her marriage with Duke Charles. He was surely pragmatic enough to appreciate that his recommendations would not always be heeded,[24] and that as Edward grew in stature he would, like all kings, make his own decisions. But he had probably not anticipated the extent to which Elizabeth's relatives would contrive to ingratiate themselves into the royal circle and become the King's trusted councillors and the companions of his leisure. Woodhouse, Edward's fool, might jest that he had 'passyd thorwth many cuntrees of your realm and in placys that I have passid the Ryvers been soo hie that I coude hardly scape thorw theym',[25] but Warwick could never have forgotten that it was he who had made Edward king while the Woodvilles were fighting for Lancaster, and found it intolerable that their influence should now be as great, if not greater, than his. The strains caused by this ill feeling can only be glimpsed in the records, but as early as January 1468 the Earl refused a summons to attend the King at Coventry as long as Earl Rivers and Lords Scales and Herbert remained with him. It was only after the intervention of friends and a meeting between Archbishop Neville and Rivers at Nottingham that Warwick agreed to comply with the order; and although he unbent sufficiently to speak cordially with Herbert and other members of Edward's circle, there was no reconciliation with Rivers and Scales. It is almost certainly no coincidence that, in the same month, the Woodville family seat at the Mote, Maidstone, was attacked by a mob and pillaged, and, in the words of Robert Fabyan, 'many murmurous talys ran in the cite atwene therle of Warwyk & the Quenys blood'. Elizabeth must have been aware of these tensions, but as the year 1469 dawned, she could have had no inkling of what troubles lay ahead.

3

Disaster and Recovery

King Edward's underlying problem was that by 1469 his 'honeymoon' with his subjects was long over and many of them were disappointed that his government had failed to fulfil their expectations. A number of contemporaries can be found complaining that the taxes which he demanded in order to raise armies had not led to campaigns and victories,[1] and there was dissatisfaction that little had been done to curb the lawlessness of Henry VI's reign. Edward had, admittedly, instituted an Act of Parliament designed to reinforce the restrictions on noblemen who retained private armies and reduce the duress and violence associated with them; but an exemption for what was tacitly described as 'lawful service' meant that a great nobleman like William, Lord Hastings, was still able to retain men on a large scale by larding his contracts with limiting phrases such as 'lawful and reasonable causes', 'as right, law, and conscience requireth', and 'according to the King's laws'. The Earl of Warwick had, of course, been very much a part of the new government in the early 1460s, but the more disillusioned he became and the further he distanced himself from it, the more ordinary people could regard him as a potential 'leader of the opposition' to the policies of the Crown.

The troubles which broke out in Yorkshire in April and June 1469 were in some measure a reaction to these and to other more local dissatisfactions, and whether or not Warwick was himself party to them they gave him an opportunity to convince his royal master that it was the Nevilles, and not the favoured Woodvilles, who were the real props of his throne. The first risings, led by obscure individuals known as Robin of Redesdale (or Robin Mend-All) and Robin of Holderness, were dispersed by John Neville, Earl of Northumberland, but by the end of June a new, and altogether more sinister, insurrection (including known supporters of the Nevilles) had taken their place. Its leader, another 'Robin of Redesdale', was probably Sir John Conyers of Hornby, Warwick's cousin by marriage, and it is possible to speculate that Edward had taken such scant notice of the earlier troubles that the Earl had concluded that only a more serious challenge would bring him to his senses. He could not rebel personally, of course – open disloyalty would have driven the King further into the hands of the Woodvilles and threatened his own position among the nobility – but he may have thought that a successful proxy uprising would allow him to step in at an appropriate moment and rescue his grateful master on his own terms.

Early in June Edward set out on a pilgrimage to Bury St Edmunds and Walsingham in East Anglia accompanied by his brother Richard, Duke of Gloucester, Earl Rivers, Lord Scales, and other members of his wife's family. He was sufficiently alarmed by the eighteenth of the month to issue orders for the raising of troops and the collection of war materials, but did not begin to move northwards via Fotheringhay (Northamptonshire), Stamford, Grantham and Nottingham until the first week in July. Fresh reports of the rebels' growing strength reached him at Newark, and he fell back on Nottingham to await the arrival of forces under the command of the Earls of Pembroke and Devon. He also learned, or feared, that it would be his (Woodville) councillors who would bear the brunt of the insurgents' fury (the slaughter of Richard II's advisers during the 'Great Rebellion' of 1381 was an obvious parallel), and he accordingly sent Earl Rivers and his son John to seek safety in Wales (or, according to MacGibbon, Grafton) and Lord Scales to Norfolk. Warwick, meanwhile, used the hiatus to marry his elder daughter Isabel to George, Duke of Clarence, on 11 July (it would be interesting to know what prospects he held out to his new son-in-law to persuade him to effectively desert Edward), and the next day issued a list of grievances placing Rivers, Jacquetta and their sons at the head of a group of royal supporters who, it was claimed, had 'causid oure seid sovereigne lord to geve of the seyd lyvelode and possessions to them above theire disertis and degrees' and 'to estrainge the true lordis of his blood from his secrete councelle'.[2] They called upon their supporters to meet them horsed and harnessed at Canterbury on 16 July, when, they said, they would take steps to lay their petition before the King.

Edward had found Elizabeth awaiting him on his arrival at Fotheringhay, and would have returned with her to Norfolk almost immediately if events had not demanded his attention elsewhere.[3] They agreed that she would undertake the journey alone, however, and soon plans were being made for her arrival in Norwich, the Mayor expressing great concern that his city observe the proper formalities 'by cause this shuld be hir first comyng hedir . . . she woll desire to ben resseyved and attendid as wurshepfully as evir was Quene a fore hir'.[4] Messengers were dispatched to ascertain precisely when and along which roads she intended to travel and to keep track of her progress, and a committee appointed to oversee the preparations which extended to repairing the crest of the conduit on the north side of St Andrew's churchyard! Elizabeth arrived with her daughters and entourage on 18 July, entering the city by the Westwick Gate where she was received by the Mayor and corporation. A stage had been constructed near the gate and covered with red and green worsted, adorned with figures of angels, scutcheons and banners of her arms and those of her husband, and it was here that she was greeted and entertained by the angel Gabriel (played by a friar), two patriarchs, twelve apostles, and sixteen virgins in mantles with hoods. There were also two giants made of wood and leather and stuffed with hay, their crests glittering with gold and silver leaf, and a pageant depicting the Salutation of Mary and Elizabeth, one of the themes employed at her coronation celebrations. The significance of this was duly explained to the Queen in a speech made by Gilbert Spirling, and we may suppose she listened politely and attentively, disguising her boredom in a suitably royal manner. The party then proceeded to the gates of the Friars Preachers, where another decorated stage had been erected, and here, seated in the great chair of St Luke's Guild that had been brought from the Cathedral, Elizabeth listened to Mr 'Fakke' and his boys singing. Heavy rain then interrupted the pageantry, and the royal party retired to their lodgings at the Friary (where dry clothes were provided for them) while local people tried to save what they could of the valuable coverings and decorations before they were completely ruined![5]

It is not known how long Elizabeth remained, or intended to remain, in Norwich, but the chamberlains' accounts indicate that she was still there in mid-August and it is unclear when she returned to London. King Edward seems to have remained largely inactive during the two to three weeks he remained at Nottingham. He may have thought that Pembroke and Devon would be able to deal with Robin's army, which had now moved around him and was marching southwards, and perhaps believed that he would be able to placate Warwick and Clarence when they met. In the event, however, the royalist forces were defeated by the northerners at Edgecote, in Oxfordshire, on 26 July, the King's chances having been marred by a dispute about billeting which divided Pembroke's and Devon's contingents; and Edward, who left Nottingham three days later, apparently still unaware of what had happened, was intercepted by Archbishop Neville at Olney on the road to London. There seems little doubt that he could have avoided capture, but perhaps still underestimated the anger of those who, until very recently, had been among his closest allies and friends.

Warwick now acted swiftly and ruthlessly. The Earl of Pembroke and his brother Sir Richard Herbert, who had been captured at Edgecote, were beheaded at Northampton the day after the battle, Devon was murdered at Bridgewater, and Earl Rivers and Sir John Woodville were likewise taken (either beyond Severn or at Grafton) and executed outside Coventry on 12 August. There is no evidence that they were formally tried and condemned – indeed, it is difficult to see how capital charges could have been brought against them when they were supporting a king who Warwick himself recognised – and their deaths and the allegation that Jacquetta had used sorcery to make Edward marry her daughter,[6] were really private acts of vengeance designed to remove the barrier which had developed between the Earl and his royal master. Word of the fate of her father and brother must have been brought to Elizabeth at Norwich within a few days of their executions, and would have plunged her, and those with her, into mourning. But grief may have soon given way to anger and a determination that Warwick and her brother-in-law Clarence would receive what she regarded as their just deserts.

With Edward in his custody, Warwick was now *de facto* master of the kingdom, but he soon found himself beset by problems he had not anticipated. The dislocation of the government, and the resulting uncertainty, gave several noble families the opportunity to use their private armies of retainers to settle old scores with their neighbours, and the obvious dissension among the Yorkists encouraged Sir Humphrey Neville of Brancepeth to proclaim King

Henry on the northern border. Warwick was forced to abandon the Parliament he had recently summoned (an assembly which the Milanese ambassador to France thought would declare Edward a bastard and give the crown to Clarence), and found that he had great difficulty in raising troops to suppress the uprising. There were, it seems, many who wished the Earl to have his rightful place in the royal council chamber, but few, if any, who thought it proper that he should hold the King a prisoner and rule through him. This realisation caused him to release Edward (whereupon they jointly raised the forces needed to defeat the Lancastrians), and the King then summoned his brother Gloucester and other noblemen and councillors to join him, and announced his intention to return to London.

Edward might now have called Warwick and Clarence to account for their lawless activity but preferred instead to offer them the hand of friendship and reconciliation. John Neville was required to exchange his earldom of Northumberland for the title of Marquess of Montague and extensive lands in Devon (to allow the heir of the Percy family to be restored to his ancestral title) while Warwick lost some of the offices he had granted to himself during the recent troubles. But their positions were otherwise respected and on 5 January 1470 the King created George Neville, John's son, Duke of Bedford, and arranged his betrothal to Princess Elizabeth. The idea of her daughter being married to the nephew of the man who had murdered her father and brother would have been anathema to Elizabeth Woodville, and the prospect of being obliged to receive the Nevilles as friends, to smile graciously upon them regardless of her true feelings, may have led to harsh words with the King.

Warwick's achievement had been to eliminate some of his Woodville rivals and to bring the Nevilles closer to the throne if Edward left no son to succeed him; but no formal reconciliation could restore him to the position of intimacy and authority he had enjoyed in the early days of Yorkist government and, inevitably, his thoughts again turned towards ruling through Clarence. His opportunity came when Richard, Lord Welles and Willoughby, his son Sir Robert Welles and his brothers-in-law Sir Thomas de la Launde and Sir Thomas Dymmock (who effectively represented the Lancastrian interest in Lincolnshire) ransacked Gainsborough Old Hall, the home of Edward's Master of the Horse, Sir Thomas Burgh, and drove him out of the shire. On 4

March 1470 Edward announced that he would deal with the trouble personally, and the prospect of the King approaching Lincolnshire and Yorkshire with a powerful army struck fear into the hearts of those who had recently been pardoned for their involvement with Robin of Redesdale. The result was that Sir Robert Welles proclaimed himself 'grete capteyn of the comons of Linccolne shire' and called on his followers to resist King Edward who, he claimed, was 'comyng thidre to destroie the comons of the same shire'. Edward did not immediately connect Warwick and Clarence with the uprising for on 8 March he sent them commissions to raise troops on his behalf in Warwickshire and Worcestershire; but there was no doubting their complicity when four days later he clashed with and defeated the rebels at the Battle of Empingham (or 'Lose-Cote Field'). The Lincolnshire men are said to have advanced shouting '*A Clarence! a Clarence! a Warrewike!*' Some of them wore the Duke's livery, and Sir Robert Welles and the other leaders are said to have admitted under interrogation that they were 'partiners and chef provocars of all theire treasons'[7] and that they intended to replace Edward with Clarence. The King still hoped to avoid an open breach with his brother and his father-in-law, who he probably thought would make 'a timely and discreet submission' now their schemes had been stymied. He stopped short of proclaiming them traitors, merely ordering them to disband their forces and wait upon him; but this led only to an increasingly acrimonious correspondence in which they refused to obey him until they received safe conducts and pardons. Edward finally lost patience and told them bluntly that unless they submitted by 28 March they would be formally indicted of treason, whereupon they fled northwards (hoping, perhaps, that Thomas, Lord Stanley, Warwick's brother-in-law, would assist them) and then, disappointed, took ship for Calais. Warwick's problem throughout all his machinations had been that the peerage as a body had declined to support a cause 'based on nothing more appealing than personal ambition and wounded pride'.[8] Even his brother John had remained loyal to King Edward, and it is possible to share Elizabeth Woodville's relief that her enemies had chosen to cross her husband openly and that her opinion of them was increasingly his too.

Warwick and Clarence were refused access to Calais (John, Lord Wenlock, the Earl's deputy, was favourably disposed towards him but dare not succour him under such circumstances), and after spending some two months preying on shipping in the Channel they dropped anchor, laden with booty, at the mouth of the Seine. Their arrival presented Louis XI with a golden opportunity to mount a challenge to King Edward in the hope of destroying the dangerous Anglo-Burgundian alliance, and before long Louis was spinning his web around the Earl and his bitterest enemy and now fellow-exile, Queen Margaret. He brought them together at Angers where, on 22 July, after much persuasion and soul-searching, Margaret pardoned Warwick for all the wrongs he had done the House of Lancaster (keeping him on his knees for a full fifteen minutes) and then received his homage and fealty as a faithful subject. It was agreed that Margaret's son, Prince Edward, would marry Warwick's younger daughter, Anne, when the Earl had restored Henry VI in England, and Warwick and Clarence, who must have been at least dimly aware that his hopes of becoming the next king of England had receded, began to prepare for an invasion. Edward did not, as some continental writers thought, ignore the Duke of Burgundy's efforts to warn him of the impending danger – indeed, all reasonable precautions seem to have been taken – but he was at the mercy of the inability of his own and the Duke's ships to blockade his enemies into French ports for a long period, and could do nothing to prevent the winds which ultimately scattered his own ships from blowing Warwick and Clarence to the coast of England. In late July there was a new rising in northern England led by Henry, Lord Fitzhugh of Ravensworth, another of Warwick's brothers-in-law, and although this was defeated Edward found himself in Yorkshire, far from his capital, when Warwick, Clarence, the Earl of Oxford and Jasper Tudor, the Lancastrian Earl of Pembroke, landed at Dartmouth and Plymouth and proclaimed King Henry on 13 September. Edward moved southwards with his own company (which included his brother Gloucester and Lords Rivers and Hastings) and summoned the Marquess of Montagu to join him; but when he reached the vicinity of Doncaster or Nottingham he received word that the Marquess had turned his coat and joined his brother Warwick. John Neville seems to have considered his promotion an inadequate recompense for the loss of the princely earldom of Northumberland, and his defection, and the popular welcome given to Warwick and the Lancastrians, left Edward with little alternative but to seek safety in flight. A dash across Lincolnshire brought the royal party to King's Lynn, where Rivers had influence, and they sailed for Burgundy on 2 October. It is said the King was almost drowned in the Wash and was later pursued and nearly captured by some hostile Hanseatic vessels; but he and his friends were well received by Louis de Gruthuyse, Duke Charles's governor, when they landed at Alkmaar, and were provided with money and accommodation in Holland.

When news of Warwick's return to England reached Queen Elizabeth in London she began to provision the Tower to withstand a siege. But when it became clear that the rebels were advancing in strength and resistance was hopeless she and her mother and three daughters entered the Westminster sanctuary the day before her husband fled abroad. She sent the Abbot to the Mayor and aldermen of the city urging them not to resist the Earl's followers or do anything which might cause them to invade the Abbey 'to despoil and kill her';[9] and two days later the Tower was peacefully surrendered to the rebels and the captive King Henry released. Elizabeth, who was nearly eight months pregnant, was justifiably afraid of the consequences of any upheaval. She knew only too well that Warwick blamed her, more than anyone, for his loss of influence, and although ladies were not often punished or victimised in the Wars of the Roses she could not assume that, in her case, her sex would save her from the fate of her father and brother. The Earl did not wish King Henry's restoration to be characterised by violence and bloodshed, however, and although the proclamation which he and Clarence had issued when they landed had exempted those they considered 'capitall ennemyes' from a general pardon they subsequently ordered that:

no manne, of what degree or condicion so evur he bee, presume, atempte or be soo hardy to defowle or destrouble the churchis or holy places of seintewaries (sanctuaries) of Westmynster and Seint Martynes (where the Bishop of Ely and other Yorkist supporters had sought safety) withinne the city of London or elleswhere. Ne vexe, troble spoyle, robbe in damage or hurte any mynister, servaunte, inhabitante or soiornaunte (sodjournant) withinne the seide hoole places in thaire bodyes or goodis movablis or unmovablis, for any maner cause or quarrell olde or newe, contrary to oure saide soveraigne lordes lawes and his peax (peace), uppon peyne of detthe.[10]

Indeed, far from seeking to punish Elizabeth 'the Qwen that was' (as John Paston the youngest laconically described her),[11] the new government paid Elizabeth, Lady Scrope, £10 to attend her (perhaps, in some measure, to supervise her) and she was allowed to receive gifts from the Abbot and 'half a beef and two muttons a week for the sustentation of her household' from a London butcher, John Gould.[12]

The Westminster sanctuary is described by Miss Strickland (relying on Dr Stukely, who had seen it) as 'a gloomy building . . . a massive structure, of sufficient strength to withstand a siege . . . which occupied a space at the end of St Margaret's churchyard (and) had a church built over it in the form of a cross'.[13] Within these powerful walls Elizabeth was allowed to prepare for the birth of her fourth child by King Edward, and on or shortly after 1 November (the exact date is uncertain) was successfully delivered of a son. The boy was baptised Edward after his absent father, the Abbot and Prior of Westminster and Lady Scrope standing godparents, and the enlarged family then adapted to the cramped conditions of their new abode as well as they were able while they waited on the turn of events. The hapless King Henry was lodged in the apartments which Elizabeth had prepared for her lying-in, while the Kingmaker concerned himself with the business of government; but he soon found that his triumph had not given him full authority or solved all his problems. King Edward and Richard of Gloucester were attainted and the brutal John Tiptoft, Earl of Worcester, executed; nonetheless, Warwick saw no alternative but to conciliate the majority of peers who had served the Yorkist government, allowing them to keep their former Lancastrian properties. This was obviously unacceptable to those lords who had suffered forfeiture and exile for their loyalty to King Henry, and many Yorkists still feared that, sooner or later, perhaps when Queen Margaret and her son returned to England, she would be likely to restore and reward her 'natural' supporters. This uncertainty extended to George, Duke of Clarence, who had benefited substantially from the 'Yorkist' land settlement, and Edward began to use the good offices of their mother and sisters to persuade his brother that his prospects were decidedly gloomy once Margaret recovered her authority. Edward was also assisted by King Louis's decision to declare war on Burgundy in December. Duke Charles had hitherto maintained a strict neutrality (ignoring Edward, although he was living in his territories) in order to minimise the risk of a joint attack by the King of France and his new English allies; but French hostility forced him to re-think his policy and at two meetings at the beginning of January 1471 he agreed to privately supply Edward with the means to recover his kingdom. These resources, three or four ships and 50,000 florins (£20,000) allowed the fugitive King to hire other vessels and the services of Flemish gunners and made his return to England an imminent probability rather than a distant hope.

It is likely that Edward and Elizabeth were able to secretly exchange messages during their separation and that she had learned of Duke Charles's agreement to assist her husband and of the family pressures being brought to bear on Clarence. She would initially have had few grounds for optimism – Queen Margaret's long exile and Henry VI's six years of incarceration would have given her no reason to suppose that her own troubles would be of short duration – but the new year brought hope that her discomfort and anguish would soon be over. Edward sailed on 11 March hoping to land in East Anglia, where he could expect help from the Woodville connection and the Dukes of Norfolk and Suffolk; but on reaching Cromer he was informed that the region was in the grip of the Earl of Oxford and decided to make for the Humber. The fleet, briefly scattered by adverse weather, brought Edward ashore at Ravenspur on 14 March, and he was reunited with the rest of his company, numbering perhaps 1,200, next day. The early signs were not promising. Kingston upon Hull, which had Lancastrian sympathies, refused to admit him, and he and a small number of followers gained access to York only after declaring (in imitation of Henry Bolingbroke, seventy-two years earlier) that he had come only to claim his father's Duchy. Both the Marquess of Montague and the Earl of Northumberland could have destroyed the little army, but neither of them moved decisively at this crucial moment. Northumberland, whom Edward had restored to his title, may have feared that he would again lose it to John Neville if Warwick remained master of the kingdom, and John himself may have been hampered by the strength of Percy influence in the region and by his own, almost hopeless, conflict of loyalties between his King and his brother. Their inactivity allowed Edward to gather recruits as he moved southwards via Doncaster (he soon cast off any illusion that his purpose was other than to reclaim his kingdom), but when he reached Nottingham he learned that

Warwick was in arms at Coventry and that the Earl of Oxford and the Duke of Exeter were shadowing his flank at Newark. A feint to the east caused Oxford and Exeter to retire southwards, and the Yorkists then marched rapidly on Coventry, where Warwick shut himself up and refused both an offer of pardon and a battle. George of Clarence, who had been in the West Country when Edward landed, was now marching up from Burford (Oxon), and on 3 April the brothers met and were formally reconciled. Initially Clarence may not have rated Edward's chances very highly, but having learned that the Earl of Shrewsbury and Lord Stanley had made no move to assist Warwick, and that influential Lancastrian peers like the Duke of Somerset and John Courteney, the heir to the earldom of Devon, were on the south coast awaiting the arrival of Queen Margaret, he decided to commit himself. He too tried to persuade Warwick to either fight or surrender, and when this was again unavailing Edward decided to strike out for London. Control of the capital (and its Lancastrian King) offered him obvious advantages, but he may also have been influenced by an overwhelming desire to see and rescue Elizabeth and their new-born son. The Londoners, who were inclined to favour him, admitted him on 11 April, and after recapturing Henry VI and a brief crown-wearing ceremony, he was reunited with his family. The 'kynge', says a contemporary chronicler:

> than went to the Qwene and comfortyd hir that had a longe tyme abyden and sojourned at Westmynstar, asswringe hir parson only by the great fraunchis of that holy place, in right great trowble, sorow, and hevines, whiche she sustayned with all mannar pacience that belonged to eny creature, and as constantly as hathe bene sene at any tyme any of so highe estate to endure; in the whiche season natheles she had browght into this worlde, to the Kyngs greatyste joy, a fayre sonn, a prince, where with she presentyd hym at his comynge, to his herts synguler comforte and gladnes, and to all them that hym trewly loved and wolde serve. From thens, that nyght, the Kynge retornyd to London, and the Qwene with hym, and lodged at the lodgynge of my lady his mothar; where they harde devyne service that nyght, and upon the morne, Good Fryeday; where also, on the morn, the Kynge tooke advise of the great lords of his blood, and othar of his counsell, for the adventures that were lykely for to come.[14]

The first 'adventure' was the approach of Warwick, Oxford, Exeter, and belatedly, Montague, who had pursued him hotly and whose forces reached St Albans the same day. Edward gathered his men and marched out to confront them, and on reaching Barnet on Saturday evening was informed that the Lancastrians were drawn up along a ridge of high ground about half a mile north of the town. Despite being outnumbered, next morning, Easter Sunday, he attacked at daybreak, moving forward under cover of a heavy mist. The Yorkists fought valiantly, but were being worsted until some of the Earl of Oxford's men, returning to the field after routing Lord Hastings's contingent, came up against their own forces who in the murk mistook Oxford's badge of a star with streams for the King's 'sun in splendour' and attacked them. Their cries of 'treason' led to general demoralisation (the old Lancastrians still had less than total confidence in their new Neville allies), and this, with the death of Montagu, turned the tide of battle in Edward's favour. The Kingmaker attempted to escape but was captured by some Yorkists and killed before anyone in authority could save him. Elizabeth, awaiting news in London, would have been mortified when fugitives from Hastings's contingent reached the city and rumoured that all was lost for her husband; and she then had to endure several hours of anxiety until one of his gauntlets was delivered to her as a token between them that all was well.[15]

King Edward returned to his capital in triumph, but almost immediately received word that Queen Margaret and her son, after various delays, had landed at Weymouth on the very day the Battle of Barnet had been fought. She and her friends soon raised a substantial army from the western counties (it is likely that many ordinary people still regarded Henry VI as their rightful king notwithstanding that a majority of powerful magnates supported the Yorkists), and Edward, fearing that this enthusiasm would be matched by pro-Lancastrian uprisings elsewhere in England, moved quickly to bring them to battle. His primary aim was to secure the crossings of the River Severn (to prevent his enemies from joining forces with Jasper Tudor's Welsh supporters and drawing strength from Cheshire and Lancashire), and the refusal of the governor of Gloucester to admit them forced them to march on to Tewkesbury, where they arrived, exhausted, on the evening of 3 May. Edward's forces had themselves marched thirty-six miles that day in order to catch the Lancastrians, but this notwithstanding he ordered them into action next morning. There seems little doubt that this battle was won by the superior generalship of Edward and Richard, Duke of Gloucester. The Duke of Somerset left his strong defensive position in the hope of striking a decisive blow against them, but was driven back up the hill and his forces routed when 200 spearmen the King had stationed at the corner of Tewkesbury Park to prevent an ambush attacked his flank. Edward then destroyed the Lancastrian centre, killing Margaret's son, its nominal commander, in the pursuit which followed, and the left wing succumbed in turn. Somerset and perhaps a dozen others who had no hope of pardon sought sanctuary in Tewkesbury Abbey, but Edward forcibly extricated them and had them executed in the market place on Monday 6 May. Queen Margaret, who had awaited news of the battle at a house called Payne's Place, west of Tewkesbury, also sought refuge in 'a powre religiows place'[16] (traditionally, Little Malvern Priory), and found herself in Yorkist custody within a matter of days.

The King, and by extension his family, had been seriously threatened by these last, diehard supporters of House of Lancaster, but their crimes did not justify his violation of the sanctuary. Edward was regarded by his contemporaries as a regal yet affable figure. Thomas More describes him as 'princely to behold, of hearte couragious, politique in counsaile . . . in peace juste and mercifull, in warre sharpe and fyerce, in the fielde bolde and hardye', and Dominic Mancini adds that 'he was easy of access to his friends and to others, even the least notable . . . so genial in his greeting, that if he saw a newcomer bewildered at his appearance and royal magnificence, he would give him courage to speak by laying a kindly hand upon his shoulder'.[17] But he could, as Mancini also remarks, 'assume an angry countenance (and) appear very terrible to beholders' and it was clearly this aspect of his personality which gained the upper hand at Tewkesbury and perhaps again when, in later years, he executed Clarence and disinherited young George Neville and the Countess of Warwick. Edward may not have been the easiest of men to live with, and it is significant that, on this occasion, Elizabeth was not present to intercede with him in a way that perhaps only she could.

The Battle of Tewkesbury completed King Edward's triumph over his enemies, but did not end the danger to his Queen. Almost immediately, word reached the victorious army that Thomas Neville, the 'Bastard of Fauconberg' (an illegitimate son of Warwick's late uncle, William Neville, Lord Fauconberg and Earl of Kent), had landed in southern England and was fermenting a new uprising in his father's titular county. The rebels reached London on 12 May and demanded entry; but the Mayor and leading citizens, fearful of pillage, decided to resist until the King could come to their rescue. The city levies, stiffened by the retinues of Earl Rivers and the Earl of Essex, spent the next three days resisting both the Bastard's land forces and bombardment from his flotilla; and the situation remained dangerous until Rivers and a picked force of men carried the attack to the enemy from a postern in the Tower and drove them across the fields to Poplar and Stepney with heavy casualties. Elizabeth and her son and daughters were with her brother in the Tower 'likly to stand in the grettest joperdy that evar they stode' as the contemporary writer has it;[18] and it is probable that she took counsel with the warriors as the battle raged around her and watched with no little trepidation as her brother hazarded the best of their forces in a direct attack. A defeat might well have culminated in the Bastard finishing the massacre of the Woodvilles begun in Robin of Redesdale's rebellion; and although his forces were discomfited rather than defeated, the arrival of an advance guard from the King's army effectively ended the rebellion. Edward again entered his capital to popular acclaim on 21 May, and King Henry, whose personal incompetence had not prevented others from using him to threaten the Yorkist dynasty and who no longer had a son to succeed him, died in the Tower that night.[19]

The twenty-five months from April 1469 to May 1471 are one of the most dramatic periods of English history. Edward IV had suffered insurrection, disloyalty, imprisonment, and exile, while Elizabeth had experienced the murder of her father and brother, the birth of her son in sanctuary, and had been besieged in the Tower while her husband hazarded his life in battle. There is no evidence that, throughout all this, she behaved with anything but a queenly dignity which won the admiration of loyal contemporaries. No writer saw fit to criticise her, and William Alyngton, the Speaker of the Commons, 'declared before the Kinge and his noble and sadde counsell, thentente and desyre of his Comyns, specially in the comendacion of the womanly behaveur and the greate constance of the Quene, he beinge beyonde the See'.[20] King Edward remains the only English monarch deposed by force of arms who was successful in recovering his kingdom, thanks in part to a measure of good fortune. It is clear that if Warwick, Queen Margaret, and the Bastard of Fauconberg had been able to coordinate their military activity the outcome might have been very different, and more direct and decisive action by the Kingmaker in the days immediately after Edward's landing could have ended his challenge still earlier. Edward succeeded because he conducted his campaign with great energy and resolution; and it is interesting to compare his behaviour here and in the Lincolnshire rebellion with the apparent lethargy which led to his capture in Robin of Redesdale's uprising after a battle fought in his name in which he played no part. Warwick's conduct is also hard to fathom. His involvement in the Lincolnshire troubles was more than a figment of the imagination of Yorkist propagandists (the rebels' confessions, if exaggerated, can hardly be dismissed as worthless),[21] but it is difficult to see what opportunities he hoped to gain from Sir Robert Welles's victory in March 1470 that Robin of Redesdale's success had not given him eight months earlier. The whole episode raises more questions than it answers, but if, as Professor Ross suggests, it 'brought out the best in Edward',[22] perhaps it brought out the best in Elizabeth too.

4

A New Beginning

King Edward's first task on recovering his kingdom was to deal with those who had opposed him. Several minor leaders were executed and a number of towns, lords and bishops were obliged to buy pardons, but the retribution meted out to those who had supported Henry VI's restoration was strictly limited. The Bastard of Fauconberg was pardoned in June 1471 (although he was executed for another offence three months later); and George Neville, Archbishop of York, remained on good terms with Edward until he was suddenly arrested on the night of 25 April 1472. He had probably been intriguing with the fugitive Earl of Oxford; and was sent to join him in Hammes castle after Oxford's abortive attempt to seize St Michael's Mount in Cornwall in February 1474. The Archbishop was released to enjoy what little life and wealth remained to him in November, but Oxford only regained his liberty when he escaped ten years later. Henry Holland, Duke of Exeter, was sent to the Tower,[1] whereupon his wife, Edward's sister, promptly divorced him and married her lover, Sir Thomas St Leger; and Queen Margaret was lodged in the same prison until King Louis ransomed her in 1475. It is not known if Elizabeth visited or otherwise saw her vanquished rival, but she would surely have sympathised with her for the loss of her husband and her only child at Tewkesbury (a sympathy sharpened by the realisation that her own family might have suffered a similar fate in other circumstances); and Miss Strickland may not be inaccurate when she asserts that 'the imprisonment of queen Margaret was at first very rigorous, but it was, after a time, ameliorated through the compassionate influence of Edward's queen'.[2] Margaret fared little better when she gained her liberty: no sooner had she surrendered her lands and rights in England to Edward to obtain her release than Louis deprived her of her French inheritance as the price of her rescue, and she lived in comparative penury on the small pension he allowed her until her death in 1482. Jasper Tudor held out for a time in Pembroke castle but then escaped to Brittany taking his nephew, Henry, with him, thus beginning fourteen years of exile beyond the Yorkist kings' reach.

King Edward's second, and more pleasant, task was to reward those who had remained loyal to him during this difficult period. Richard, Duke of Gloucester, and William, Lord Hastings, who inherited Warwick's authority in the north and the west midlands respectively, were the principal beneficiaries of his generosity, but he did not forget the lesser individuals who had helped him or those who had assisted his Queen. Margery Cobbe, her midwife, and Domenico de Serigo, her doctor, were given annuities of £12 and £40 respectively; Thomas Milling, Abbot of Westminster, who had sheltered the royal family, was appointed the infant prince's chancellor and, three years later, preferred to the bishopric of Hereford; and John Gould, who had supplied Elizabeth with beef and mutton, was granted leave to load a royal ship, the *Trinity of London*, with 'oxehides, ledde, talowe, and all other merchandises except staple ware'.[3] But however much Edward appreciated the risks taken by his own subjects, he probably felt an even deeper sense of gratitude towards Louis de Gruthuyse, who had received him cordially in his darkest hour when even Duke Charles, his brother-in-law, had stood aloof. Gruthuyse was invited to England in September 1472, created Earl of Winchester, and lavishly entertained by the Yorkist court. Edward and Elizabeth greeted him personally on his arrival at Windsor Castle, Bluemantle Pursuivant recording that:

when he had spoken w^t the Kinges good grace and the quene, he was accompanied to his chamber by me lorde Chamberlein (Hastings), Sir John A Parre, w^t dyuers moo . . . . When they had sopte, my lord chamberleyn had hym againe to ye Kinges chamber, and incontinent the Kinge had hym to ye quenes chamber, wher she sat plainge w^t her ladyes at the morteaulx (a game resembling bowls), and some of her ladyes and gentlewomen at the closheys (closh, or ninepins) and daunsing. And some at dyuers other games accordinge. The whiche sight was full plesant to them. Also ye Kinge daunsed w^t my lady Elizabethe, his eldest doughter. [The following evening] the quene dyd order a grete banket in her owne chambre. At the wch banket were the Kinge, the quene, my lady Elizabethe the Kinges eldest doughter, the Duches of Excester, my lady Ryuers, and the lorde Gruthuse, settinge at oone messe, and at the same table sat the Duke of Bokingham, my lady his wyff, w^t diuers other Ladyes, whose names I have not, my Lorde Hastinges, Chamberleyn to the Kinge, my lorde Barnes (Berners), chamberleyn to the quene, John Grutehuse son to ye forsaid lorde, Mr George Bart, secretory to the Duc of Burgoine, Loys Stacy, usher to the Duke of Burgoine, [and] George Mytteney: also certeyn nobles of the kinges owne courte. Item, there was a syde table, at the wch sat a grete vewe of ladyes, all on ye one syde. Also in the vtter chamber sat the quenes gentlewomen all on one syde. And at the other syde of the table agenest them sat as many of the lorde Gruthuse servauntes: as touchinge to ye abondant welfare, lyke as hyt ys accordinge to soche a banket. And when they had sopt, my Lady Elizabeth, the Kinges eldest doughter, daunsed w^t the Duke of Bokingham: and dyuers other ladyes also. And aboute ix of the clocke the king and the quene w^t her ladies and gentlewomen brought ye sayde lorde Grutehuse to iij chambers of Pleasance, all hanged and besyne w^t whyt sylke and lynnen-clothe, and all ye flowers couered w^t carpettes. There was ordeined a bed for hym selff of as good downe as coulde be thought, the shetes of Raynes, also fyne fustyan, the counterpoyne cloth of gold furred w^t ermyne, ye tester and ye seler (canopy) also shyning clothe of gold, curtens of whyt sarsenette: as for his bed shete and pelowes [they] were of the quenes owen ordinaunce. In ye ij^{de} chamber was an other of astate, the wch was alle whyt. Also in the same chamber was made a couche w^t fether beddes, hanged w^t a tent knit lyke a nett; and there was ye coberd. Item, in the iij^{de} chamber was ordeined a bayne (bath) or ij, wch were covered w^t tentes of whyt clothe. And when the Kinge and the quene, w^t all her ladyes and gentlewemen, had shewed hym these chambres, they turned againe to theire owne chambres, and lefte ye said lorde Grutehuse there, accompanied w^t my lorde chamberleyn, wch dispoyled hym and wente bothe to gether in the bane.[4]

Gruthuyse's reception and ennoblement were appropriate rewards for the good service he had rendered, but were also part of the process of publicly re-establishing the Yorkist dynasty. The King and Queen went to Canterbury on pilgrimage in September 1471 (Sir John Paston wrote that 'nevyr (were) so moche peple seyn in pylgrymage hertofor at ones, as men seye'),[5] and there were crown-wearing ceremonies on Christmas Day and again on Twelfth Night, although Elizabeth did not wear hers on the latter occasion 'because she was grete with childe'.[6] Their son was created Prince of Wales on 26 June 1471 (probably as soon as was possible in the circumstances), and twelve days later was given his own council headed by his mother, the Archbishop of Canterbury, the Dukes of Clarence and Gloucester, and Lord Rivers. They were all charged to advise and counsel him until he reached the age of fourteen, but the day-to-day running of his affairs was placed in the hands of a sub-committee empowered to take decisions 'with the advice and express consent of the Queen'.[7] King Edward clearly felt that his wife was the best person to undertake this supervisory responsibility, which she fulfilled, apparently entirely satisfactorily, for the next twenty months (until a separate household was created for the Prince at Ludlow in Shropshire), notwithstanding the deaths of her mother, Jacquetta, in May 1472 and her newborn daughter, Margaret, shortly before Christmas.

It is impossible to estimate how much Elizabeth owed to her mother's encouragement and influence, but there must be a distinct likelihood that without it, she would have found her task considerably more daunting. Jacquetta had made the practical arrangements for the royal wedding and helped the young couple meet secretly in the months which followed; she had been present on all the great state occasions of her daughter's reign and at her confinements;[8] and she had joined her in sanctuary in her darkest hour in 1470 and assisted in the successful delivery of Prince Edward. She was undoubtedly Elizabeth's closest confidant, and the charges of witchcraft brought against her by the Earl of Warwick in his moment of triumph, however baseless, indicate that he regarded her as a shrewd and potentially dangerous political operator.[9] The Sir Thomas Cook affair suggests she was among the most ruthless of the Woodvilles, although the citizens of London had had cause to be thankful that her personality and diplomacy had helped prevent Queen Margaret's undisciplined army from entering the city after the Lancastrian victory at the second Battle of St Albans in 1461. She had the craft, and the mettle, of a great medieval lady, and it is possible that without her Elizabeth would not have become Queen.

The Prince's household at Ludlow, dominated by his governor Earl Rivers, was essentially part of the process by which the King sought to control the regions through the influence of powerful, locally based, noblemen. Neither William Herbert, Earl of Pembroke (whose father had been executed after Edgecote), nor Henry Stafford, Duke of Buckingham, his fellow Woodville-in-law (whose estates in the area made them the more obvious choices) seem to have been highly regarded by Edward; and by February 1473 it had become apparent that only royal intervention could reduce Wales and the Marches to order. Elizabeth's influence over her son was inevitably diminished by this decision, but she remained wholly committed to his interests. She accompanied him to Ludlow in the spring of that year, and although pregnant with Prince Richard (who was born at Shrewsbury in August) also went with him to Hereford to help investigate a spate of robberies and murders both there and in Shropshire.[10] Sir John Paston heard reports that she would spend Easter with the King at Leicester, but she was still at Ludlow on 30 April and her return to London may have been still further delayed.

It has been suggested that Elizabeth and her brother used the disorder in Wales to persuade Edward that the creation of a family hegemony in the region would be in the best interests of the kingdom.[11] Earl Rivers, it is claimed, ruled the area as a personal fiefdom, and he and his sister not only held two of the three keys to the Prince's coffers but packed the boy's now enlarged council with Woodville supporters. These accusations are not unlike some others which allegedly illustrate the vaunting ambitions of the Queen and her relatives, relying on a similarly biased interpretation of the available evidence. There were certainly occasions when Rivers issued instructions under his own seal or associated his nephew in his decisions as an afterthought, but such actions only reflected the reality of the situation and do not imply an abuse of power. It is true that he appointed two of his councillors as deputy butlers and used the Prince's patronage to strengthen his position in East Anglia; but only a fool or a saint would have failed to reward his own followers or benefit personally when the opportunity arose.[12] In the same way, there can be no doubt that he and the other resident keyholder, John Alcock, Bishop of Rochester, the Prince's tutor and president of his council, kept a tight grip on the council's finances, but again, there is no suggestion that they behaved improperly and Rivers sometimes used his own money to pay his nephew's bills. The extended council consisted, initially, of twenty-five members, seven of whom (including Clarence, Gloucester, Hastings and the Archbishop of Canterbury) were either too elderly or too committed in other areas to play a significant part in the administration of the Prince's baliwick. This still left eighteen working members, of whom only four, Elizabeth, Rivers, Sir Richard Haute and Sir John Fogge, were members of the extended Woodville family, and only three others besides Alcock who were associated with them: Abbot Milling of Westminster, Edward Story, Bishop of Carlisle, Elizabeth's confessor, and Richard Fiennes, Lord Dacre of the South, her steward and master forester in her lordship of Pevensey. They had proportionately greater representation on the smaller committee which ran the day-to-day affairs of the principality (Rivers, Alcock, Haute, Dacre and Bishop Story were all members), but even here their numbers were matched by Thomas Vaughan, the Prince's chamberlain, William Alyngton, a former Speaker of the Commons, Walter Devereaux, Lord Ferrers of Chartley, and the lawyers Richard Martyn (who was destined to become Bishop of St David's) and John Sulyard.[13] There is, moreover, no evidence that men like Fogge, a long-time royal servant, or Milling, were more committed to the Woodvilles than they were to the King and the good of England, and it is significant that of seven individuals added to the council after 1473 (to replace those who had died or retired) only Richard Grey, Elizabeth's younger son by her first marriage, might have been chosen for his family connections. There can be little doubt that these men were appointed primarily for their ability rather than for their commitment to a Woodville agenda, and Rivers and his friends would surely have set about acquiring land in the region if they had intended to bring the principality and the Marches permanently under their own authority.[14] It seems likely that if Edward IV had assigned this role to another nobleman or connection it would have been deemed a reasonable and necessary way of establishing effective government in the region, but because he chose, or allowed, the Woodvilles to undertake the responsibility there is an almost automatic assumption that they were up to no good!

The same might be said of the King's decision to use Thomas Grey, Richard's elder brother, to establish royal authority in the West Country. Here, the old Lancastrian leaders of the region, the Hungerfords and the Courteneys, had perished in the recent conflicts along with the Yorkist Earl of Devon; and although local men such as Thomas Bourchier (who had married Devon's widow), and Sir Thomas St Leger were dependable, the Duke of Clarence, the one powerful magnate in the area, was not. Edward initially sought to bolster royal authority by obtaining Elizabeth's agreement to appoint influential local figures, men like Sir Roger Tocotes, to the stewardships of her properties in Wiltshire, Dorset and Gloucestershire, but even this was not, apparently, enough. Thomas Grey had been appointed to commissions in Wales and the Marches in 1473 and 1474 (although he was never a member of the Prince's council), but in 1474 the King and Elizabeth persuaded Lord Hastings to allow him to marry Hasting's step-daughter, Cecily Bonville, heir to the west country baronies of Bonville and Harrington, and the next year he was created Marquess of Dorset. His mother's first attempt to provide him with a westerly inheritance had faltered when Anne Holland died within a year of their marriage; but it may have been this earlier connection with the region which prompted the King to choose him to serve the royal interest in the baliwick and endow him with the status and lands needed to establish his credibility. Elizabeth's hopes of inheriting the Exeter estates if his marriage to Anne Holland (for which she had paid 4,000 marks) proved childless – she had persuaded the King to grant her the reversion of lands which would normally have passed to the Crown if and when the girl died without issue – had been dented by an arrangement dated 26 August 1467 which settled the inheritance on Anne but gave a prior residual interest to her mother, Duchess Anne, and the heirs of her body. The result (which could hardly have been foreseen at the time) was that Duchess Anne's daughter by Sir Thomas St Leger (another Anne) became entitled to succeed to her mother and half-sister's properties, and this may explain why, in 1474, Elizabeth was careful to provide that Richard, her second son, would marry Cecily if Thomas pre-deceased him, and that the £2,500 she paid for the arrangement would be recouped by her collecting the revenues of the Bonville and Harrington properties until her daughter-in-law reached the age of sixteen.[15] There can be no doubt that she looked after both her own and her sons' interests, but these are hardly valid grounds for criticism. Thomas, as Edward IV's stepson and the future King's half-brother, was always likely to be entrusted with high office, and although little is known of his tenure of the western counties his length of service, and the lack of complaint or upset, would suggest that he ably fulfilled the role.

The Queen and some of the more senior members of her family clearly played a major part in the re-establishment and consolidation of King Edward's rule after the troubles of 1470–71, but the process was not without its difficulties and did not eliminate the friction which had characterised the Yorkist court in the previous decade. Earl Rivers had asked permission to go on a pilgrimage almost before the dust of the re-adeption had settled, and Edward, who regarded the request as singularly ill-timed when so much remained to be done in England, deprived him of the captaincy of Calais and appointed Lord Hastings. Rivers responded by spreading rumours that Hastings would deliver the stronghold to Louis XI; and More records that he was so successful that Hastings was briefly 'farre fallen into the kinges indignacion, and stode in gret fere of himselfe'.[16] Hastings was the King's boon companion and most faithful servant, and it is probable that only Elizabeth could have convinced her husband, however momentarily, that he was likely to betray him. Her resentment may have stemmed from their dealings shortly before her second marriage, but, according to More's account, she also 'specially grudged, for the great fauoure the kyng bare hym, and also for that shee thoughte hym secretelye familyer with the kynge in wanton coumpanye'.[17] Hastings was some twelve years the King's senior and Elizabeth may have regarded him as a man of the world who could have influenced her husband for the better but was instead leading him astray. Thomas Grey is said to have quarrelled with Hastings 'because of the mistresses whom they had abducted, or attempted to entice from one another',[18] but they were undoubtedly rivals for their royal master's affections and it may have been an ageing favourite's fear of a younger supplanter that led Hastings to suborn informers and seek to damage reputations at court. It is likely that the John Edwards who in August 1482 confessed before the Council at Westminster that he had traduced Dorset and Rivers before, and obviously under pressure from, the royal council at Calais, was one of his agents, and the fact that Rivers had Edwards's admission that the accusations were groundless copied for circulation reveals the by now public nature of the feud.[19]

It is, of course, possible that these differences were no more than isolated incidents, and some writers have argued that they should not be regarded as part of an ongoing quarrel. Hastings, it is suggested, would not have allowed Thomas Grey to marry his stepdaughter if he had been completely alienated from the Woodvilles, and he cooperated, apparently amicably, with them on a number of occasions during the 1470s. He and Dorset worked together as trustees in the settlement of a dispute between John Brooke, Lord Cobham, his mother and her second husband,[20] and he nominated both Grey brothers for election to the Order of the Garter.[21] Elizabeth, moreover, gave his sister, Elizabeth Donne, and his sister-in-law (Anne, the wife of his brother Ralph) places among her ladies,[22] again implying that relations between them were not as strained as is sometimes suggested. The most likely explanation, however, is that their mutual obligation to serve Edward IV, and their presence at his court, required them to preserve at least a veneer of affability, and although Mancini's 'deadly feud'[23] may owe something to the gossip he had heard during his brief time in London, it is impossible to dismiss the knowing Croyland writer's comment that 'there had long existed extreme ill-will between the said lord Hastings and them'.[24]

But however much the Hastings–Woodville/Grey quarrel disturbed the royal polity in the early and mid-1470s, there can be no doubting the King's difficulties in containing the struggle between his two brothers, the Dukes of Clarence and Gloucester, for the lion's share of the Kingmaker's estates. Edward initially granted the Earl's personal, entailed, Neville lands to Gloucester, and the general inheritance, including the vast Beauchamp-Despenser birthright of his countess, to Clarence in right of his wife Isabel, although there were others who had valid claims to them. George Neville, Duke of Bedford, was heir to his uncle's entailed properties; Anne Neville, Isabel's younger sister, was entitled to a half share of the general inheritance; and the Countess of Warwick, whose lands were being re-distributed as though she were in some way responsible for her husband's treason, was in sanctuary at Beaulieu Abbey in Hampshire, and far from dead! Gloucester apparently felt that his unswerving loyalty to his brother merited a larger share of the lands than he had been given, and he decided to marry the widowed Anne Neville (who was living in Clarence's custody) in order to pursue her claims. Anne may not have found the proposal unattractive – she would have come to know Gloucester well in the years he had trained under her father at Middleham Castle and he was clearly the only potential husband who might successfully challenge her sister and brother-in-law – but Clarence was determined to keep what he had been given. He is said to have concealed Anne as a kitchen maid until Gloucester sought her out, rescued (or abducted) and married her, probably between mid-February and the middle of March 1472. Sir John Paston informed his younger brother that:

> yisterday (16 February) the Kynge, the Qween, my Lordes of Claraunce and Glowcester, went to Scheen to pardon; men sey, nott alle in cheryte; what wyll falle, men can nott seye. The Kynge entretyth my Lorde off Clarance ffor my Lorde of Glowcester; and, as itt is seyde, he answerythe, that he may weell have my Ladye hys suster in lawe, butt they schall parte no lyvelod, as he seythe; so what wyll falle can I nott seye.[25]

Elizabeth's part in this is uncertain, but Professor Hicks points out that she renewed a stewardship worth £100 a year to Gloucester on 23 February and so may have joined her husband in pressurising Clarence to compromise.[26] The result was that on 18 March Clarence agreed to surrender some properties to his younger brother and received in return a more secure title in others. He was formally created Earl of Warwick and Salisbury a week later, and among other perquisites became Great Chamberlain of England in Gloucester's place.

This might have been the end of the matter, but Gloucester was still dissatisfied.[27] The agreement seems to have held for some fifteen months, but in May 1473 the Countess of Warwick was allowed to leave sanctuary and went to live with Gloucester and her younger daughter in northern England 'men seye by the Kynges assent, wherto som men seye that the Duke off Clarance is not agreyd'.[28] There were rumours that Edward had restored the lady to her inheritance (which included much of what Clarence had retained under the 1472 settlement), and that she had then conveyed it to Gloucester, by which Clarence clearly felt his position threatened. Sir John Paston reported that by November 'ffor the most part (those) that be abowte the Kyng have sende hyddr ffor ther harneys, and it (is) seyd ffor serteyn, that the Duke off Clarance makyth hym bygge in that he kan, schewyng as he wolde but dele with the Duke of Glowcester; but (he added) the Kyng ententyth, in eschyewying all inconvenyents, to be as bygge as they bothe, and to be a styffeler atweyn them'.[29] It is possible that Edward had been told, or suspected, that Clarence had been in treasonable correspondence with his wife's kinsmen, the Archbishop of York and the Earl of Oxford, and that this is why he allowed Gloucester to undermine the agreement; but when it became apparent that there was no evidence to connect Clarence with the rebels, Edward decided that the earlier settlement must prevail. Clarence and Gloucester were recognised in Parliament as the legitimate heirs of the Earl of Warwick in May 1474, and Acts were passed which deprived the Countess of Warwick of her personal properties (she was effectively declared to be legally deceased) and prevented young George Neville from succeeding to the entailed lands. The King and his brothers needed no lessons in sharp practice from the Woodvilles, and the whole episode shows them in a thoroughly bad light.[30]

King Edward thus settled, or at least appeased, the domestic difficulties which attended his restoration, but foreign considerations loomed equally large on his agenda. England's already difficult relationship with France had been further soured by the help King Louis had given the Earl of Warwick, and Edward was more than ever inclined to ally with Burgundy and Brittany, the two remaining semi-independent French feudatories, on the basis of mutual self-interest. He thought that if English troops assisted the two Duchies when Louis threatened their independence, they would join with England in a tripartite alliance against France and this would allow him to open a new phase of the Hundred Years' War. The complex series of negotiations in which the three states engaged between 1471 and 1475 need not concern us, but they were often more difficult than might have been expected. Both Charles the Bold and Duke Francis of Brittany were happy to accept English aid in resisting King Louis's predatory ambitions towards them, but they were, in the last resort, Frenchmen, and could not quite bring themselves to deliver France to an enemy. Parliament granted large sums to finance the great enterprise, but the collection of these was complicated by successive postponements of the invasion and Edward boosted his resources by requiring his wealthier subjects to pay additional subventions called 'benevolences'. These were ostensibly gifts in lieu of military service which the donors willingly offered their grateful sovereign, but there can be little doubt that Edward leaned heavily on some reluctant payers and the word became synonymous with unwarranted exactions thereafter. His preparations were complete by the early summer of 1475, and, the unreliability of his allies notwithstanding, what was described by a contemporary as the 'finest, largest, and best appointed force that has ever left

England'[31] was ordered to assemble at Barham Downs, near Canterbury. The Prince of Wales, now four and a half, was brought to London on 12 May and officially appointed head of state (with the title Keeper of the Realm) during his father's impending absence; and the government was placed in the hands of a council of prelates, peers and officials headed by Archbishop Bourchier of Canterbury and Bishop Alcock, who was also appointed temporary Chancellor while Bishop Rotherham of Lincoln was abroad. Earl Rivers had contracted to join the army with two knights, forty lances and 200 archers,[32] and so the Prince was transferred to the custody of his mother, who was allowed approximately £2,200 a year to maintain him and the remaining members of his household.[33] Elizabeth would have been concerned for the safety and success of her husband, but she was surely pleased that the turn of events had, however temporarily, reunited her with their elder son.

Edward left Canterbury for Sandwich on 20 June, and the same day sealed a will he had prepared in anticipation of his departure. He bequeathed his soul to 'allmighty God and to his glorious Moder oure Lady Saint Marie, Saint George, Saint Edward, and all the holy Companie of heven', and asked to be buried in St George's Chapel, where a silver and gilt (or at least copper and gilt) effigy and other remembrances were to be provided for him. He arranged for the payment of his debts, for the completion of St George's, and for the distribution of alms to the value of £200 annually 'for evermore', and made provision for his wife and younger son and his daughters' marriages. Cecily, his third daughter, who was now six years old, had been betrothed to the two-year-old Prince James of Scotland in October 1474 (principally to ward off trouble in the north during his absence), and he ordered that her dowry of 20,000 marks – 2,000 a year for the first three years and 1,000 thereafter, payable at St Giles's Church in Edinburgh every 3 February – be remitted accordingly. He was well aware of the fragility of such arrangements, however, and empowered the Queen and the Prince of Wales to settle the unpaid portion on any other husband they might choose for her if the present scheme faltered. The Princesses Elizabeth and Mary (and the unborn child the Queen was then carrying, if a girl) were to have 10,000 marks each if they accepted the husbands which Elizabeth Woodville and Prince Edward selected for them, but if they married contrary to their mother's and brother's wishes and were 'thereby disparaged' the money was to be used to pay the

King's debts instead. He named 'oure said derrest and moost entierly beloved wiff Elizabeth the Quene' as his foremost executor, and charged the others to respect her personal property 'catelles stuff beddying arrases tapestries verdours stuff of housholde plate and jouelx and all other thing which she now hath and occupieth, to dispose it freely at her will and pleaser without let or interruption'. She was also to be allowed to keep such of his own chattels 'as she shall thinke to bee moost necessarie and convenient for her' (only the ornaments and books he had bequeathed to St George's Chapel were excepted), and to divide others between their two sons 'by her discrecion', 'the Prince (of Wales) to have the preferrment in such therof as shal seme to her discrecion moost necessarie and convenient for his astate'. This is again testimony to the confidence which Edward placed in his wife's guardianship of their family's interests, and there is little doubt that he envisaged a significant role for her if he failed to return.[34]

In the event, the invasion amounted to little more than a brief incursion. Duke Francis of Brittany, who had promised Edward 8,000 troops as recently as 16 May, failed to join him, and the Burgundian army was engaged in a long and debilitating siege of the city of Neuss in the archbishopric of Cologne. Edward hoped that Duke Charles would abandon this in favour of their joint enterprise, but when he finally appeared, having kept the English waiting for ten days in Calais, it was with only a small bodyguard. The King knew that he could not seriously challenge the French without the support of his allies, but a venture which had cost so much to finance could not be abandoned before it had entered enemy territory. He therefore accepted Duke Charles's suggestion that the army should march eastwards through his Burgundian lands to Peronne, from which point they would then advance into France proper, to the town of St Quentin, which the Count of St Pol, Elizabeth's uncle, had promised to surrender to the English. The plan was then to proceed to Rheims for Edward's coronation before King Louis's forces, which had been stationed in Normandy in anticipation of an English attack in that direction, could intervene. But the Duke signally refused to allow the English to enter any of his towns, the Count of St Pol reneged on his undertaking and fired on the army at St Quentin, and the news that Rheims was heavily fortified and the King of France was threatening his supply lines left Edward with little alternative but to negotiate. He was perhaps fortunate that Louis also desired a peaceful outcome, and the two Kings opened discussions as soon as Duke Charles left to rejoin his army. They met at Picquigny on the Somme, near Amiens, on 29 August and concluded agreements which provided for a seven years' truce, for free trade between their two countries, for the marriage of the Dauphin and Princess Elizabeth, and for Edward to leave France on receiving 75,000 crowns (about £15,000) from Louis, who would continue to pay him 50,000 crowns (£10,000) annually for the rest of his life. The Dukes of Burgundy and Brittany were to be allowed to join the truce, but Charles the Bold angrily rejected the offer. He ignored his own failure to support the enterprise and instead accused Edward of reneging on their alliance by making a separate peace.[35]

King Louis's readiness to bribe the English to leave France is somewhat puzzling, but he clearly thought it to his country's advantage. An orderly withdrawal was preferable to a war of attrition, and there was the possibility that when Edward returned home without spoils of war or victories, his disappointed taxpayers would depose him. It is true that some 2,000 or more Englishmen who wanted battle and booty offered their services to the Burgundians; but the nobility had been sweetened with gifts and pensions, the merchants were pleased with the new trading arrangements, and there was apparently little general dissatisfaction with the outcome. When Elizabeth welcomed Edward home at the end of September she greeted a husband who, thanks more to good fortune than good judgement, was considerably wealthier than when he had left.[36]

5

Elizabeth the Queen

King Louis's pension allowed Edward to avoid asking Parliament for money (another factor which would have commended the 1475 agreement to his subjects), and permitted the royal couple to enjoy the most regal and secure phase of their reign. Elizabeth's personality and attitude to her role as queen are matters of opinion which have been, or will be, discussed in the appropriate places, but contemporaries who criticised her on other grounds were unanimous in their praise of her appearance. Dominic Mancini wrote that Edward had fallen in love with her because of her 'beauty of person and charm of manner', and Thomas More described her as 'both faire, of a good favor, moderate of stature, wel made and very wise'.[1] The surviving panel portraits of her are probably derived from a lost original, but they closely resemble the contemporary image in the north window of the Martyrdom Chapel of Canterbury Cathedral and are based on an authentic likeness. It is true that the high, plucked or shaven forehead, the large eyes, the straight nose tapering to a small pointed chin, and the long, graceful neck are all consistent with contemporary notions of ideal beauty, and whether or not the artist, or artists, has been guilty of some exaggeration, there can be no doubt that Elizabeth wished to be portrayed in this manner. In Plates 1 and 9 she is shown wearing a fashionable, tight-fitting dress with cloth of gold collar and cuffs and with her low-cut neckline modified by a band of cloth known as a *piece*. Her hair is worn tucked into a small, box-like cloth of gold cap overlaid by a veil which descends to just above her eyes, again emphasising her high forehead. She wears an elaborate quatrefoil jewel attached to a wide necklace, and another ornament, apparently suspended from a cord, which lays on her breast. There is, however, no corroborative evidence that a second decoration would have been worn in this manner (the style did not become popular until the Tudor period), and Frederick Hepburn suggests that it was an elaborate clasp or buckle which secured a wide belt immediately beneath the closing of her dress. A Tudor copyist may, he thinks, have failed to appreciate the existence of the belt, and was confused either by a lace worn to hold the *piece* in position or faint lines indicating a gauze scarf.[2] Her clothes then, were stylish and queenly, and complemented a *presence* which was undoubtedly admired.

Dress and beauty were only a beginning, however, and Elizabeth would soon have learned that she was expected to be more than a mere ornament of the court. We have already noticed a number of occasions – her coronation and churching ceremonies, her refounding of Queens' College and her part in the welcome given to Louis de Gruthuyse – when she fulfilled her own role and complemented that of her husband; but there were other responsibilities which demanded her attention and which could enhance her reputation as an able and prudent consort. The most informal of these, and therefore the hardest to glimpse in practice, was the giving of advice and counsel, a duty which flowed naturally from her close, personal relationship with her husband. Contemporaries would have thought this entirely appropriate – the Earl of Warwick probably suspected that she had encouraged Edward to favour her family in the marriage market and persuaded him to ally himself with Burgundy, but he had no real grounds for complaint in the matter since the final decision always lay with the King. The monarch was expected to choose between the various courses of action proposed to him; it was only when he proved incompetent to do so and allowed the Queen (or another councillor) to actually determine and drive his policy that the bounds of acceptability were exceeded. Elizabeth in all probability offered advice on these and other matters and there were undoubtedly occasions when that advice was taken; but she did not play Queen Margaret to her husband's King Henry and no one thought him clay in her hands.

Elizabeth, like other medieval queens, maintained her own, separate household, although officials could be transferred between hers and her husband's and the Queen's ladies might sometimes be married to the King's gentlemen. The costs of her household were met principally from the income from her dower properties, which amounted to about £4,500 per annum.[3] This was considerably less than the 10,000 marks (just under £6,700) which Joan of Navarre, Henry IV's second wife, and Henry V's bride,

Katherine of Valois, had received earlier in the century; but was in keeping with King Edward's determination to restore the Crown's solvency after his predecessor's mismanagement. Elizabeth's estates, the majority of them Duchy of Lancaster properties, were worth just over £6,100 gross and although prior charges reduced this to the £4,500 actually received by her Treasurer, John Forster, the income they yielded was more consistent than the customs duties and grants from the Exchequer which had formed part of Margaret of Anjou's notionally larger dower. The only evidence for Elizabeth's management of her finances derives from a single household account for the year 1466–67, which may be usefully compared with a similarly chance survival from Queen Margaret's reign dated 1452–53.[4] While we cannot assume that the years in question were necessarily average or typical, the overriding impression is that the Yorkist queen spent her smaller income more judiciously and that her establishment was altogether more modest and tightly run. She managed with fewer staff (seven maids-in-waiting to Margaret's ten, for example); her auditors regularly reduced claims for expenses; and although many fees were traditional her employees often received smaller payments than those engaged by her predecessor whenever there was scope for discretion. There were some extravagances – £14 10s spent on sable furs and £54 on goldsmith's wares, for example; but whereas Queen Margaret received over £7,500 (including nearly £3,000 arrears) in 1452–53 and still had a working deficit of £24, Elizabeth was left with a surplus of nearly £200 after meeting her expenses from her net receipts of £4,540 (which incorporated arrears of only £220) in 1466–67.[5]

These figures should not be taken too literally, however, since Forster, like most medieval accountants, would have been more concerned to demonstrate his honesty than to provide a full or complete record. We do not know how Elizabeth spent his two largest disbursements – the £919 paid to her Chamber to cover personal expenses and the near £1,200 allocated to her Great Wardrobe which was responsible for buying clothes and other materials – since he was quit when he had handed the money over; and there were other factors which did not directly concern him but would have worked in her favour at the beginning of her reign. Elizabeth's expenses were smaller because she did not (as yet) employ a full staff in 1466–67 (certain servants were not allocated to Queen Margaret until some time after her coronation), and it is probable that since the King and Queen were often together, some of Elizabeth's costs, the food for her attendants and other charges which could not be easily separated, were initially borne by the King's household. Margaret of Anjou had paid her husband £6 rising to £7 daily to compensate for this, something which Elizabeth did not do in the year in question; but an oblique reference in the Black Book of Edward IV to the effect that 'if hit please the king and hur highness hit hath byn vsed by quenez to pay a certen dayly for theyre dietes, whan she cumith to this court'[6] could imply that she was required to contribute to their maintenance after 1471–72.

What is clear though is that Elizabeth's lands, supplemented by grants from the Exchequer, provided her with the bulk of her income, and that perquisites like the above and sundry receipts, from sources such as Queen's Gold and wardships, were comparatively minor. Queen's Gold, described as an additional 'one-tenth of the value of any voluntary fine made in any of the king's courts', and which we have already noticed in connection with the Thomas Cook affair, had yielded Queen Eleanor of Castile £1,564 in 1289–90, more than she received from her estates; but it seems to have so fallen into abeyance (perhaps because it was seen to be a somewhat arbitrary and therefore unfair imposition) that Queen Margaret collected only £53 1s 4d in 1452–53 and Elizabeth a mere £37 in 1466–67. It is worth noting, however, that whereas Margaret pursued fifty-nine claims in the year of her account and was successful in only sixteen of them, Elizabeth obtained money from ten of just eleven such writs issued by her clerk Oliver Dynham. But whatever her talent for targeting suitable cases, her income from this source dwindled to a paltry £6 13s 4d in 1481–82 (the other year for which a figure is available) and it can never have been very substantial.[7] The same is true of wardships, although it may be noted that Elizabeth was allowed 500 marks (£333 6s 8d) a year by King Edward to maintain the young Duke of Buckingham and his brother in her household, of which she paid John Giles, whom she hired to teach them grammar, a mere £6 over a year and three-quarters!

Elizabeth's household was headed by her chamberlain, John Bourchier, Lord Berners, younger brother of the Earl of Essex, who received £40 a year for his services. The same sum was paid to each of her two senior ladies-in-waiting, her sister Anne Bourchier (now the wife of the Earl's son and heir) and her sister-in-law,

Elizabeth, Lady Scales, to her doctor Domenico de Serigo, and to her brother John Woodville, her master of the horse. Her two stewards, or carvers, Sir Humphrey Bourchier (Lord Berners's son), and Sir James Haute, another kinsman, received 40 marks; three more junior ladies-in-waiting, Lady Alice Fogge, Lady Joanna Norris, and Lady Elizabeth Overdale, received £20 each; Edward Story, her confessor, was given £10, the same sum that was divided between her three minstrels; and other damsels and attendants received amounts which ranged between £10 and 5 marks. Also fee'd were more mundane but indispensable officials like Forster, who served as receiver-general as well as treasurer; his chief assistant, Thomas Holbeche, clerk of the receipt; William Kerver, keeper of the great wardrobe, and Elizabeth's secretary, John Aleyn, soon to be replaced by John Gunthorpe. They were joined by Dr Roger Radcliff, her chancellor, whose warrants issued under her great seal facilitated the administration of the household, the law officers, John Dyve, her attorney-general, and Robert Isham, her solicitor-general (Isham had supported her in her dispute with Lady Ferrers during her widowhood), besides others, squires and the husbands of her ladies, who attended her court on a more casual or daily basis. She clearly used some of the offices within her gift to favour her relatives, but there is no evidence that their rewards were excessive (in the sense that they exceeded the fees paid to the equivalent staff in Queen Margaret's establishment) or that they did not fulfil their designated roles.

The real question, however, is to what extent did Elizabeth participate personally in the administrative and decision-making procedures in her household? Did she spend long hours discussing weighty problems with her officers and check their accounts (as her daughter, Queen Elizabeth of York did, for example), or is Professor Myers correct in his assumption that 'there is no reason to suppose that she understood finance beyond the usefulness of money for gratifying her desires'.[8] Myers thought that John Forster rather than Elizabeth was primarily responsible for the 'good housekeeping' which characterised her accounts in 1466–67; but it seems unlikely that senior employees like John Dyve and Roger Radcliff would have had their fees reduced or their expenses limited unless the Queen herself was closely involved in the process. The medieval aristocracy was characterised more by a rigorous competence than by dilatoriness when it came to managing their finances, and the notion that

Elizabeth was a rather frivolous lady who merely spent what her officials gathered is not supported by the available evidence. When she heard that Sir William Stonor (with whom she had previously been on good terms[9]) had been hunting deer in woods that formed part of her property, her stern and uncompromising response would have left him in no doubt of the consequences if the offence was repeated:

> To our trusty and welbeloved Sir William Stonor, knyght.
> By the Quene
> Trusty and welbeloved, we grete you wel: and where as we understand by report made unto us at this tyme that ye have taken upon you now of late to make maistries withynne our fforest and Chace of Barnewod and Exsille, and that in contempt of us uncourteisly to hunt and slee our deer withynne the same to our grete mervaille and displeasir, we wol ye wite that we entend to sew suche remedy therynne as shall accorde with my lordes laws. And whereas we herthermore understand that ye purpose under colour of my lordes Commyssion in that behalf graunted unto you, as ye sey, hastly to take the view and reule of our game of dere withyn our said fforest and Chace, we wol that ye shew unto us or our Counsell your said Comission, if any suche ye have. And in the mean season that ye spare of huntyng withynne our said fforest or Chace, as ye wol answere at your perill. Yoven under our signet at our Maner of Grenewiche the first day of August.
>
> Elysabeth[10]

Elizabeth's council consisted of her senior officials, her chamberlain, treasurer, stewards, secretary and attorneys, together with Duchy of Lancaster administrators and noblemen, who were not members of her household but who had connections with her personally or with her estates. The Queen, as one of the greatest landowners in England, needed expert guidance in the management of her properties, particularly with regard to the maintenance of their values, the settlement of disputes arising upon them, and the distribution of patronage and 'good lordship' in certain areas. It is likely that in Hertfordshire and East Anglia, where she had substantial holdings, her 'connection' was regarded as one of the dominant forces in the region, and there were undoubtedly those who brought their petitions to her because she was a great lady in a local as well as a national context. Her influence almost certainly led to the appointment of John Forster and her brother Anthony to the Bench in Hertfordshire, and Dr Horrox has suggested that 'the queen's interest in East Anglia was regarded as the main instrument of royal authority there by 1475'.[11] We have already noticed the Paston family's efforts to engage her assistance in 1469, but two years earlier she had taken the part of one Simon Bliaunt, a local Yorkist, who was then trying to evict the Pastons from the Fastolf manor of Hemnals in Cotton. The Earl of Oxford (who was also influential in the region) had apparently persuaded Bliaunt to allow him to appoint two arbitrators to examine the rival claims on the understanding that he would intervene personally if they failed to deliver their verdict by Easter. But Oxford (who seems to have been the Pastons' preferred patron when he was not in prison or exile for his adherence to Lancaster) had subsequently shown no inclination to displace his clients, and so Bliaunt appealed to the Queen.[12] Elizabeth's letter to the Earl is again typical of her firm, no-nonsense approach to the great and the good in her husband's kingdom, and is worth quoting in full:

To oure right trusty and enterly beloved cosyn, Th'Erll of
Oxon

BY THE QUENE

Ryght trusty and entierly beloved cosyn, we grete you well, lattyng you wete [know] how it is commen un to oure knowlege that where as ze [ye] newly entred upon oure welbeloved Symon Blyant, gentilman, in to the maner of Hemnals in Cotton, descended and belongyng unto hym by right of enheritaunce, as it is seid, ze ther upon desired the same Symon to be agreable for hys part to put all maters of variance thenne dependyng atwene hym and oon Sir John Paston, Knyght, pretendyng a title unto the seid maner into th'award and jugement of two lenered men, by you named and chosen as arbitrours atwene them; and in case that the same arbitrours of and upon the premisses neither yave oute nor made suche awarde be for the brekyng up of Pasche [Easter] terme nowe last passed, ze of your owne offre graunted and promysid unto the seid Symon, as we be enformed, to restore hym forwyth there upon unto hys possession of the seid maner. And how it be that the same Symon, at youre mocion and for the pleasir of youre lordshyp, as he seith, aggreed un to the seid compromyse, and ther upon brought and shewed hys evydence concernyng, and sufficiently provyng hys ryght in the seid maner un to the seid arbritrours and that they have not made nor yolden out betwene the said parties any suche awarde; yet have not ze restored the same Symon unto hys possession of the seid maner, but contynuelly kepe hym owt of the same, wich, yf it so be, is not only to hys right grete hurt and hinderaunce, but also oure mervaile. Wherfore we desire and pray you ryght affectueusly that ze woll the rather at the contemplacion of thees oure lettres, shew unto the said Symon, in hys rightfull interesse and title in the seid maner all the favorable lordshyp that ze goodely may, doyng hym to be restored and put in to hys lawfull and peasible possession of the same, as fer as reason, equite, and good conscience shall require, and youre seid promise, in suche wyse that he may undyrstond hym selfe herynne to fare the better for oure sake, as oure verray trust is in you.

Yeven under oure signet at my Lordes Palois of Westminster, the xxv. day of Juyn

ELEZEBETH[13]

Sir John Paston had for some years been one of Edward IV's courtiers (he and his younger brother had been among those chosen to escort Margaret, the King's sister, on her journey to Burgundy) and there is no doubt that Elizabeth could take a firm line against individuals who enjoyed her husband's favour. When the three-year-old Prince of Wales visited Coventry (once the Kingmaker's stronghold) in April 1474 the mayor and leading citizens donned green and blue to welcome him, staged tableaux in his honour, and presented him with a gilt cup. Elizabeth was undoubtedly grateful for this loyal and generous reception, and in September gave the members of the corporation and their wives twelve bucks from her forest and park of Fakenham (Norfolk) 'to be evenly distributed among them'. Their relationship was clearly very cordial, and when in November she received word that Reginald Buckley, one of her husband's servants, had been disturbing the peace in the city, she wrote ordering his imprisonment until such time as the King could judge and punish him in the appropriate manner. She promised to take the matter up with Edward, and made it clear that not only would neither of them tolerate lawless behaviour by their followers but any who thought that royal service conferred immunity from prosecution would find they were mistaken.[14] No more is heard of the matter; the citizens were presumably satisfied with the result.

Elizabeth also intervened in the domestic affairs of those who regarded her as their 'good lady', usually, we may suppose, because members of her affinity asked for her assistance but sometimes at the request of others. Another letter in the Stonor collection indicates that a daughter of the family had been placed in a great household, possibly that of the Duchess of Suffolk, against the wishes of her parents, but at the Queen's insistence. Elizabeth had apparently responded to a request from the Duchess (her sister-in-law) to send the girl to her ('we knowe ryght wele it cam nat of her selfe', wrote her mother), and had been annoyed when the Stonors proved reluctant to accept the arrangement 'wherwith the quene was ryght gretly displisyd with us both'. The daughter subsequently asked to be allowed to return home because, surprisingly, she found herself unwanted in the Suffolk household ('me thynk thay sshuld nat be so wery of yow, that dyd so gret labour and diligence to have yow', wrote her mother), but although her parents sympathised with her they did not dare interfere with the existing arrangement. Her best course of action, they suggested, was to ask the Duchess to release her 'so that my housbond or I may have writyng fro the quene with her awn hand, and ells he nor I neyther dar nor wyll take upon us to reseyve yow, seyng the quenys displesyr afore: for myn housbond seyth he hath nat wyllyngly disobeyde her comaundment here afore, nor he wyll nat begynne nowe'.[15] We do not know the end of the story or even precisely when it happened (although it may have been as much as a decade before the spat over Barnwood), but Elizabeth's apparent high-handedness does not imply that she was careless of the girl's well-being. Many letters have survived in which children complain of the treatment they endured in other households – even the future Edward IV and his brother wrote to their father complaining of the 'odious rule and demeaning' of Richard Croft and his brother who, Charles Ross suggests, had bullied them in the establishment in which they were all residing[16] – and Elizabeth would have taken the view that she had provided the young lady with an excellent opportunity to mix and mingle with the 'right' people. What the incident does make clear is that, even in comparatively routine matters, her associates knew that she was not to be trifled with and treated her with considerable respect.

It may not be strictly accurate to refer to Elizabeth as a 'builder' since all renovations undertaken at the royal palaces would have been very much a matter for her husband, but it is likely that she helped to plan and to supervise the changes made to her own apartments, and that she discussed the proposed improvements with the master mason who was also the architect. Although the surviving evidence is fragmentary, she may have requested the bay window which was added to her great chamber at Windsor in 1477–8, and the creation of what Simon Thurley has termed a 'Queen's Side' for her use at Westminster.[17] The withdrawing chamber and wardrobe built for her in 1464 were supplemented by 'the making of a grete chambre unto oure derest wif the quene in her logging (lodging)' and a 'prive kechon',[18] although the date of the warrant authorising the expenditure (6 November 1482, only five months before the death of her husband) meant than she would have had little, if any, time to enjoy them. Major improvements were also undertaken at Eltham, which although never an official residence, was much favoured as a country mansion large enough to accommodate the court and important visitors in some comfort. Edward constructed brick-built rooms for himself and his wife at right angles to his new great hall (in the shape of a letter 'T' with the hall representing the upright), and it is possible that it was Elizabeth who requested the incorporation of two apparently novel features into her wing. These were an articulated facade incorporating a sequence of five-sided bay windows and chimney breasts, which terminated in a gallery which did not connect different parts of the building (as was usual) but simply served as a 'sitting room' with spectacular views over the Thames Valley. The King's underlying purpose was clearly to turn old, uncomfortable palaces into more luxurious dwellings with private quarters for himself and his family (an idea which he, and especially his wife, may have borrowed from Sheen, which had been redeveloped along these lines by their Lancastrian predecessors), and it would be remarkable if Elizabeth did not encourage and advise him in these matters and add what may be described as a 'woman's touch'.[19]

We have already noticed Elizabeth's encouragement and patronage of learning, and her personal literary interests can be gauged from four books associated with her which have survived the passing of the centuries. The first is an *Hours of the Guardian*

Angel, which contains an illustration of a lady presenting the book to a crowned queen and a dedicatory poem in English in which the first letter of each line forms the acrostic 'Elizabeth'. There is no evidence that Elizabeth Woodville especially favoured the fifteenth-century cult of All Angels or the Guardian Angel in particular (although her vicissitudes of fortune might have inclined her to do so); but a fraternity dedicated to the Virgin and All Angels had established a chapel and hospital across the river from Sheen Palace and two of its members were Thomas Luyt, an attorney of the Duchy of Lancaster (from which the Queen, as we have seen, drew some of her revenues), and his wife Joan. Anne Sutton and Livia Visser-Fuchs have suggested that Joan Luyt, who lived at St Bartholomew's Hospital, where there was a tradition of devotional literature and book production, may be the lady presenting the volume in the illustration, and that although the queen *could* be Elizabeth of York there is no reason to doubt Dr J.G.G. Alexander's conclusion that the style can be dated to between 1475 and 1483.[20]

The other three volumes are secular, stories of legend and chivalry which were read chiefly for amusement but which many contemporaries believed were a part of history. The first is a copy of Caxton's translation of the *Recuyell of the Histories of Troy*, which contains a portrait of the great pioneer presenting the work to Margaret of Burgundy and a curious late fifteenth-century inscription written in one hand:

> This boke is mine quene elizabet late wiffe unto the
> moste noble king edwarde the forth off whose
> bothe soolis y be seche almyghty Gode
> Take to his onfinyght mercy above. Amen.
> > Per me Thomam
> > Shukburghe iuniorem

Dr Sutton and Ms Visser-Fuchs suggest that Thomas Shukburgh may have copied the now lost original legend (down to 'elizabet') and then added what follows, but without pausing or using punctuation to clarify the sense. Elizabeth may not have owned the remaining two books personally, but she undoubtedly knew and approved of them. One is another Caxton publication, the story of Jason and the search for the Golden Fleece, presented to her son Prince Edward by the King's 'licence and congye and by the supportation of our most redoubted liege lady, most excellent princesse the Quene'. The other, a collection of romances in French written on vellum, is considerably older, and included stories of the Grail, of Joseph of Arimathea, Sir Lancelot and King Arthur, together with an extract from the Tristram cycle written on paper (since removed). The collection belonged at one time to Sir Richard Roos who bequeathed it, on his death in 1482, to his niece Eleanor, Elizabeth's damsel and the wife of Sir Richard Haute her kinsman. The Woodville family's interest in the volume is apparent from the inscriptions *elysabeth the kyngys dowther* and *cecyl the kyngys dowther* at the beginning, by the repeated signature of *Jane grey* (who Sutton and Visser-Fuchs suggest may be identified with Elizabeth's sister Joan, or Jane, who married Anthony Grey of Ruthin but who may be the more famous Lady Jane who spent some time in Queen Catherine Parr's household), and by the name *E Wydevyll* on the last flyleaf. This may be Edward Woodville (the Queen is unlikely to have signed herself as anything but Elizabeth after 1465), but the book was clearly a favourite within the family and Eleanor Haute could have presented it to her before Edward IV died in April 1483.[21]

Another aspect of Elizabeth's queenship was her piety, a piety expressed in her possession of devotional literature (the *Hours of the Guardian Angel*, for example), her membership of religious fraternities, her readiness to undertake pilgrimages and to petition the Pope for special privileges, and her charitable gifts to the Church and the poor. Her activities in this sphere, like her ownership of property and her management of her council and household, resembled those of many contemporary noble ladies, but because of her special position were always on a larger and grander scale.[22] She founded a chapel dedicated to St Erasmus (the protector of sailors and women in childbirth) in Westminster Abbey, almost certainly in gratitude for the protection and care she had received there in the perilous winter of 1470–71, and took a close personal interest in the two great religious houses situated near Sheen Palace, the Carthusian charterhouse which shared its name and the Bridgettine Abbey of Syon. In 1479 she gave the new prior of Sheen, John Ingilby (who was to become one of her executors) forty-three acres of land from her manor, two years after she had secured the right to attend services at all the order's houses which had been founded by kings or queens of England; and the following year she and King Edward named their last child Bridget, in honour of the Swedish saint who had taught that only the rightful heir could save his kingdom from destruction. Among the religious organisations she patronised were the London Skinners Company's Fraternity of Our Lady's Assumption, the Holy Trinity Guild, Luton, and Christchurch Cathedral, Canterbury (in some cases members of her household were already associated with these bodies or followed her lead and joined afterwards), and in March 1466 she obtained the royal licence to establish a fellowship of the Trinity intended to support sixty priests at Leadenhall in London. She and the King went on pilgrimage to the shrines of St Mary of Walsingham (Norfolk) and St Thomas of Canterbury on a number of occasions,[23] Elizabeth riding side-saddle after the new aristocratic fashion. She probably enjoyed the conviviality and camaraderie of these excursions as much as Chaucer's pilgrims, but they were nonetheless characterised by an underlying seriousness of purpose and by the belief that, whether queen or commoner, they were pleasing to God. Lastly, in 1480–81, she personally petitioned the Pope to allow her subjects to say the devotions appropriate to the newly proclaimed feast of the Visitation in private (because two other important feasts were already being observed near the same date in England) without forfeiting any spiritual benefits. The Pope went so far as to allow special indulgences to those who devoutly said the Angelical Salutation three times daily 'because the queen desires the devotion of the faithful of the realm for the said salutation to be increased'.[24]

But Elizabeth's intervention was not confined to purely spiritual matters: she was also expected to assist her subjects in practical ways, not least by mitigating the masculine harshness of her husband's policies in imitation of the intercessory role of the Queen of Heaven. It is no coincidence that in two of the illustrations in this book (the portraits in the Skinners' Fraternity book and the *Hours of the Guardian Angel*) she is shown robed and crowned, her fair hair loose and flowing, in imitation of contemporary depictions of the Virgin, and it would have seemed natural to seek her intercession when there seemed little hope of moving King Edward. The extent to which a queen might fulfil this role depended upon the personalities and relationship of the royal couple and the opportunities presented to the queen – few could hope to emulate Philippa of Hainault who had famously pleaded with her husband, Edward III, for the lives of the burghers of Calais – but Elizabeth certainly intervened successfully on one recorded occasion when she helped the Merchant Adventurers obtain a rebate of part of the £2,000 the King had demanded from them when their payments of tunnage and poundage fell into arrears. The Adventurers' first protest led only to the brusque retort that 'the lordes (of the Exchequer). . . had non such auctoritie or power to deminysshe any peny of the ij Mli. by the Kyng named & sett for to haue, And if it were xl Mli. (£40,000) it were the Kynges right for to haue it'. They consequently appealed to Elizabeth, the Marquis of Dorset, and Lord Hastings, and the next Company court, or assembly (held on 13 December 1478), was told of:

> verrey grete labour made by mean of the quenes good grace, the lorde Marques, the lorde Maister & the lorde Chaumberleyn (Hastings) & other gentilles &c. But specially by the quene. And as William Pratt reporteth, the lorde Chaumberlayn is oure verrey good speciall lorde and aviseth us to applie oure laboure still unto the quenes grace & to the lorde Marques, and he will helpe whan tyme cometh what he can doo or may do for vs. Wherfor John Mathew was desyred for to go unto the quenes hous and there for to comen with suche parsones of his acquayntaunce so that the mater may be remembred unto the quenes grace, thrugh whom we trust in god to haue helpe & comforte &c.

They heard on 8 January that 'hit hath pleased the quenes good grace so to laboure & pray for vs unto the Kynges grace that at the instance of her prayer, of the said ij Mli. is released vc (500) marcs'; but negotiations continued and three days later she had won them a second rebate of 500 marks or a third of the total sum.[25] We have already noticed how Elizabeth's mother, Jacquetta, had played the part of the queen in this context when, with other ladies, she had gone out to ask Queen Margaret not to attack London after the Earl of Warwick's defeat at the second Battle of St Albans in 1461. Margaret had, of course, been 'standing in' for her husband King Henry, leading his armies while he was in Yorkist custody, and it was not inappropriate for Jacquetta, who had once been England's second lady, to adopt the role which the Queen had vacated until normality could be restored again.

Elizabeth would also have been responsible for many small acts of charity or kindness, many of them gifts to ordinary people, paid for out of her chamber or 'privy purse'. The financial records of her chamber have all perished, but a single account (for the year March 1502 to February 1503) survives from the reign of her daughter, Queen Elizabeth of York. The younger Elizabeth, it is clear, received a stream of petitions from individuals who had money problems of one kind or another, and donated sums which ranged from payments for the burial of executed felons to provision of a dowry for a girl about to enter a convent. William Pastone, 'page of the Quenes beddes' was provided with forty shillings to help buy his wedding clothes, and small amounts of cash were given to retired servants and to poor people generally, sometimes in response to a small gift, often of food, from the petitioner to the Queen. 'A poure woman that brought a present of apuls from Hownslowe to the Quene to Richemounte' was rewarded with twenty pence, and the same sum was given to 'a pore man in aulmouse somtyme being a servant of King Edward the iiij'.[26] Elizabeth Woodville's subjects must have looked to her for assistance in such matters, and there is no reason to doubt that she fulfilled their expectations in the same manner as her daughter was to do. In sum, she undoubtedly owed much to her able lieutenants; but she was plainly at the helm of her administration and much more than just the spender of her funds.

6

The Last Years of King Edward

The quiet of the years after 1475 and his newfound financial security allowed King Edward to attend to a matter which had been on his conscience for his entire reign. His father, Richard, Duke of York, and younger brother, Edmund, Earl of Rutland, had been killed at the Battle of Wakefield in 1460, and although Edward had removed their heads from Micklegate Bar (York) after his victory at Towton, their remains still lay where the Lancastrians had buried them, probably in the priory of St John the Evangelist near Pontefract Castle. He had subsequently arranged for a number of churches to say prayers for them, but it was not until July 1476 that he gave orders for their bodies to be exhumed and brought southwards with due ceremony prior to their re-interment in appropriately splendid tombs in the collegiate church at Fotheringhay, which he had refounded in 1462.[1] The bodies were taken up on, or about, 21 July and placed in coffins on elaborate roofed hearses decorated with heraldic and religious symbols and surrounded by candles. Rutland's coffin may have been covered by a pall displaying his arms, but his father's was adorned with a lifelike effigy arrayed in a dark blue royal mourning gown with a white angel holding a crown behind – or over – his head to symbolise that he had been king as of right. The funeral procession, which passed through Doncaster, Blyth, Tuxford, Newark, Grantham and Stamford, was headed by Richard, Duke of Gloucester, accompanied by the Earl of Northumberland, Lord Stanley and other peers, a number of kings of arms, heralds, pursuivants and 400 poor men on foot carrying large torches, all wearing black clothing and hoods. The coffins and the effigy were born on two carriages draped with black velvet, and York's was pulled by seven horses, again trapped to the ground in black.[2] The churches in the several towns had been prepared to receive the cortège (the bishops and abbots accompanying it apparently rode ahead to ensure that all was in readiness), and it was formally received by members of the local guilds and religious orders and watched over by sixty men with torches at night. In each place dirige (or matins) was said shortly after midnight followed by a requiem mass before departure, and alms were distributed to the poor.

The procession arrived at Fotheringhay on Monday 29 July at between two and three in the afternoon, and was met by the senior clergy who had gathered for the occasion. King Edward was waiting with his brothers and a great assembly of noblemen at the entrance to the cemetery, and the procession paused while he respectfully kissed his father's effigy.[3] The appropriate obsequies were then observed after which the King, represented by Lord Hastings, and Elizabeth, represented by Lord Dacre of the South (who had replaced Lord Berners as her chamberlain) laid seven and five pieces of cloth of gold across the body in the form of a cross. This process was repeated at the requiem mass held the next day, 30 July, the dukes and earls present each offering five and three pieces respectively, after the King and Queen. York's knightly achievements, a coat of arms, and a shield, sword and helmet, were then ceremonially delivered up (and may have been hung over his tomb after the burial), and his harness was offered by Lord Ferrers of Chartley, who rode a black-trapped warhorse displaying the full arms of England (again symbolising the Duke's regal status) to the choir entrance. Edward then offered the mass penny and bowed to the catafalque, followed by Elizabeth, two of their daughters (presumably Elizabeth, now ten, and Mary, nearly nine), and ambassadors from France, Denmark and Portugal. A contemporary described the Queen as 'dressed all in blue without a high headdress' (blue was the royal colour of mourning) and noted that she 'made a great obeisance and reverence to the said body'.[4] The coffins were then lowered into their graves, and the formal, religious, part of the ceremony brought to an end.

The banquet which followed was a magnificent affair. There were few occasions when so many of the great and the good were gathered together, and Edward seized the opportunity to display his new-found wealth. Large numbers of guests (one writer says 1,500, not including the royal household) were accommodated in canvas pavilions built for the occasion, up to 5,000 people who came to receive alms were given a penny, and 'there was enough to drink and eat of wine and meat for everybody'.[5] We have no knowledge of how the feast was ordered, but a surviving treasurer's account records the provision of thirty-one tuns of ale, forty-nine beef cattle, 210 sheep, ninety calves, and 200 piglets besides fish and poultry. The whole process, from the planning of the procession to the feeding of such a multitude, was a triumph of organisation. Everyone seems to have been in the right place at the right moment, and few who were present can have failed to be impressed by their royal master's ability to command, his largesse and by the general magnificence of the event.

Observers of this act of filial piety were doubtless gladdened by the apparent concord which now existed between the royal brothers, but hopes that the dissensions of the past decade had been buried were premature. The Duke of Clarence seems to have been a shallow individual who found it difficult to be a king in waiting, and the birth of two sons to King Edward had only increased his frustrations. He could not forget that a Lancastrian parliament had named him heir-presumptive in succession to Henry VI and his immediate offspring, and every imagined slight only increased his resentment that fate had denied him the crown. Matters were brought to a head by the death of his wife, Duchess Isabel, on 22 December 1476, and the unexpected slaying of Duke Charles of Burgundy at the Battle of Nancy on 5 January. It was apparent that only a marriage between Mary, the Duke's heiress, and a powerful and well-resourced foreigner could prevent the Burgundian lands from being swallowed up by King Louis, and Margaret of York, (Charles's widow) suggested her brother Clarence. Clarence found the prospect of becoming duke (or perhaps even king) of Burgundy immensely attractive, but his brother refused even to consider it. Edward was unwilling to jeopardise his lucrative agreement with France – or countenance potentially unlimited military expenditure – to win Clarence a continental empire, and may have been influenced by a rumour (spread, apparently, by King Louis) that the Duke would ultimately use his new power base to challenge him for the throne of England. It was perhaps only when Louis suggested that the Dauphin (who was already promised to Princess Elizabeth) should marry Mary that Edward retaliated by proposing Elizabeth's brother, Earl Rivers, whose wife, Elizabeth Scales, had died four years earlier. Miss Scofield thought that Edward had 'parted with his senses' and that 'he had again allowed his judgement to be overruled by his wife's ambition for the advancement of her family';[6] but neither the relatively impoverished Anthony Woodville nor the six-year-old Dauphin were likely to win Mary's approval. Both Kings were master tacticians who could afford to make rival offers which they knew were unlikely to be accepted; and it was again policy, rather than Elizabeth's influence, which led Edward to refuse the King of Scotland's offer of his sister Margaret as a bride for his brother because, he said lamely, Clarence was still mourning for Duchess Isabel. The King had forgiven, rather than forgotten, the Duke's treasons, and recognised the danger of his gaining authority in a foreign land.[7]

The result was that Clarence all but withdrew himself from the Court and the Council chamber, and began to behave in a lawless and generally provocative manner. In April he seized Ankarette Twynho, a former servant of Duchess Isabel, on suspicion of poisoning her mistress, and brought her to Warwick to be tried with one John Thursby, whom he claimed, had poisoned his infant son Richard. They were convicted by a 'packed' jury and summarily executed, an event which may or may not be connected with the subsequent trial of one of Clarence's supporters, Thomas Burdet of Arrow Park (Warwickshire).[8] Burdet and two associates, John Stacy and John Blake of Merton College, Oxford, were accused of conspiring against the King and the Prince of Wales (the charges ranged from using sorcery to disseminating seditious documents), and Burdet and Stacy were hanged at Tyburn in May. Clarence could (and should) have distanced himself from a convicted traitor, but instead had Burdet's dying protestation of his innocence read before a startled and bemused Council. No self-respecting king could tolerate such open insubordination, and the Duke was arrested and sent to the Tower on, or shortly after, 10 June. He was tried and condemned in Parliament in January 1478 where, the Croyland writer tells us, 'not a single person uttered a word against the duke except the king (and) not one individual made answer to the king except the duke'.[9] Edward still seemingly hesitated; but after ten days had passed, William Alyngton, the Commons' Speaker, came to the House of Lords to formally ask for the implementation of the sentence and Clarence was executed privately on 18 February possibly, as tradition has it, by being drowned in a butt of malmsey wine.

Historians have long wondered why King Edward dealt with his brother in this harsh and largely unprecedented manner when prison and the loss of his estates might have brought him to his senses. True, Clarence had made a thorough nuisance of himself, but some of his accusations – that the King was illegitimate, for example – were old chestnuts and hardly merited the supreme penalty. There were undoubtedly those who, for their own purposes, wanted to sow seeds of dissension between the brothers – the Croyland writer refers to 'flatterers running to and fro, from the one side to the other, carrying backwards and forwards the words which had fallen from (them) even if they had happened to be spoken in the most secret closet';[10] and Dominic Mancini thought that one of the principal stirrers was Elizabeth who, he says, had 'concluded that her offspring would never come to the throne unless the duke of Clarence were removed, and of this she easily persuaded the king'.[11] Professor Hicks has argued that the Woodvilles 'constituted the most powerful faction' in the parliament that attainted the Duke,[12] but it is dangerous to assume that all those who were connected with the Queen, by marriage or in other ways (and there were many of them), were automatically in her pocket. William, Lord Hastings, would probably be surprised to find himself described as a Woodville sympathiser (because his stepdaughter had married the Marquess of Dorset), and it is unlikely that all members of the 'family' were on good terms with one another or shared the same political opinions.[13] Richard of Gloucester is said to have objected to his brother's execution, but he used the opportunity to persuade King Edward to adjust the Warwick settlement in his favour and his regrets, as Professor Hicks remarks, 'ring hollow'.[14] Elizabeth may still have harboured resentment against Clarence for his part in her father's and brother's executions (it is interesting that one of the Duke's last wishes was to make restitution for the injuries and grievances he had inflicted on her parents), and she may have genuinely feared for the future if her husband died before her son attained his majority. But Parliament could not have been 'packed' (with royal, rather than specifically Woodville supporters) nor Clarence finally executed without the King's personal approval, and this particular buck stops with him.[15]

It was earlier in 1476, shortly before the Clarence business began to move towards its gruesome climax, that Elizabeth received word that Anthony, her brother, who was travelling in

Italy with other noblemen including the Earl of Ormond and John, Lord Scrope of Bolton, had been robbed of his jewels and plate some twelve miles from Rome. Anthony Woodville would probably have preferred a life of pilgrimage and knight-errantry to the routine of his 'day-job' as the Prince's governor, but such journeys were not without danger. The attack caused the Earl to 'retorn to Rome ffor a remedy', and his sister may have had to wait anxiously for reassurance that all was well.[16]

A rather different problem which taxed the King and Queen during this period was the marrying of their large brood of children into suitably endowed and well-connected families. We have already noted the arrangements made for Elizabeth and Cecily, while Margaret and George died in 1472 and 1479 respectively. No plans were made for the two youngest, Catherine (born 1479) and Bridget (born 1480) in their father's lifetime, but detailed negotiations centred on their sisters Anne and Mary and their brothers Edward and Richard. Anne was affianced to Philip of Burgundy (infant son of Mary and her new husband, Archduke Maximilian, the heir to the Holy Roman Empire) in 1480, and Mary was contracted to King Frederick I of Denmark in 1481. Professor Ross thought that no earlier arrangements had been made for Mary because she was regarded as 'first reserve' for her sister Elizabeth; but her premature death on 23 May 1482 (aged fourteen) may imply that she had always been sickly, and the delay was at least partly for this reason. In Anne's case King Edward exploited the Archduke's need for English backing to avoid promising a dowry and insisted that Maximilian pay an annual sum equivalent to the French pension in the event of a breach with King Louis!

If the alliances which these unions were intended to create were potentially valuable, the marriages of the Prince of Wales and the Duke of York held out still greater possibilities. A match between the Prince and the Infanta Isabel, daughter of Ferdinand and Isabella, was being considered from as early as the winter of 1476, but the birth of a son to the Spanish monarchs two years later made the prospect less attractive, and Edward turned to the rich ducal house of Milan. He proposed that his son marry a daughter of Duke Galeazzo Maria, who had been murdered in 1476; but the Duke's widow, Bona of Savoy (whose hand had once been offered to Edward himself) was hostile, mainly because she and her advisers feared the English would demand too high a price.

The King then opened negotiations with the Duke of Brittany, and in 1481 it was agreed that Prince Edward would marry Anne, the Duke's eldest daughter and eventual heiress, in eight years time when she reached the age of twelve. The contract provided for the substitution of a brother or sister if either child did not live to fulfil it personally, and it was agreed that Anne's dowry should be 100,000 crowns, to be increased to 200,000 crowns if the Duke had a son between then and the date of the marriage. If he had a son *after* the marriage, the boy was to marry one of King Edward's daughters, whose dowry would be provided not by her father but by the Duke! The King was rapidly gaining a reputation for avarice – a Breton writer commented that 'to marry his daughters without dowries was the objective which this miser set before himself in the last years of his life'[17] – and there can be little doubt that the same motive prompted his decision to wed his younger son Richard to Anne Mowbray, heiress to the Duchy of Norfolk. Her father John, the fourth and last Mowbray Duke, had died in 1476, and although some of his lands were burdened by dower interests (including those of Duchess Catherine, the second Duke's and John Woodville's widow), Anne would ultimately acquire the whole vast inheritance. The marriage between the four-year-old groom and his five-year-old bride was solemnised in St Stephen's Chapel, Westminster, on 15 January 1478, and, like Elizabeth's coronation and the re-burial of her father-in-law, was one of the great ceremonial occasions of her reign. The contemporary observer recorded how on:

the fourteenth day of January, the high and excellent Princesse (Anne) came to the place of estate, in the King's great chamber at Westminster, and there, according to her high and excellent estate, had a void (repast) after the forme and estate of this famous realme of England; accompanyed with many great estates and degrees, dukes and earles, and barons, and with great abundance of ladies and gentlewomen; and the Princesse before rehearsed was led by the right noble Count, Rivers. And on the morne, on Thursday the fifteenth day of the same moneth, this high Princesse before rehearsed came out of the Queenes chamber at Westminster, and so proceeded through the Kings great chamber, and into the White Hall, and so proceeded into Saint Stephens Chappell, being attended by great estates and many ladyes and gentlewomen, my lord the noble Count of Lincolne ledd her on the right hand, and upon the second hand the noble Count Rivers. And at her entry into the chappell before rehearsed, which was richly garnished with tappetts (carpets) of azure culler, inramplished (covered) with flower de luces of gould curiously wrought; and also a little space within the dore of the same chappell, there was an imperiall of cloth of gould, in manner of a canopie; and under the saide canopie was the King, the Queene, and my Lord the Prince, and the right high and excellent Princesse and Queene of right, Cicelie Mother to the Kinge, the Lady Elizabeth, the Lady Mary, the Lady Cicely, daughters to the King our Soveraigne Lord; and there was my said Lady received by Doctour Goldwell, Bishop of Norwiche. And when hee had received her in at the chappell dore, intending to proceed to her wedding, Doctor Cooke spake, and said that the high and mighty Prince Richard Duke of Yorke ought not to be wedded to that high and excellent Princesse, for that they were within degrees of marriage; the one at the fourth, the other at the third; for which cause hee defended (forbad) the espousalls, without that there were a speciall lycence from the Pope, and dispensacion from the Pope for the said neerenes of blood.

Then Doctour Gunthorpe, Deane of the Kings Chappell shewed an ample bull of authority, that they might proceede to the contracte and matrimony before rehersed. Thereupon the said Bishoppe of Norwiche proceeded to the marriage, and asked who should give the Princesse to the church and to him; and the King gave her, and so proceeded to the high altar to masse.

Then was there great number of gould and silver cast amongest the comone people, brought in basons of gold, by the high and mighty Prince the Duke of Glouc(ester); and after were accomplished the appurtenaunces of the said marriage; and after, spices and wyne, as appertayneth to matrimoniall feastes.

From the Chappell of Saint Stephen, led the said Princesse of this feast, the Duke of Gloucester upon the right hand, and upon the second hand the Duke of Buckingham; and so proceeding to the Kings greate chamber; and there, the second estate at the bord was the Bishopp, that did the appurtenaunces before rehersed. On the second hand, the third estate at the bord sate the Dutchesse of Buckingham, and the Dutchesse of Norfolke mother to the Princesse of the feast. And then, at the first side table, satt the Marquis of Dorsett; the length of the same table accomplished (occupied) with ladyes and gentlewomen; and at the other end, my Lady of Richmond, and many ladyes and gentlewomen; and all the Parliament chamber, of ould tyme called Saint Edwards chamber, on both sides tables, and there satt ladyes and gentlewomen. And after the second course, Minstrells, as appertayneth to such high estate. And then Kings of Armes and Herauldes, thankeing her highnes for her largesse; and then the Kings of Armes and Herauldes, to their cry, as appertayneth.

And after the surnapp made, and wash, then the avoyd (repast), marvellous reverently, with famous estates. The presse was soe great that I might not see to write the names of them that served; the abundance of the noble people were so innumerable.[18]

Three days later, on Sunday 18 January, the King created twenty-four new knights of the Bath, and a great tournament was held at Westminster the following Thursday in the presence of the royal family, noblemen and ladies, and foreign ambassadors. The Marquess of Dorset, Lord Richard Grey, Earl Rivers (who was 'armed in the habitt of a White Hermite'), Sir Edward Woodville and Sir Richard Haute all participated, and Haute was among the prizewinners, receiving a gold 'E' (standing, presumably, for Elizabeth) set with a ruby from Princess Elizabeth of York. The ceremony was in part a celebration of the wealth and might of the ruling dynasty, and is testimony to the continuing (and perhaps still growing) power of the Woodvilles and the prominence they enjoyed in its midst.

Unfortunately, the little bride died on 19 November 1481, a few days short of her ninth birthday, leaving the descendants of her father's great aunts, John, Lord Howard and William, Viscount Berkeley, co-heirs to her estates and, by extension, the titles of Duke of Norfolk, Earl of Nottingham and Earl Warenne. King Edward had no intention of allowing the normal laws of inheritance to operate to his son's disadvantage, however, and, in a move reminiscent of his deprivation of the Countess of Warwick, arranged for Parliament to give Richard a life interest in his wife's legacy with remainder to his own heirs. William, Viscount Berkeley, had previously surrendered his rights to the King as the price of his release from bonds totalling £37,000, but John, Lord Howard, was denied his expectations until Richard of Gloucester became king in 1483.

This short-lived marriage was the only one which the royal parents arranged with one of their own subjects and the only one to be brought (albeit temporarily) to fruition. The subsequent breakdown in the accord with Scotland terminated the 'engagement' between Prince James and Princess Cecily, and when Louis XI and Maximilian came to terms at Arras in December 1482 they agreed that the Dauphin would marry the Burgundian couple's little daughter Margaret, not Princess Elizabeth. The Prince of Wales (and his brother) disappeared into the Tower long before his intended bride, Anne of Brittany, reached marriageable age (she eventually married the Dauphin), and the events of 1483–85 – the overthrow of the House of York little more than two years after the death of King Edward – inevitably diminished their siblings' prospects. Princess Elizabeth subsequently married King Henry VII, but her sisters, as Professor Ross has it, 'had to be content with an earl, a viscount and a gentleman, a knight and a nunnery'.[19]

These marriages were matters of national policy which the Queen could encourage, or discourage, only within very limited parameters, but she doubtless approved of her brother Anthony's proposed union with Princess Margaret of Scotland and was, it seems, still determined to secure the Holland inheritance which she had intended for the Marquess of Dorset. King James III had suggested in 1478 that a marriage between Rivers and Margaret (who had recently been disappointed of Mary of Burgundy and George of Clarence respectively), would further strengthen Anglo-Scottish relations, and it was agreed that the couple would become man and wife at Nottingham the following October. But by then Scottish raids across the border were again becoming commonplace (thanks, probably, to Louis XI's efforts to revive the 'auld alliance') and the arrangement was buried in the debris of the ensuing war. The loss of the Exeter lands had probably long irked Elizabeth, and in the last months of her husband's life she sought to recover them for her Grey family by arranging for Dorset's son (another Thomas) to marry the new Holland heiress, Anne St Leger. She paid the King 7,000 marks for the match (Richard, her second son by her first marriage, was to receive an annuity of 500 marks from the properties), but again, Edward's death, and the drama which unfolded, frustrated her intentions. She was undoubtedly ready to do all she could to improve the wealth and prospects of all her brothers, sisters and children; but what has been termed avarice would have been criticised as dilatoriness if she had failed to look after their interests when she had the chance.

The birth of Bridget in November 1480, when Elizabeth was forty-three, was destined to be the last of her twelve known pregnancies. The little princess was christened by Edward Story, now Bishop of Chichester, with all the usual ceremony, the honour of carrying her being given to Lady Margaret Beaufort assisted by the Marquess of Dorset. Lord and Lady Maltravers (Elizabeth's sister Margaret), brought up the rear of the procession, he carrying a basin with a towel about him and she with 'a rich chrisom pinned over her left breast'. Cecily, Duchess of York (the baby's grandmother), Princess Elizabeth and William Waynfleet, Bishop of Winchester stood sponsors, and their 'great gifts' were carried before the child when she was returned to her mother's chamber.[20]

The regularity with which Elizabeth bore her children is the best possible evidence that she retained her husband's affection (and her ability to influence him), notwithstanding his many liaisons and infidelities. Edward IV did not formally acknowledge his bastards, still less bring them to court and award them titles, so the record of his amours is extremely patchy. His only known mistresses were Elizabeth (Jane) Shore (of whom more presently), and Elizabeth Lucy (formerly Wayte) the mother of his son Arthur (Plantagenet), immortalised in the *Lisle Letters*.[21] Two daughters are mentioned, an Elizabeth said to have married a member of the Lumley family, and Grace, who may have been brought up by Queen Elizabeth and who was one of those who accompanied her body to Windsor, but these were probably only the tip of the iceberg. King Edward was a larger than life character with huge appetites: the chronicler Gregory remarked that, even before his marriage, 'men mervelyd that (he) was so longe withoute any wyffe, and were evyr ferde that he had be not chaste of hys levynge (living)'.[22] Thomas More wrote that 'hee was of youthe greatlye geven to fleshlye wantonnesse, from whiche healthe of bodye, in greate prosperitye and fortune, wythoute a specyall grace hardelye refrayneth', and Mancini's comment that 'he had been most insolent to numerous women after he had seduced them, for, as soon as he grew weary of dalliance, he gave up the ladies much against their will to the other courtiers' implies that his habits changed little in the course of his reign. Louis XI jocularly told him at Picquigny that he would be pleased to welcome him to Paris 'and that if he would come and divert himself with the ladies, he would assign him the Cardinal of Bourbon for his confessor, who he knew would willingly absolve him . . . for he knew the cardinal was a jolly companion.'[23] Edward's contemporaries were either mildly scandalised or amused by his behaviour, but they did not condemn it or express moral outrage. Mistresses and illegitimate children were seen as the inevitable consequence of human frailty, and the King's pleasures could be winked at providing the ladies in question did not influence policy. Elizabeth, the 'wronged' wife, could doubtless have taken umbrage on many occasions, and it is to her great credit that she had the strength of character to overlook her husband's infidelities and retain her hold over him even when well into the medieval equivalent of middle age.

Life, indeed, went on much as usual for the royal couple in these last few quiet years of King Edward's lifetime. In September 1481 they visited Magdalen College, Oxford, at the invitation of the founder, William Waynfleet, accompanied by the King's sister, Elizabeth, Duchess of Suffolk, whose son, Edmund, was studying there. They arrived from Woodstock on 22 September shortly after sunset, and a numerous and excited crowd bearing torches conducted them to the College where Queen Elizabeth's brother Lionel, the newly elected Chancellor, received them with an oration. The next day the President made a short congratulatory speech asking the King to deal favourably with the University and College, and Edward was pleased to give suitable assurances and to join a procession of the fellows. On 24 September he attended the public disputations before hearing Chancellor Lionel deliver the divinity lecture he had recently founded, and then, says an historian, 'after the King had visited several parts of the University and heard scholastical exercises he departed with great content'.[24] It is easy to imagine the King being thoroughly bored by these proceedings, and listening resignedly with his mind on other matters. But perhaps Elizabeth, whose interests seem to have been more intellectual and cultural, enjoyed the visit, and took pleasure in her younger brother's new role.

It is likely that, by Christmas 1482, the King's health was already beginning to deteriorate, but the celebrations at Westminster were apparently even grander than usual. Edward appeared, says the Croyland continuator, 'clad in a great variety of most costly garments, of quite a different cut to those which had usually been seen hitherto in our kingdom . . . (so) as to give that prince a new and distinguished air to beholders', and although he does not mention Elizabeth in this context it can be assumed that she was also attired in the latest fashions.[25] The writer was sufficiently moved to remark that 'you might have seen, in those days, the royal court presenting no other appearance than such as fully befits a most mighty kingdom, filled with riches (and) boasting of those sweet and beautiful children, the issue of his marriage with Queen Elizabeth'.[26] The nature of Edward's last illness remains a mystery – suggestions have ranged from the effects of his libidinous lifestyle to appendicitis – but the decline in his health continued and he took to his bed at Eastertide, 28–30 March. Thomas More records, presumably with some degree of accuracy, that although he attempted to effect a reconciliation between the Woodvilles (in the person of the Marquess of Dorset) and Lord Hastings his efforts were unavailing; they wept and forgave one another in his presence, but their hearts, says More, 'were far asonder'.[27] Miss Scofield remarks on the fact that Elizabeth 'though she had been in no merely nominal sense the head of the Woodville faction'[28] was not, apparently, present on this occasion, but it appears to have been an exclusively male gathering and More drew no conclusions from her absence himself.

Edward died on 9 April. His body was first shown to the assembled lords and leading citizens and then embalmed and dressed for the official laying in state in St Stephen's Chapel. The funeral service was held in Westminster Abbey on 17 April, and the next day the body was taken via Sion Abbey and Eton to St George's Chapel, Windsor, where two days later he was laid to rest. A number of accounts of these obsequies (compiled, in the main, by heralds) have been printed by James Gairdner in his *Letters and Papers Illustrative of the Reigns of Richard III and Henry VII* (2 vols., 1861–3), but they unfortunately tell us nothing about Elizabeth saving that Lord Dacre, her chamberlain, offered the mass-penny for her. It is probable that she was present, at some time, at every stage of the proceedings, but court etiquette would have prevented her from taking an active part in them. Edward's last will has perished, but it is likely that it followed the lines of the document he had drawn up in 1475.[29] He probably proposed a senior role for his brother

Gloucester in the event of a minority[30] and several near contemporaries thought that he had committed his kingdom and children entirely to him. But it is unlikely he would have stipulated that Elizabeth and Anthony Woodville should play no further part in the upbringing of Prince (now King) Edward and his siblings, and the assumption may owe something to Gloucester's own propaganda and his subsequent seizure of power. It is true that Elizabeth was not among the executors who subsequently met to prove the will, and, inevitably, she was bound to surrender some of her former prominence and dignity; but there is no evidence to support the suggestion that her husband, for reasons which are as uncertain as they are inexplicable, had entirely dispensed with her services. Her devotion to Edward was obvious and she had fulfilled her role impeccably. Her beauty had not occasioned any scandal (in striking contrast to two of Henry VIII's English consorts), and those who had feared the worst in those now far-off days of the 1460s had learned to respect, and admire, a lady who had proved herself to be everything an English queen should be.

7

Elizabeth and Richard III

King Edward's death was destined to change Elizabeth's fortunes more dramatically than either she or any of her contemporaries could have anticipated. The differences which had soured her family's relationship with Hastings and her own distant – and possibly cautious – association with Gloucester[1] meant that the parties would now watch each other closely, but most observers expected them to follow the example of the infant Henry VI's counsellors sixty years earlier and ensure their personal rivalries did not threaten the succession. The problem in this case was that the twelve-year-old Edward V, who had been brought up largely by his mother's family, would soon be able to play a major role in government[2]; and many lords who had experienced, or who knew of, the consequences of King Henry's domination by a noble faction feared that he would use his growing authority to favour the Woodvilles to the detriment of others.

When King Edward died, Elizabeth, together with some members of her family and William, Lord Hastings, were in London; the Prince of Wales (now Edward V) was with his uncle, Anthony, Earl Rivers, in the Welsh Marches at Ludlow; and Richard, Duke of Gloucester, who, we may suppose, expected to be appointed Protector, was on his estates in northern England. A large number of senior peers and clergymen who were members of the Council had assembled in the capital for the late King's funeral, and it was they who now assumed responsibility for the realm pending the establishment of a permanent government for their new sovereign. They agreed that, following the precedent of 1422 when Duke Humphrey of Gloucester had been denied the full authority his brother Henry V had devised for him, Duke Richard would become the senior member of the Council of Regency which would govern after the coronation, which they fixed for Sunday 4 May.[3] Elizabeth allegedly urged Rivers to bring the young King to London as quickly as possible and with as large a force as he could muster, but Hastings, fearing a Woodville dominated government, threatened to retire to Calais unless the number of troops was limited and wrote to Gloucester stressing the need for decisive action on his part. There can be no doubt that Elizabeth wished to see her son crowned before anything could frustrate it, but, faced with Hastings's recalcitrance, she immediately adopted the role of peacemaker and sought to reassure him that she was not planning a coup. The well-informed Croyland continuator recorded that she 'most beneficiently tried to extinguish every spark of murmuring and disturbance'[4] with the result that both sides agreed, if somewhat reluctantly, that the young King's escort should be limited to 2,000 men.

When Richard of Gloucester heard of his brother's death he asked the nobility and gentry of Yorkshire to swear an oath of fealty to his nephew and wrote to Elizabeth and the Council to assure them of his good intentions before setting out on his own journey to the capital. He arranged to meet his ally, Henry Stafford, Duke of Buckingham (the Queen's brother-in-law and former ward), at Northampton on 29 April and made contact with the royal party which had reached Stony Stratford further south. Earl Rivers and Lord Richard Grey rode back towards Northampton to greet the Dukes and perhaps offered them hospitality at Grafton, conveniently situated nine miles from Northampton on the Stony Stratford road. The four lords passed a pleasant evening; but next morning Rivers and Grey were dramatically arrested and Gloucester and Buckingham rode to Stony Stratford to inform the King that a conspiracy had been uncovered and detained other members of his entourage. The young King defended his counsellors bravely – they had, he said, been given him by his father and he had complete confidence in them. But he realised that the Dukes were demanding rather than requesting his compliance, and could only watch as his friends were committed to northern jails.

As soon as word of the events at Northampton and Stony Stratford reached London the Woodvilles tried, unsuccessfully, to raise an army to recover the initiative, and Elizabeth, the Marquess of Dorset, Prince Richard, and Elizabeth's five daughters again took sanctuary at Westminster.[5] Thomas Rotherham, now Archbishop of York and Lord Chancellor, was so alarmed when he heard the news that he immediately rose from his bed and went to assure Elizabeth of his loyalty by presenting her with the Great Seal. He found her surrounded by:

> muche heavinesse, rumble, haste and businesse, carriage and conveyaunce of her stuffe into Sainctuary, chestes, coffers, packes, fardelles (bundles), trusses, all on mennes backes, no manne unoccupyed, somme lading, somme goynge, somme descharging, some commynge for more, some breakinge downe the walles to bring in the nexte (nearest) way . . . The Quene her self (says Thomas More) satte alone alowe on the rushes all desolate and dismayde, whome the Archebishoppe coumforted in the best manner hee coulde, shewinge her that hee trusted the matter was nothynge soo sore as shee tooke it for.[6]

Rotherham quickly realised his mistake and sent to Elizabeth, asking her to return the Seal to him; but he had displayed his support for the Woodvilles too openly and was replaced as Chancellor (by Bishop John Russell) even before Gloucester and the King reached London. Duke Richard continued to protest his loyalty to his nephew and sought to reassure the peers that he wanted nothing but the place in government his brother had desired for him. But he had shown himself to be more ruthless and decisive than his enemies, and had, regardless of whether he or they knew it, taken his first step on the road to the throne.

The King and the two Dukes reached London on 4 May, Gloucester secured his own appointment as Protector, and the coronation was rearranged for Sunday 22 June. The Dukes brought with them four wagonloads of arms which, Gloucester claimed, the Woodvilles had intended to use against him, but his attempt to have Rivers and the other detained members of the faction executed immediately was rejected by the Council. The moderate majority took the view that since he had not been appointed Protector when the conspiracy against him (if conspiracy there was) had been hatched his enemies could not be condemned as traitors, and Duke Richard, who wished to be seen to be acting entirely properly, bowed to their decision. He contented himself with securing the allegiance of all but two of a fleet of ships which had sailed under the command of Sir Edward

Woodville the day before his sister took sanctuary (their captains were threatened with outlawry if they refused to return to port) and then turned his attention to gaining possession of Prince Richard who, he argued, must be present when his brother was crowned. His attempts to persuade Elizabeth to cooperate with him were unsuccessful – Simon Stallworth reported on 9 June that the Council met at Westminster 'butt there wass none that spake with the Qwene'[7] (any longer) – and two days later he wrote to the city of York, to Lord Nevill of Raby and probably to other loyal northerners asking them to 'eide and assiste us ayanst the Quiene, hir blode adherentts and affinitie, which have entended and daily doith intend, to murder and utterly distroy us and our cousyn, the duc of Bukkyngham, and the old royall blode of this realme . . .'[8] It seems likely that he had finally concluded that however he might extend his protectorate, the day would come when Edward V and his mother's family would possess the kingdom, and the only certain way of preventing this was to become king himself. There can be little doubt that this is why, at a meeting of the Council held on Friday 13 June, William, Lord Hastings, who until then had worked closely with Gloucester, was suddenly and dramatically accused of conspiring with Elizabeth, bundled out and executed without any semblance of a trial. The only thing which could have brought Hastings and Elizabeth together was their mutual loyalty to the young Edward; and although a 'conspiracy' to crown the rightful king was in no sense treasonable it sufficed to remove the one man who, with his powerful Midlands-based retinue, had both the will and the means to oppose him. This was the second time within six weeks that Gloucester had used the excuse of a plot (for which there is no corroborative evidence) to eliminate his opponents; but it is possible that Elizabeth had turned to Hastings after her own negotiations had faltered, and that they had begun to plan a counter-coup using the good offices of Edward IV's mistress Jane Shore. This lady, who was also the sometime lover of both Hastings and Dorset, may have carried secret messages between them, and was afterwards made to feel the full weight of Gloucester's displeasure by being branded a harlot and sentenced to do penance through the streets.[9]

On 16 June the Westminster sanctuary was surrounded with soldiers, and Thomas Bourchier, the aged Archbishop of Canterbury, and other lords were delegated to make one last attempt to persuade Elizabeth to surrender her younger son to them before Gloucester resorted to force. More's description of this scene, written thirty years afterwards, must be at least partly conjectural, but there is no reason to doubt his assertion that the Archbishop relied chiefly on the arguments that it was desirable for the two brothers to be together and that Prince Richard could not claim sanctuary because he had not been threatened by anyone or committed a crime. Elizabeth raised many objections, pointing out that the same sanctuary had once protected her equally innocent elder son, and declaring that, legally, she was her son's guardian and no more obliged to surrender him than any other part of her possessions. The Prince, she said, had recently been ill and had real need of his mother, and she poured scorn on the suggestion that the young King was lonely and wanted his brother for a playfellow. The Archbishop 'perceiving that the quene waxed ever the lenger the farder off, and also that she began to kindle and chafe and speke sore biting wordes against the protectour' told her bluntly that he would personally guarantee the Prince's safety if she surrendered him to them, but that if she refused 'he never entended more to move her in that matter, in which she thought that he, and all others also save herselfe, lacked either wit or trouth'. Elizabeth, realising that she and her children risked being abandoned to whatever fate Gloucester might devise for them, and believing that the Archbishop and some of the peers present 'as she fered lest they might be deceivid, so was she well assured they would not be corupted', decided with this to release her son into their keeping, reminding them as she did so of the trust her husband had placed in them and cautioning them that 'as farre as ye thinke that I fere to muche, be you wel ware that you fere not as farre to little'. 'And therewithall she said unto the child: "Farewel, my own swete sonne, God send you good keping, let me kis you ones (once) yet ere you goe, for God knoweth when we shal kis togither agayne." And therewith she kissed him, and blessed him, turned her back and wept and went her way, leaving the childe weping as fast.'[10]

The Prince was sent to join his brother in the Tower of London, and with the Council suitably cowed by the fate of Hastings, Gloucester issued orders for the execution of Rivers, Richard Grey and the others arrested at Stony Stratford. The Protector was now acting as another king, and on Sunday 22 June, six days after the surrender of Prince Richard, Ralph Shaw, a Cambridge doctor of theology, preached a public sermon at St

Paul's Cross in London suggesting, again, that Edward IV had been illegitimate and questioning Edward V's right to the succession. The theme was taken up by the Duke of Buckingham in speeches to the Mayor and aldermen on 24 June and to an assembly of lords and gentry the following day, but was then abandoned, possibly because no one believed it and because of the great offence it must have given to Edward's and Gloucester's mother. The Protector's allies also argued, either concurrently or later, that it was King Edward's marriage, rather than the circumstances of his birth, which was invalid, because, they said, Elizabeth and her mother had used sorcery and witchcraft to ensnare him, the marriage had been conducted secretly, without the assent of the peers, in a 'profane place', and he was already pre-contracted to another lady, the Lady Eleanor Butler.[11] Most of these allegations can be dismissed without comment – the King was not, strictly speaking, obliged to marry in public nor seek the consent of the great men of the kingdom, and sorcery was a predictable allegation in such circumstances – but the last charge, the pre-contract, based on information which the Protector had received from Robert Stillington, the careerist Bishop of Bath and Wells, was more serious. The canon law position was that such an agreement was only a little less binding than marriage and precluded union with a third party for as long as it remained in being. This, it was claimed, meant that Edward IV and Elizabeth had never, in fact, been legally married, and that all their children were illegitimate and could not succeed to the throne. Edward, Earl of Warwick, the executed Duke of Clarence's son, was debarred by his father's attainder, and Richard, Duke of Gloucester, was therefore, by a process of elimination, the true heir of York.[12]

The circumstances of Elizabeth's second marriage had always been less than satisfactory, but this alleged impediment, which was apparently known only to Stillington and which would have given much ammunition to erstwhile opponents of the union, appears to have surprised everyone. The matter was never properly examined (the Duke of Gloucester declined to refer it to the jurisdiction of an ecclesiastical court) and it is difficult to avoid the conclusion that it was (at best) an example of the kind of technical objection often used to dissolve an unwanted marriage. The prohibited degrees of marriage were more widely drawn in the medieval period than is the case nowadays, and the fact that marriages between members of noble or local gentry families who were already closely related were commonplace meant that many were, strictly speaking, illegal. A papal dispensation could be obtained of course, and providing that the couple wished to remain married their union was unlikely to be questioned; but if one of the parties wished to end the arrangement, the easiest, and most convenient, solution was to 'discover' that he (or she) had never been legally contracted to the other. It is inconceivable that Edward and Elizabeth were aware of the existence of a potential objection to their own marriage and the legitimacy of their children. The Yorkist claim to the throne was based on strict primogeniture, and the King and Queen could have formally married again (and therefore placed their unborn eldest son's right beyond question) after the Lady Eleanor Butler died in 1468. That they did not do so is some indication that King Edward attached no importance to whatever undertaking, if any, he had given the Lady Eleanor; and Elizabeth was probably as bemused by this revelation as everyone else.

But even if the objection was valid, and the King and Queen had allowed themselves to be lulled into a false sense of security, it is still possible to argue that Edward V, who had been recognised as heir apparent throughout his father's lifetime, did not have to be deposed. Bastardy, whether real or technical, had not prevented William the Conqueror from becoming King of England in 1066, nor would it prevent Queens Mary and Elizabeth from succeeding in the next century, notwithstanding that their father, Henry VIII, had questioned the validity of his marriages to both their mothers. Elizabeth I, bastardised in 1536 but crowned in 1558, did not need to have the stigma of her illegitimacy set aside because her coronation had automatically cancelled any impediment in her title; and there was no reason why the same criteria could not have been applied to Edward in 1483. Gloucester's modern apologists argue that he was acting from the highest of motives when he deposed his nephew; but it is plainly suspicious that an objection which had previously lain dormant should be resurrected at the very moment he made his bid for the throne.

It is possible that the Duke, like other powerful figures in history, found the temptation of the crown irresistible, but it is more likely that there were other, essentially personal, considerations that now outweighed the loyalty he had earlier shown to his brother and family. Gloucester's northern Neville estates had, as we have seen, been taken from George Neville, whose father, John, Marquis Montague, the Kingmaker's brother, had been slain on the Lancastrian side at the Battle of Barnet. The grant had given the Duke and his wife Anne, Warwick's daughter, a full title in the properties while George or his heirs lived, but had provided for it to be reduced to a life interest (to protect the residual rights of other members of the Neville family) if the young man died without issue. George did, in fact, die childless, on 4 May 1483, and Gloucester (who may have heard that he was seriously ill towards the end of April) would have been well aware that those who would have inherited the lands in other circumstances would be quick to challenge even his life interest if his position appeared to be weakening. He would be bound, also, to draw a parallel between his own situation and that of his predecessor as Duke of Gloucester, Duke Humphrey, who, it was suspected, had been murdered, probably with the connivance of Henry VI and his Beaufort relatives, at Bury St Edmunds in 1447. The Queen and her supporters had apparently agreed with the Council's decision to recognise Gloucester as the senior member of the Council of Regency which would have effectively governed when Edward V was crowned; but his relations with the reigning King and another branch of his family were potentially as fraught as Duke Humphrey's, and there could be no certainty that the Woodvilles's cordiality would last. But this being said, the charges which Richard brought against them – that they had been storing arms in preparation for a coup and that Elizabeth, Dorset, and Sir Edward Woodville had misappropriated Edward IV's treasure[13] – appear to have no foundation in reality, and, whatever Gloucester's fears for the future, it seems plain that he was more threatening than threatened in the summer of 1483.

The Duke of Gloucester's success in gaining the throne owed much to his ability to take decisive action, and this facet of his character clearly surprised many of those who had known him in the years leading up to his brother's death. Edward IV's confidence in him had proved to be entirely unwarranted (whatever role in government he had envisaged for him), and Rivers and Hastings, who were both experienced and astute politicians, had walked blindly into the traps prepared for them. Only Elizabeth, if her flight into sanctuary and her reluctance to surrender Prince Richard are true indicators, perceived the danger which Gloucester posed to the young King, and did her best to organise resistance within the limited range of options available to her. Both Mancini and the

Croyland continuator refer to the Woodvilles's unsuccessful attempt to raise troops when word of the events at Stony Stratford reached London,[14] and it is interesting that the Queen could not command even the limited amount of backing needed to deprive Gloucester of possession of her elder son. This may owe something to her family's general unpopularity, but was perhaps not unrelated to her gender and to aristocratic perceptions of her queenship. When the young King told the Dukes of Gloucester and Buckingham that he had complete confidence in the peers of the realm and the Queen, his mother, Buckingham allegedly retorted that 'it was not the business of women but of men to govern kingdoms, and so if he cherished any confidence in her he had better relinquish it'.[15] Her failure – the realisation that, although the equal of Gloucester in foresight and determination she could do nothing to change the situation – undoubtedly contributed to the state of dismay in which Archbishop Rotherham discovered her; but it is clear that she did not give in to a sense of grief and helplessness and instead tried to regain the initiative, even approaching her old enemy, Hastings, and when that failed, standing courageously alone against the ploys used to persuade her to surrender Prince Richard. It may be fairly said that, whatever the roles played by the principal parties, and regardless of whether they were deceived or deceivers, Elizabeth alone emerges with credit and dignity from this sorry affair.

The Duke of Gloucester became King, as Richard III, on 26 June. Elizabeth remained in sanctuary, and her two sons by King Edward disappeared into the recesses of the Tower. Many books have been devoted to this, the most famous of all historical mysteries, but all that can be said with certainty is that the boys were progressively 'removed from men's sight'[16] as Mancini has it, and had disappeared, apparently completely, by the autumn of 1483. These events must have alarmed and dismayed many of the lesser nobility – knights and gentry – who had loyally served the Princes' father, and before the summer was over there were rumours of plans to rescue both them and their sisters 'in order that, if any fatal mishap should befall the said male children of the late king in the Tower, the kingdom might still, in consequence of the safety of the daughters, some day fall again into the hands of the rightful heirs'.[17] The girls could hardly have been taken from the sanctuary and smuggled abroad without Elizabeth's agreement and cooperation, and she was undoubtedly also party to a more serious challenge to King

Richard which broke out in October. This, known as 'Buckingham's Rebellion', was predominantly a rising of southern gentry supported by the Marquess of Dorset (who had escaped from the Westminster sanctuary) together with the Queen's brothers, Richard and Bishop Lionel Woodville, and latterly, the Duke of Buckingham. It is uncertain why Buckingham, who had effectively masterminded Richard's seizure of power, now turned against him; but it is possible that, like other kingmakers (the Percies in 1403, for example) the considerable rewards he had received still fell short of his expectations, and that John Morton, the wily Bishop of Ely (who had been arrested with Hastings and assigned to Buckingham's custody), persuaded him that Edward V's restoration would make him the real power in the country. Their plans, the Croyland writer tells us, were checked by a rumour that the young King (and, presumably, his brother) had died violently,[18] whereupon Morton proposed that they transfer their allegiance to Richard's exiled Lancastrian rival, Henry Tudor, Earl of Richmond. Polydore Vergil records that one Lewis, a Welsh physician who attended both Elizabeth and Henry's mother, the Lady Margaret Beaufort, carried messages between them when he visited them in his professional capacity, and it was agreed that Henry would marry Elizabeth's eldest daughter, Elizabeth of York, when he secured the kingdom, the Queen undertaking to 'maketh hir frinds partakers of this devyse and busynes to be set forward with all spede convenyent'.[19] Vergil, who was writing under Tudor patronage, says that it was the Lady Margaret who proposed this union of the two former warring families, but she took the precaution of telling Lewis to first gauge Elizabeth's attitude by pretending that it was his own suggestion. This would seem to imply either a distinct coolness in relations between the two women, or that the Lady Margaret did not want to appear too eager to capitalise on the deaths of the Princes; but Elizabeth would have been quick to discern Margaret's involvement, and to appreciate that here was an opportunity to use Henry to turn the tables on King Richard, much as she had tried to use Hastings in June. Unfortunately, her plans again came to nothing. The uprising in Kent began prematurely, King Richard appeared to be well informed of the rebels' intentions and moved decisively against them, and heavy rains prevented Buckingham from crossing the Severn into England. Henry Tudor's little fleet was scattered by gales and returned to Brittany where he was joined by Dorset and others fortunate enough to escape the King's retribution, while Buckingham was betrayed by the servant with whom he had taken refuge and was executed in the market place at Salisbury on 2 November. The Lady Margaret might have shared his fate, but her attainder was remitted[20] and she was merely stripped of her properties. These were transferred to her husband, Thomas, Lord Stanley, who was made responsible for her future conduct and for ensuring that she had no further communication with her son.

Elizabeth did not, apparently, indicate in so many words whether or not she believed the Princes had been murdered – perhaps there was nothing she could say or her opinion went unrecorded – but there can be no doubt that, unlike those of her contemporaries who seem to have been content with hearsay, she would have spared no effort to discover the truth. It is just possible she conspired with the Lady Margaret in the belief that Henry's claim would falter if the rumour of her sons' deaths proved unfounded, but the strong probability is that she agreed to support his bid to depose King Richard (and to allow her eldest daughter to assume the mantle of heir apparent) in the sure knowledge that they had been killed. The failure of the rebellion, coming hard as it did on the discovery of her conspiracy with Hastings in the summer, placed her in an extremely difficult situation. King Richard had so far permitted her to remain in sanctuary notwithstanding the embarrassment the reproach must have caused him, but there could be no guarantee that he would allow the situation to continue indefinitely. Similarly, the sanctuary must, with the passage of time, have become increasingly cramped and uncomfortable for the six women who shared it, and the Church authorities themselves may have begun to lose patience with their unwanted guests whose presence would have constantly threatened the cordiality of their own relationship with the new ruler. There was no longer any hope of rescue, and so Elizabeth, having been formally deprived of her dower by the Parliament which met on 23 January 1484, and 'after frequent entreaties as well as threats had been made use of'[21] bowed to the inevitable and entered into discussions with the new government. The result was an agreement, confirmed 'by the most solemn and public promise that Richard could contrive',[22] sworn on holy relics before the lords spiritual and temporal and the Mayor and aldermen of London, that the Queen and her daughters would leave sanctuary, and that, in return, the new King would protect them, provide for them financially, and make suitable provision for the girls' marriages. Richard declared:

I promitte & swere that if the doughters of dam Elizabeth Gray, late calling her self Quene of England that is to wit Elizabeth Cecille Anne Kateryn and Briggitte wolle come unto me out of the Saintwarie of Westminstre and be guyded, Ruled & demeaned after me, then I shalle see that they shalbe in suertie of their lyffes and also not suffre any maner hurt by any maner persone or persones to theim or any of theim in their bodies and persones to be done by wey of Ravisshement or defouling contrarie their willes, nor theim or any of theim emprisone within the Toure of London or other prisone, but that I shalle put theim in honest places of good name & fame, and theim honestly & curtesly shalle see to be(e) foundene & entreated and to have alle thinges requisite & necessarye(te) for their exibicione and findinges as my kynneswomen. And that I shalle do marie suche of theim as now bene mariable to gentilmen borne, and everiche of theim geve in mariage landes & tenementes to the yerely valewe of CC marc [200 marks = £133 6s. 8d.] for terme of their lyves, and in like wise to the other doughters when they come to lawfulle Age of mariage if they lyff, and suche gentilmen as shalle happe to marie with theim I shalle straitly charge from tyme to tyme lovyngly to love & entreate theim as their wiffes & my kynneswomen, As they wolle advoid and ecschue my displeasure. And over this that I shalle yerely fromhensfurthe content & pay or cause to be contented & paied for thexibicione & finding of the said dame Elizabeth Gray during her naturelle liff at iiij termes of the yere, that is to wit at pasche, Midsomer, Michilmesse, & Christenmesse to John Nesfelde one of the squires for my body (&) for his finding to attende upon her the summe of DCC marc [700 marks = £466 13s. 4d.] of lawfulle money of England by even porcions. And moreover I promitte to theim that if any surmyse or evylle report be made to me of theim or any of theim by any persone or persones that than I shalle not geve thereunto faithe ne credence nor therefore put theim to any maner ponysshement before that they or any of theim so accused may be at their lawfulle defence and answere.[23]

It has been suggested that Elizabeth would never have come to terms with Richard knowing that he had killed the two princes (what mother could have done so?) and that her doing so implies either that she had discovered they were still living or that someone other than the King had ordered their deaths.[24] But she had certainly reached her agreement with Richard in the knowledge that he had ordered the judicial murders of her brother and the younger son of her first marriage, and perhaps recognised that her continuing resistance was only harming the surviving members of her family. The document, which Charles Ross says 'reeks of the queen-dowager's suspicions'[25] betrays her misgivings, but Richard's youth (he was fifteen years younger than Elizabeth) meant that there was unlikely to be another king in her lifetime, and whatever her feelings there was no alternative but to deal with him. The status of her daughters had been reduced and she herself may have been subject to supervision;[26] but she still had her understanding with Henry Tudor and the Lady Margaret, if, against the odds, Henry proved able to depose Richard, and in the meantime (and it was likely to be a long meantime) she had secured the best arrangement for herself and her daughters that she could.

There is no record of where Elizabeth and her daughters lived after they emerged from sanctuary. Some of them may have been among the children mentioned in the ordinance drawn up to regulate the King's northern household at Sheriff Hutton in July[27] (Elizabeth of York certainly became a member of this household the following year) while others may have been lodged with trusted royal supporters. They were probably invited to court on state and family occasions, and certainly joined the King and Queen to celebrate Christmas in 1484. The Croyland continuator commented disapprovingly on the 'vain exchanges of apparel presented to queen Anne and the lady Elizabeth, the eldest daughter of the late king, being of similar colour and shape'[28] which formed part of the festivities, but such expressions of cordiality were clearly designed to convince onlookers that Richard was now fully reconciled with the Queen Dowager and his late brother's family. Queen Anne seems to have fallen ill soon afterwards, and before long there were rumours that Richard intended to marry the younger Elizabeth when his wife died. Sir George Buck, one of Richard's earliest apologists, claimed to have seen a letter which the Princess wrote to the

Duke of Norfolk towards the end of February 1485 asking him to help facilitate her union with the King, whom she referred to as 'her only joy and maker in [this] world', declaring 'that she was his in heart and in thoughts, in [body,] and in all'.[29] It is likely that her mother approved and encouraged her enthusiasm – Elizabeth Woodville had already written to the Marquess of Dorset urging him to abandon Henry Tudor and return to England[30] – and that she was now somewhat cynically hoping that a marriage between King Richard and her daughter would restore her to her position at the centre of affairs. Queen Anne died on 16 March, but the union with Elizabeth did not materialise. Croyland says that two of Richard's closest advisers, Sir Richard Ratcliffe and William Catesby, told him to his face that the north had supported him principally out of loyalty to the Kingmaker's daughter, and that any new wife must be acceptable to northern, Neville, sensibilities. Their real fears were probably that a Woodville restoration would lead to retribution for their involvement in the deaths of Earl Rivers and the others arrested at Stony Stratford (Ratcliffe had been particularly active in the north during Richard's usurpation, and Thomas More alleges that Catesby had been instrumental in the destruction of Hastings), but be that as it may, the outcome was that the King was obliged to deny publicly, at an assembly held in the great hall of St John's Hospital, that the thought of marrying Princess Elizabeth had ever entered his mind.[31]

A marriage between Richard and his niece would have frustrated the ambitions of Henry Tudor (Henry had formally sworn to marry the princess in a ceremony held in the presence of his followers at Rennes Cathedral on Christmas Day, 1483), and it is possible that it was Queen Elizabeth who persuaded the King, against his better judgement, that here was a way, perhaps the only way, of regaining the support, not only of her own family but also of the majority of her late husband's followers, and that his rejection of the idea was another blow to her ambitions. It is clear that nothing she had learned since she had left sanctuary had given her any hope that either of her sons might still be living, or again, her promotion of their sister would have been unthinkable; and King Richard could only have contemplated marrying the princess, thereby acknowledging her legitimacy, if her two brothers had died. Nevertheless the hold which relatively humble acolytes like Ratcliffe (the second son of a Derwentwater knight) and Catesby (a Northamptonshire esquire) now enjoyed over the King is testimony to the weakness of his position by 1485, and Elizabeth could console herself with the thought that the situation remained fluid and the wheel of fortune could soon turn in her favour again.

It is easy to criticise King Richard's behaviour in this two-year period just as it is easy to admire Elizabeth's fortitude and determination to make the most of the hand which fate had dealt her. One factor which must not be forgotten is that it was the most ruthless, perhaps the least likeable, kings of England, who were generally the most successful. Henry I, for example, cut off the testicles and right hands of counterfeit moneyers and allowed the blinding of two illegitimate granddaughters who had been given as hostages, but has nevertheless gone down in history as a capable ruler who enjoyed the confidence of his greater subjects. It was the more ascetic, gentler monarchs, like Henry III, Richard II, and Henry VI, who either lost their thrones or came close to losing them, and it can be argued, quite reasonably, that if Richard III had not possessed a comparable streak of determination in his character he would not have found government easy even if he had won the Battle of Bosworth. Richard's fundamental problem was that he had taken the crown in a manner which was unacceptable to the majority of his subjects,[32] and if the time-servers (and there were many of them) were willing to work with him while his reign lasted, they were not prepared to go out of their way to extend it. It was against this background that Henry Tudor's invasion in the late summer of 1485 secured one of the most unlikely military victories of the Middle Ages. His small army, which included Elizabeth's brothers Edward and Richard (Bishop Lionel had died in exile and the unreliable Dorset had been left behind as a pledge for the 40,000 livres advanced by the French government), landed at Milford Haven on 7 August. It was stiffened by a contingent of French mercenaries, but the enterprise would have been foolhardy if Henry had not been assured that certain powerful figures in England would support him or would at least do nothing to assist his adversary. Historians cannot agree where, precisely, the Battle of Bosworth (or Dadlington) was fought, still less where the long-vanished marsh was located and how the contingents of the armies – including the wavering Stanleys – were deployed there. But it is clear that King Richard was the victim of treachery in that his rearguard, commanded by the Earl of Northumberland, played no part in the conflict, Lord Stanley may have been entirely absent, and Sir William Stanley launched the fatal attack that killed him. Margaret Beaufort and her agents were in no small measure responsible for her son's success at Bosworth, but Richard's death was a bonus even they could not have anticipated.[33] It allowed Henry to seize the throne comparatively peacefully, and meant that all the parties, Elizabeth included, could put the events of the previous two years behind them and begin again.

8

Elizabeth and Henry Vll

There is no evidence of how Elizabeth reacted to the news of King Richard's overthrow, although she is unlikely to have long mourned his passing. Their relationship seems to have improved in the last year of his reign and Elizabeth appeared ready to put the past behind her; but she can never have forgotten that he had eliminated many members of her family and denied her the authority and status she would have enjoyed as Edward V's mother. Richard's decision not to marry her daughter meant that she could expect no improvement in her situation in the immediate future, and she can only have welcomed the success of a contender whose supporters not only approved his proposed union with the Princess but may have insisted upon it. One of Henry's first actions was to send Sir Robert Willoughby to Sheriff Hutton to secure the persons of the younger Elizabeth and Edward, Earl of Warwick; and Elizabeth Woodville was duly restored to her title and dignity as Queen Dowager in his first Parliament which met a week after his coronation on 7 November. The Act declaring the invalidity of her marriage to King Edward was repealed, and on 5 March of the year following she received annuities and a life interest in a raft of properties in southern England in full satisfaction of her dower.[1] In reponse to a Parliamentary petition to fulfil his promise the new King married Elizabeth of York in Westminster Abbey on 18 January, although the formal papal dispensation was still awaited. It is unfortunate that no record of this ceremony has come down to us, but it was doubtless a magnificent occasion, with the Queen Dowager and the surviving members of her family prominent among the guests. The new King was, to some extent, an upstart with an uncertain future, and the Woodvilles may have felt a certain satisfaction that, in this company, the old slur of parvenu was a thing of the past.

The unexpected and fortunate nature of Henry's victory meant that, inevitably, King Richard's surviving supporters would try to reverse the verdict of Bosworth; and the new reign was only a few months old when, on 17 October 1485, the King dispatched letters to Henry Vernon and other followers ordering them to array their forces against 'certeyne oure rebelles and traitours' (including, probably, a group of the late King's adherents who are known to have taken refuge on the Furness moors in Lancashire) who, 'confedered with oure auncient enemyes the Scottes ayenst their naturall dutees and allegiances, made insurrections and assemblees of our poor subgettes in the north partis of this our realm'.[2] The chroniclers' silence would suggest that the new government was, in fact, in no immediate danger,[3] but the north, always the most distant and potentially disaffected part of Henry's kingdom, was the scene of new, more serious, disturbances in the following year. The King was probably at Doncaster when, in April 1486, he learned that Francis, Viscount Lovel, Richard III's chamberlain, had raised a revolt in the vicinity of Middleham Castle, and that other fugitives from Bosworth, notably Sir Humphrey Stafford and his brother Thomas, were fermenting trouble in Worcester and the south. The rebellion may well have surprised Henry – the evidence suggests that he had quite underestimated Lovel's determination to continue the struggle[4] – but although ill-prepared he despatched such troops as he had against the northern insurgents, giving them authority to pardon any who would lay down their arms. The strategy proved successful. Lovel, mistrusting the resolution of his followers, left them to throw themselves on the royal mercy,[5] and news of the débâcle precipitated the collapse of the risings in Worcester and elsewhere. The Furness group of rebels (who seem to have stood apart from Lovel's uprising) remained unsubdued until mid-August when they negotiated sureties for their future behaviour with the royal emissaries Sir Richard Tunstall and Sir Thomas Wortley and were duly admitted to royal favour. The new Queen had meanwhile become pregnant, and the royal couple's first child was born on 20 September and christened Arthur in Winchester Cathedral the following Sunday. Princess Cecily carried the infant, and Elizabeth Woodville stood godmother, laying him on the High Altar and presenting him with 'a riche cuppe of golde, coverede, whiche was borne by Sir Davy Owen'. Lord Stanley (now Earl of Derby), Thomas, Lord Maltravers, and the Earl of Oxford (who arrived late) acted as godfathers and gave a gold salt, a gold coffer, and 'a pere of gilte basonns, with a sayer' respectively.[6] The disturbances were over for the moment, the new heir promised hope for the future, and Henry might have felt satisfied with what had been a turbulent but successful first year.

The King was, however, destined to have little lasting peace or tranquillity, and only a few months passed before word reached England of new intrigues against him in the Irish pale. The origins of the conspiracy are shrouded in mystery, but Polydore Vergil tells us that the instigators of the trouble were a 'lowborn' priest, Richard (or William) Simons, and Lambert Simnel, the son of an Oxford tradesman, whom the clerk had chosen for his good looks and bearing and whom he had schooled to be party to his dubious schemes.[7] Simons conveyed his protégé to Ireland where the House of York had been held in special affection since Duke Richard's lieutenancy in the 1450s, and where, we are told, he 'secretly summoned a meeting of a considerable number of Irish nobles' and convinced them that Simnel was Edward, Earl of Warwick, the Duke's grandson, who had been imprisoned in the Tower since Bosworth but who he (Simons) had 'saved from death'.[8] It is, of course, highly improbable that a humble cleric could teach a youth courtly manners (where would he himself have learned them?) or, unaided, call together the Irish lords; and we may reasonably conjecture that this part of the story was designed to protect the real culprit whose complicity (and Vergil was writing twenty years after the rebellion) had been deliberately concealed. It is surely no coincidence that early in February 1487, shortly after news of the disturbances reached England, King Henry deprived Elizabeth Woodville of all her properties and confined her to Bermondsey Abbey on the unlikely grounds that she had imperilled his cause by surrendering her daughters (including Henry's intended bride Elizabeth) to King Richard some three years earlier.[9] But Henry had restored the Queen Dowager to her dignity after Bosworth in the knowledge that she had reached an accommodation with his late adversary; and the fact that he had become King of England and married her daughter proved that she had not damaged his prospects. Even Edward Hall, the most unlikely of Yorkist apologists, remarked that the disapproval which King Richard incurred when he considered marrying the younger Elizabeth himself probably assisted rather than hindered the Tudor party, and added that Elizabeth Woodville's punishment went far beyond anything which her indiscretion (committed at a time of great perplexity) deserved.[10] It is apparent from other measures then taken by the Council – the decisions to offer pardons to all offenders throughout England and to show the real Earl of Warwick to anyone who cared to see him – that the King was really concerned with the immediate conspiracy – but why should Elizabeth have supported a rebellion directed against her own daughter and son-in-law? The answer may be that she resented the authority which the change of dynasty had given to Henry's mother, the Lady Margaret Beaufort, but more particularly that Henry had been anxious to dispel any illusions that he ruled England in right of his wife. No arrangements had been made for the young Queen's coronation, and Lord Bacon (writing a century after Vergil when the matter could be discussed more openly) says that Elizabeth thought her daughter 'not advanced but depressed'.[11] Bacon believed that she was so deeply tainted with treason that 'it was almost thought dangerous to visit her, or see her';[12] but a formal prosecution would have been diplomatically embarrassing, and would have alienated some supporters of the new government (including members of Elizabeth's own family) whom Henry was reluctant to offend.

There is, however, an alternative theory that Elizabeth had no quarrel with Henry, nor he with her. The Queen Dowager, it is suggested, was moved by poor health to surrender her lands voluntarily (they were transferred to the Queen, her daughter), and she then retired to the Clare guest suite at Bermondsey Abbey – where Katherine of Valois, Henry V's widow, had spent her last few months – again of her own free will. The King continued to refer to her in suitably endearing terms in official documents, and in November 1487 proposed her as a wife for the widowed James III of Scotland, something he would hardly have done if he suspected her of treason. Elizabeth may have found the new order not entirely to her liking, but would she, it is argued, have conspired against her son-in-law (and against her own daughter and grandson) to make the son of Clarence king in his stead?

These points need to be answered in some detail, beginning with the suggestion that Henry found himself short of lands with which to endow his wife and thus persuaded Elizabeth, who was finding the cares of life increasingly burdensome, to surrender her holdings as part of an amicable 'family settlement'. But land was the principal source of wealth in the Middle Ages – schemes for increasing their acreage (by means both fair and foul) occupied the thoughts of every noble and gentle family – and it would have been unthinkable for someone in the Queen Dowager's position to willingly reduce herself to relative poverty. There is no evidence that she was unwell at this period, and illness is not a very plausible explanation given that her personal involvement in the management of her properties, her supervision of her estate officials, could have been as considerable or as minimal as she wanted. Similarly, the argument that some of these estates were customarily held by the reigning queen and were bound to be transferred to the younger Elizabeth anyway, begs the question of why Henry gave them to the Queen Dowager (instead of to her daughter, whom he was shortly to marry) at the beginning of his reign.

It is interesting to compare Elizabeth's situation with that of the Lady Margaret Beaufort, another matriarch who might, quite reasonably, have retired from public life when her son had secured the kingdom but who instead became one of the principal figures in his administration. She, too, might have taken less interest in her personal properties as she grew older, but in practice exploited them rigorously, even dunning the widows of loyal servants and pursuing small debts owed to her grandfather, John, Earl of Somerset, almost a century earlier.[13] Her house at Collyweston in northern Northamptonshire was extended at the turn of the century to become the centre of a 'court of equity',[14] a court of arbitration whose area of jurisdiction corresponded closely with her estates in the east Midlands but which nevertheless enjoyed official sanction in the sense that cases were referred to it from the King's own court. Many of the matters decided were of an essentially political nature, and Margaret's personal involvement caused one disappointed litigant, the Nottinghamshire yeoman John Hewyk, to refer to her as 'that strong whore'. She frequently accompanied the King and Queen on royal visits and progresses, and at Woodstock her lodgings were connected to her son's by a withdrawing chamber where they could be together in the utmost privacy to relax or discuss matters of state. The Spanish ambassador observed in 1498 how much Henry was influenced by his mother – her authority, he thought was greater than that of the

Chamberlain, Sir Giles Daubeney or the Chancellor, now Archbishop and Cardinal, John Morton – and the next year she abandoned her usual sign manual 'M Richmond' for the more regal 'Margaret R', although whether the 'R' stood for Richmond or Regina is uncertain.[15] When Elizabeth of York was finally crowned in November 1487 it was the Lady Margaret who accompanied her in the procession and sat at her right hand in the parliament chamber (Elizabeth Woodville was not even present); and it was again Margaret who wore the same clothes as the Queen at the Christmas festivities with 'a riche coronnall' on her head'.[16] The contrast between this and the position in which Elizabeth Woodville found herself in the last five years of her life could hardly be greater, and she was undoubtedly being punished for something. Vergil's statement that she was 'deprived by the decree of the council of all her possessions'[17] is something he would not have said about his patron's mother-in-law unless it was undeniably true.

The second point made by those who maintain that Henry's differences with Elizabeth are a mere flight of the historian's fancy is that he remained on friendly terms with her, even inviting her to court on occasion, and that he was prepared to marry her and two of her daughters to James III and his two sons. The King's goodwill, they argue, is writ large in later official references, a good example being the grant of fifty marks he allowed her on 14 December 1490 'ayenst the fest of Cristemas next commyng' in which he refers to her as 'oure right dere and right welbeloued quene Elizabeth moder vnto oure most dere wif the quene'.[18] But these phrases (and others like them) were conventional rather than personal, and failure to use them would have allowed contemporaries to seriously question the unity of the royal family. The same may be said of the meeting between Elizabeth and her kinsman, Francois, Monsieur de Luxembourg, the head of a visiting French embassy, which took place in the Queen's chamber (the royal couple were expecting the birth of their second child) in November 1489. Henry was bound to allow the Count to see Elizabeth or again risk inviting suspicion; but a private meeting at Bermondsey was, we may suppose, out of the question and he chose, instead, a semi-formal gathering, with 'my Lady the kinge's moder'[19] present to hear all that was said. Similarly, it is unlikely that Henry would have considered marrying the Queen Dowager to King James (thereby providing

1 Panel portrait of Elizabeth. Early seventeenth-century copy of a contemporary likeness. (*The Deanery, Ripon Cathedral*)

2 Edward IV, *c.* 1482. Detail from stained glass window, the Martyrdom Chapel, Canterbury Cathedral.

3 Elizabeth Woodville, *c.* 1482. Detail from stained glass window, the Martyrdom Chapel, Canterbury Cathedral.

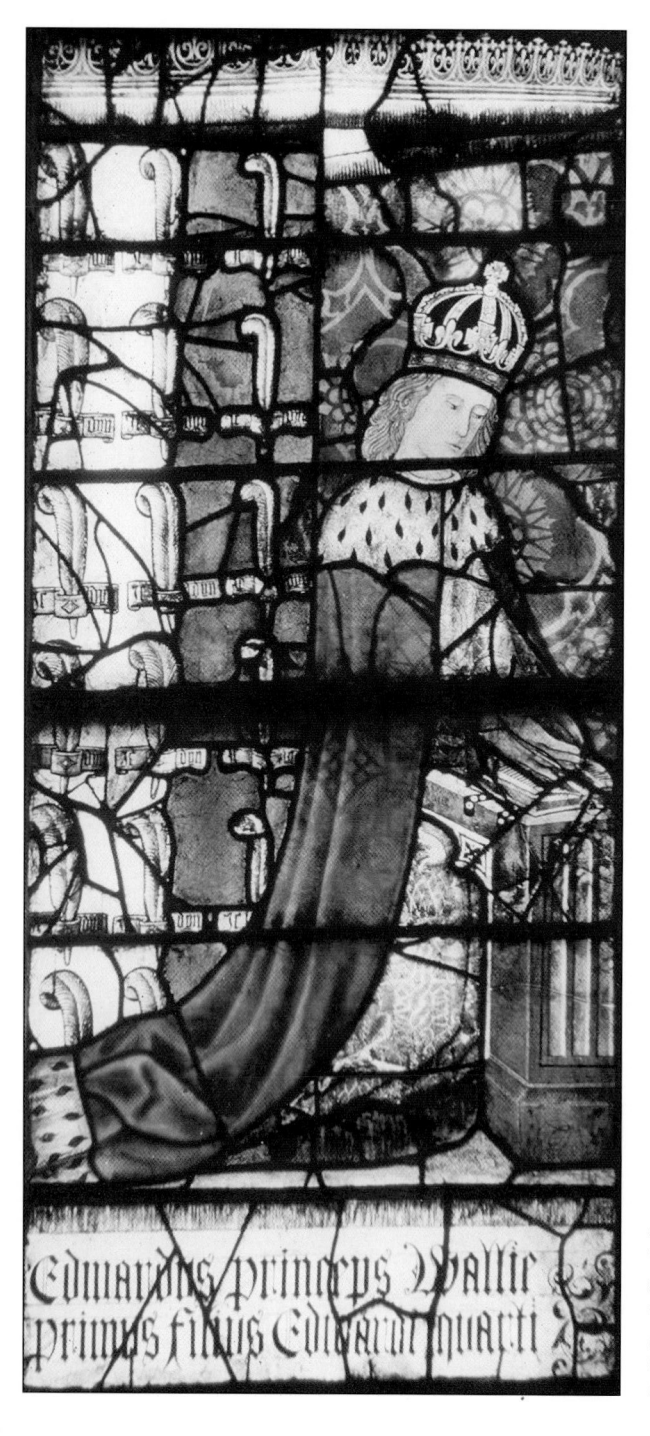

4 Edward, Prince of Wales. Detail from stained glass window, the Martyrdom Chapel, Canterbury Cathedral.

5 Richard, Duke of York. Detail from stained glass window, the Martyrdom Chapel, Canterbury Cathedral.

6 Elizabeth of York with her sisters Cecily and Anne. Detail from stained glass window, the Martyrdom Chapel, Canterbury Cathedral.

ure moost goode and gracıouse. Quene Elısabeth:
Soster vnto this oure ffraternite: Of oure blessed
Lady, and modr of mercy. Sanct Mary Vırgyn the

7 Elizabeth portrayed in her coronation robes, as a member of the Worshipful Company of Skinners' Fraternity of Our Lady's Assumption, probably *c.* 1472. The legend reads: *Oure moost goode and graciouse Quene Elizabeth, Soster unto this oure Fraternite of oure blissed Lady and Moder of Mercy Sanct Mary Virgyn the Moder of God.*

8 A lady (probably Joan) presenting an Hours of the Guardian Angel to a crowned queen, almost certainly Elizabeth Woodville. (*Liverpool Cathedral MS Radcliffe 6*)

9 Panel portrait of Elizabeth. The date 1464 was probably added later.

10 Elizabeth (lower right foreground), Edward IV, Bishop Thomas Rotherham and Cecily Neville, kneeling with other members of the confraternity before the Trinity, *c.* 1475. (*The Luton Guild Book*)

11 John Tresilian's ironwork grille for Edward's and Elizabeth's tomb, St George's Chapel, Windsor, *c.* 1481–83.

12 Effigies of Sir Edward Grey (Elizabeth's father-in-law), Elizabeth Talbot, Viscountess Lisle (sister-in-law), and Cecily Bonville, Marchioness of Dorset (daughter-in-law), from church of St Mary's, Astley, Warwickshire.

13 Elizabeth's shield bears the royal arms impaled with those of (1) Luxembourg (Pierre, Count of St Pol, her mother's father), (2) Margaret of Andria (her maternal grandmother), (3) Henry the Blond (founder of this [youngest] branch of the House of Luxembourg), (4) Susanna Orsini (her maternal great-grandmother), (5) Guy de Luxembourg (her great-great grandfather), and (6) Woodville.

14 Elizabeth's Seal, displaying arms which stress her noble descent through her mother supported by the White Lion of March and a Collared and Chained Greyhound.

15 Elizabeth's signature from a receipt for her annuity from Henry VII, 1491.

16 Panel portrait of Richard III. (*The Society of Antiquaries, London*)

17 Bronze effigy of Henry VII by Torrigiani. Henry VII Chapel, Westminster Abbey.

18 Garter Stall Plate of Richard Woodville, first Earl Rivers, 1450. St George's Chapel, Windsor.

19 Jaquetta Woodville, Elizabeth's sister, with her husband, John, Lord Strange of Knockyn and daughter Joan (the small figure). Brass, church of St John the Baptist, Hillingdon, Middlesex.

20 Incised slab depicting Sir John Woodville (d. 1415). St Mary the Virgin, Grafton Regis.

21 The church of St Mary the Virgin, Grafton Regis.

22 The 'Queen's Oak'. Potterspury, near Grafton Regis.

24 Floor tiles decorated with White Roses (below) and (**23**) the Woodville arms (above and below) found in the Hermitage Chapel, Grafton Regis (the probable site of Edward and Elizabeth's secret marriage) during excavations in 1965/6.

25 The Enthronement of Elizabeth at Reading Abbey. Oil on canvas, Ernest Board.

26 Cardinal Bourchier urges the widow of Edward IV to let her younger son out of sanctuary, J. Z. Bell.

her with a new power-base in Scotland) if he seriously suspected her of plotting; but what is overlooked is that the proposed marriages had been mooted before the Simnel rebellion, at least as early as the Three Years Truce signed on 3 July 1486.[20] It is possible to believe that Henry kept the negotiations between the two countries going in the belief that the Scots would not cause trouble on the northern border as long as there was some likelihood of a successful outcome, and that his strategy was only defeated by James III's untimely death.[21]

The third observation – that Elizabeth would never have contemplated the overthrow of her own daughter – is perhaps the most difficult to answer, but she undoubtedly resented Margaret Beaufort's influence over Henry,[22] an influence which diminished both their positions. The ideal solution, from her standpoint, was to remove the King and his overbearing mother *without* deposing her daughter, and although it was unlikely that the younger Elizabeth would be accepted as queen regnant there was nothing to prevent her from being married to her cousin Warwick once Henry was out of the way. The young Earl is said to have been simple-minded (a judgement perhaps partly based on the naivety which was a consequence of his long imprisonment), and there could be no doubt that with Warwick and Elizabeth of York crowned King and Queen of England, Elizabeth Woodville would have been the real power behind the throne. The young Prince Arthur was a problem, but recent events had shown how easily a claim could be superseded, and she could anticipate that another, more 'legitimate', grandson would soon replace him. It is impossible to know whether this plan, or another like it, actually formed in Elizabeth's mind, but it seems certain that she was actively working for Henry's overthrow and would surely have expected a large dividend in the new world she had helped to create.

The precise role which Elizabeth Woodville played in the Simnel conspiracy is, unfortunately, lost to history, but it is possible that it was she who persuaded the Irish lords to recognise the pretender – or, more specifically, to use him as a stalking-horse for the genuine Warwick – until the young Earl, her nephew, could take his place. It is unlikely that the Chancellor, Sir Thomas Geraldine, would have been 'among the first to entertain the boy'[23] and taken the lead in rallying support for him in Ireland unless he knew that behind the facade stood a powerful interest which would foster their cause in England when the moment came. There must, of course, have been other conspirators who encouraged and cooperated with Elizabeth, but their activities have left little or no trace of their identities in official records. The fact that Simnel and Simons had resided at Oxford suggests that one of the principal agents may have been John Sante, the strongly pro-Yorkist abbot of nearby Abingdon; but although an Act of Attainder accused him of conspiring with his acolytes, Christopher Swan and John Main, at Abingdon in January 1487 there is (predictably) no mention of Elizabeth and the record of their treasons is unusually vague.[24] Similarly, Bishop Robert Stillington, whose knowledge of Edward IV's pre-contract had been used to depose Edward V, was summoned to appear before Henry before 7 March because he was 'usyng certan practyses prohybyte by the lawes off holy church and other damnabyll conjuresies and conspiraes'.[25] It is interesting (but not, now, particularly surprising) to find Elizabeth cooperating with yet another of those who had so harmed her family; but the Bishop, like the Queen Dowager, was not formally indicted or punished – he could not have been tried publicly without rehearsing Elizabeth's part in the conspiracy – and was merely kept incommunicado until his death in 1491. He had been close to the Duke of Clarence, and doubtless felt a deep sense of commitment to his son.

The enthusiastic reception which Simnel received in Ireland emboldened the conspirators, and they began to draw in other likely sympathisers in England and Flanders, the most notable being Margaret, dowager Duchess of Burgundy, the Yorkist Kings' sister, who was ready to use her considerable resources in her family's interests and who was destined to trouble Henry for much of his reign. Margaret's wealth gave the rebellion a credibility it could scarcely have attained otherwise, and Bacon alleged that her influence was crucial in securing the allegiance of John de la Pole.[26] John, the Earl of Lincoln, was the eldest son of John, Duke of Suffolk and Elizabeth Plantagenet, Margaret's sister and eldest surviving daughter of Richard, Duke of York. His uncle, King Richard, had arguably regarded him as his heir apparent (in preference to the Earl of Warwick) for at least a few months before the Battle of Bosworth; and although events had seriously blighted his expectations he had been loyal to Henry Tudor thus far. He was present at the meeting of the Council which formally deprived Elizabeth, but in late March took ship for Flanders whence Lovel (who had passed the interval as a fugitive in different parts of England) had preceded him some weeks before.[27]

The Yorkist leaders must have been aware that Simnel was an impostor – Lincoln was, in all probability, one of the lords who conversed with the real Warwick when he was displayed at St Paul's in February – but they were ready to harness popular enthusiasm for the pretender and use it to further their own schemes. The Duchess Margaret paid for ships and for a force of German mercenaries commanded by Martin Schwarz, a notable soldier, and on 5 May 1487 the party landed in Dublin, ostensibly to espouse Simnel's cause. The arrival of foreign troops further emboldened the Irish nobles, and on 24 May the lad was 'crowned' King Edward VI in Christchurch Cathedral before a congregation which included the head of the Geraldine clan and Henry's titular representative in Ireland, Gerald Fitzgerald, Earl of Kildare. We do not know whether Kildare had been involved in the conspiracy from the outset, or alternatively had responded to its progress: but he was very much a law unto himself in Ireland and his influence ensured that a substantial number of his countrymen were in Lincoln's company when the rebels landed on Piel Island, off the Furness Peninsula, on 4 June.

When King Henry first heard of Lincoln's departure and of what was intended, he immediately caused the Duke of Suffolk to accompany him on a progress of East Anglia, no doubt to catch the mood of this vulnerable region and dissuade the Duke's well-wishers from assisting his son. He cautiously placed the Marquess of Dorset in honourable confinement 'to preserve him from doing hurt either to the King's service or to himself'[28] as Bacon has it, and then, like King Richard before him, established his headquarters in the Midlands, at Coventry, where his supporters from other parts of England could more readily join him until he had surer knowledge of his enemies' plans. When it became clear that Lincoln had sailed for Ireland, and that there would be no immediate descent upon England, he retired to Kenilworth with a smaller retinue; and it was there that news of the landing at Furness reached him, probably not earlier than 7 June.[29] He at once summoned those of his followers who, for convenience sake, were waiting in readiness in their respective counties, and by the time he reached Leicester on Sunday his army may already have boasted one duke (Jasper Tudor, now Duke of Bedford), three earls (Oxford, Devon and Shrewsbury), Viscount Lisle

(Elizabeth's brother-in-law by her first marriage),[30] the Lords Grey of Codnor, Powis and Ruthin, Lords Ferrers of Chartley and Hastings, and probably most of the sixteen knights bachelor who are known to have joined him from south of Trent.[31] But the success of the muster was threatened by indiscipline – a 'great nomber' of 'harlatts and vagabonnds'[32] had attached themselves to the army and were causing disorder among the soldiery – and by rumours spread by rebel agents 'sett atwene the place of the ffeeld and many of the kyngys subgettys which were cummyng toward hys grace, shewing unto theym that the kyng had lost the ffyeld & was ffled'.[33] Henry 'ressonabley fylled' the prisons at Leicester and Loughborough with troublemakers 'wherfor ther was more reste . . . and the better rule'[34] in the army, but he could do little to counter the rumours 'by which subtyll meane many a trewe man to the kyng turnyd bak'.[35] Bacon's suggestion that some of the gentry simply 'used' the stories to excuse their absence from the coming conflict is entirely plausible,[36] but there can be little doubt that others genuinely hesitated and that one large contingent may even have fled. The French chronicler Molinet tells how, a few days afterwards, a force which Lord 'de Veals' (probably Lord Welles, the King's uncle) had gathered in southern England and which was marching to Henry's assistance, suddenly fell back through London in panic.[37] The Yorkists who were in sanctuary in the city assumed that the King had already been defeated and proceeded to rob his well-wishers and cry for Warwick – clear evidence that the royal hold on the capital was still tenuous. Elizabeth may have heard the commotion from within the walls of the Abbey and listened with barely suppressed excitement while the monks murmured apprehensively and wondered what the future would bring.

The main royal army had meanwhile continued its march northwards, but did not reach the vicinity of Nottingham until Wednesday evening, the foreward camping 'under a hille to Notynham warde'[38] after experiencing difficulty in finding a suitable site. The King retired to a 'gentilmannes place' in Ruddington, three miles south of the city, his own men lodging in the village and 'in a bene felde to Notingham warde'.[39] Their sluggish progress may have been due partly to the indiscipline and uncertainty we have already noticed, but it is also probable that Henry was reluctant to close with the rebels until he had joined forces with the large contingent of Stanley retainers who were approaching under the command of Lord Strange. This 'great hoste', described by an eyewitness as well equipped and 'inow (enough) to have beten al the Kings enemies',[40] duly arrived the next morning; but we may reflect that had they delayed their muster and march by as little as thirty-six hours then Lincoln would have caught Henry ill-prepared. The rebels passed by Southwell (some fourteen miles north-east of Nottingham) on Friday, and were clearly advancing as rapidly as possible. Their march from Furness to Masham (where Simnel signed letters), a distance of at least seventy miles, much of it over rugged country, had been accomplished within four days of landing; and they had covered the sixty-odd miles from Bramham Moor (where they had scattered a small royalist force under Lord Clifford) to Southwell, again in rather less than four days. Lincoln clearly hoped that any Tudor contingents not deterred by his agents would be caught off their guard by his resolute progress; but if news of Strange's arrival dismayed him, the royal forces were not, apparently, reassured. The King had already hanged several rumour-mongers from an ash tree on 'Notyngham Brygge Ende' on Wednesday evening, but their removal did not prevent a 'great skrye' (a commotion, or panic) from disturbing the army on the nights of both Thursday and Friday (the eve of the battle) and 'whiche causede many cowards to flee'.[41] The episode shows that Henry, like Richard before him, could not rely on all those who accompanied him to the battlefield, and there was every possibility that a bold stroke by determined rebels would again succeed.

The Earl of Lincoln crossed over to the south bank of the Trent at Fiskerton and drew up his forces on a ridge before Stoke village, either late on Friday or in the early hours of Saturday 16 June. The ridge lay astride the Fosse Way (along which the royal army was approaching) and was protected on the west by a steep escarpment which fell almost to the river from the edge of the plateau. We do not know precisely how many men he had with him – estimates vary from as few as 5,000 to as many as 20,000 – but the figure of 8,000 mentioned in the November Act of Attainder may be tolerably accurate.[42] These he concentrated together into a single ward, or 'battle' (as opposed to the customary three corps into which the King's forces were divided) probably in the hope of striking decisively at the royal vanguard before the centre and rear wards could be deployed. Again, there is no reliable estimate of the strength of the royal army, but the author of the York House Books thought that 10,000 men were committed to Oxford's command in the foreward, and this is broadly consistent with Bacon's apparently well-informed comment that Lord Strange and the Earl of Shrewsbury brought 'at least' 6,000 of their followers to the Tudor's service *'besides the forces that were with the king before'*[43] (my italics). Molinet, who may have gleaned some of his particulars from rebels who fought in the battle and who afterwards escaped to the Continent, says that Sir John Savage (another Stanley kinsman) commanded 1,200 outriders on Oxford's left while Sir Edward Woodville led a contingent of 2,000 horsemen (presumably mounted infantry) on the right flank of the vanguard. Sir Edward would not have been given this command if Henry suspected him (or the Woodville family in general) of being behind his present difficulties, and there seems little doubt that on this occasion Elizabeth had acted for primarily personal reasons and essentially alone.

Our knowledge of the ensuing battle is scanty even by medieval standards and must be reconstructed on the basis of a few chance comments which are by no means indisputable as fact. It is, however, probable that, as at Bosworth, Oxford began his advance very early in the morning and that Lincoln allowed the royal foreward to labour some distance towards him before launching his offensive, at approximately '9 of the clok'.[44] The two armies engaged in a fierce hand-to-hand conflict in which the German and Irish contingents in general, and Martin Schwarz in particular, are said to have distinguished themselves by their valour:[45] but the Irishmen, who wore little or no body armour and were armed only with 'skaynes' (knives) and 'mantelles',[46] began to fall like 'dull and brute beastes'[47] before the royal billmen and archers, their slaughter striking no little terror into the hearts of the residue of Lincoln's men. The forces which Sir Thomas Geraldine had brought from Ireland are sometimes depicted as an ill-equipped rabble bent on plunder. But a mere gang of brigands would not have stood their ground in such difficult circumstances (still less have marched through England with such relative speed and discipline), and there can be little doubt that they were, in fact, seasoned warriors whose weapons, although crude by English standards, were those which they customarily used.[48] The struggle continued for some three hours until at length Oxford rallied his forces – or perhaps brought up a few reinforcements – and broke the rebels' resistance with a vigorous charge. Lincoln perished in the furious onslaught (notwithstanding that Henry had wanted him spared for interrogation), and with him fell Schwarz and Geraldine and most of their few prominent knightly supporters. Simnel and Simons were captured and duly consigned to oblivion, the boy, with wry humour, to the royal kitchens, and his priestly mentor to jail. Lovel alone of the leaders eluded his pursuers and found refuge at his house on the Windrush in Oxfordshire, but it seems that death overtook him there suddenly, possibly before the end of the year.[49] The Yorkist party had been crushed, and, although pretenders continued to trouble Henry for more than a decade, the threat was never as serious again.

The failure of the rebellion may be attributed partly to Henry's own coolness under pressure, partly to the fact that his aggrandisement of the hitherto ambivalent Stanleys had left them with little alternative but to uphold his government, and partly to Lincoln's inability to persuade more than a handful of Englishmen to take his part. There were doubtless many former retainers and well-wishers of Warwick the Kingmaker in the northern counties who would have welcomed his grandson's coronation; but they were understandably wary of the foreign-backed pretender and perhaps suspected the Earl's intentions. The Yorkists who broke sanctuary in London are said to have shouted for Warwick rather than Lincoln: and while this may merely reflect the fact that the rebellion had been organised on behalf of Warwick, it does not suggest that Lincoln was tacitly regarded as the 'natural' king. Indeed, it may be thought unlikely that the conservative English aristocracy – or at least a significant part of them – would have permitted the heir of the great house of Neville to be superseded by a man who (notwithstanding his close kinship with the Yorkist branch of the royal family) was still only the great-great-great-grandson of a Hull merchant. Vergil is adamant that Lincoln intended to seize the crown in the event of victory however, and Bacon may not be far from the truth when he notes that the Yorkist leaders had formally agreed to replace Simnel with the 'true Plantagenet' (whatever that meant), *wherein the Earl of Lincoln had his particular hopes*[50] (my italics). It may be that a rebel victory at Stoke would not have ended the Wars of the Roses nor produced the outcome desired by Elizabeth Woodville. Rather, it would have resulted in a three-cornered power struggle between the partisans of Neville and

Tudor and a rump of the Yorkist faction which adhered to Lincoln, a conflict which would have weakened the body politic and left England prey to the ambitions of the King of France. The fact that Henry defeated his enemies and established his dynasty may not have been an unmitigated blessing for his countrymen, but the alternatives, like Churchill's alternatives to democracy, were, arguably, all potentially worse.

The Simnel rebellion was effectively Elizabeth's last throw of the political dice, and the remaining five years of her life were spent in involuntary retirement, behind the walls of the Abbey or its manor, with little distraction from her daily routine. There is nothing to suggest that she was kept incommunicado – the Marquess of Dorset and her daughters doubtless visited her, and perhaps Dorset told her of the magnificent new house he was building in Leicestershire, which now lies in ruins in Bradgate Park. A visit to Bradgate, to see this fine property in the making, would have given her no small pleasure, but her only respite from her boredom was (as far as is known) her presentation to the French ambassadors in November 1489. King Henry provided her with an annuity of 400 marks (£266 13s 4d) payable in four quarterly instalments which was increased to £400 in February 1490,[51] but it is uncertain how much of her living was 'found' for her, or conversely, how much of the sum went into the monks' coffers. The Abbey's charter required it to provide hospitality for guests of the Clare family,[52] and Edward IV was descended from the Clare heiress, Elizabeth de Burgh and Lionel, Duke of Clarence; but it is unlikely that the abbot would have welcomed (or would have been willing to bear) the full expense and responsibility of her confinement by the end of the fifteenth century.[53] In any event, the sum was still less than the 700 marks (£466 13s 4d) she had received under the terms of her settlement with King Richard, and even then was not always paid promptly. Elizabeth signed a receipt for £30 on 31 May 1491 which was 'in party of payment of CC^{li} (£200) due to me at ester last past as hyt aperyth be my annuete grauntyd be the Kyng',[54] and her will leaves little doubt that, throughout her 'retirement', her resources (perhaps with good reason) never exceeded her immediate needs.

Elizabeth's last years were further saddened by the deaths of her two remaining brothers. Sir Edward was killed at the Battle of St Aubin du Cormier on 28 July 1488 while lending covert

English support to the Duke of Brittany; and Richard, the third and last Earl Rivers, died on 6 March 1491. Richard seems to have been something of a political lightweight – neither Edward IV nor, for that matter, Henry VII, had given him any meaningful office although Edward had once tried to have him appointed prior of the English Hospitallers – and he was apparently unmarried and childless. He bequeathed his property to the Marquess of Dorset, 'desiring him that there might be as much underwood sold, in the woods at Grafton as would buy a bell, to be a tenor at Grafton, to the bells then there, for a remembrance of the last of the blood'.[55] The extinction of the direct male line of the Woodville family may be blamed partly on the effects of war and political miscalculation, but closer examination shows that, in common with many other noble lineages, they were finding it increasingly difficult to produce sons.[56] Three of Elizabeth's four brothers (not counting the celibate Bishop Lionel) had died violently, but, with the exception of John (who was, in any case, married to a much older lady), they had survived well into middle age without leaving sons to succeed them, and would probably have had no greater success in the matter if they had lived longer and died in their beds.

Elizabeth's constitution had always been robust – the record contains no hint of illness or delicacy – but it seems that her health began to fail as she approached her mid–fifties, and on 10 April 1492 she made her will. The document is short, more like a will made *in extremis* than the last testament of a Queen Dowager, but the twists and turns of fortune had left her with precious little to bequeath:

In Dei nomine, Amen. The Xth daie of Aprill, the yere of our Lord Gode M cccc LXXXXII. I Elizabeth by the grace of God Quene of England, late wif to the most victoroiuse Prince of blessed memorie Edward the Fourth, being of hole mynde, seying the worlde so traunsitorie and no creature certayne whanne they shall departe from hence, havyng Almyghty Gode fresh in myndy, in whome is all mercy and grace, bequeith my sowle into his handes, beseechyng him, of the same mercy, to accept it graciously, and oure blessed Lady Quene of comforte, and all the holy company of hevyn, to be good meanes for me. I'tm, I bequeith my body to be buried with the bodie of my Lord at Windessore, according to the will of my saide Lorde and myne, without pompes entreing or costlie expensis donne thereabout. I'tm, where I have no wordely goodes to do the Quene's Grace, my derest doughter, a pleaser with, nether to reward any of my children, according to my hart and mynde, I besech Almyghty Gode to blisse here Grace, with all her noble issue, and with as good hart and mynde as is to me possible, I geve her Grace my blessing, and all the forsaide my children. I'tm, I will that suche smale stufe and goodes that I have to be disposed truly in the contentac'on of my dettes and for the helth of my sowle, as farre as they will extende. I'tm, yf any of my bloode will of my saide stufe or goodes to me perteyning, I will that they have the prefermente before any other. And of this my present testament I make and ordeyne myne Executors, that is to say, John Ingilby, Prior of the Charterhouse of Shene, William Sutton and Thomas Brente, Doctors. And I besech my said derest doughter, the Quene's grace, and my sone Thomas, Marques Dorsett, to putte there good willes and help for the performans of this my testamente. In witnesse whereof, to this my present testament I have sett my seale, these witnesses, John, Abbot of the Monastry of Sainte Saviour of Bermondsey, and Benedictus Cun, Doctor of Fysyk. Yeven the day and yere abovesaid.[57]

Elizabeth placed all her confidence in the two senior surviving members of her family, the Queen and the Marquess of Dorset, and a few trusted friends. King Henry, her son-in-law, was not mentioned or appealed to, although he could, in other circumstances, have allowed her the means to at least reward those who had done her good service or make restitution to anyone she believed she had wronged. The very real poverty in which Elizabeth found herself at the end of her life can perhaps be best demonstrated by comparing her situation with that of her one-time adversary, William, Lord Hastings, who made his will at the height of his power on 27 June 1481. Hastings's testament, in the slightly abbreviated version printed by John Nichols,[58] runs to approximately 2,500 words, of which slightly more than half are concerned entirely with religious and charitable matters, 700 deal with secular affairs and legacies, and the remainder with his closing requests and instructions. In the first part he bequeathed valuables and monies to no fewer than nine named churches and religious foundations and to 'every parish church' in Leicester (there were at least five of them at this period), to pray for his soul and the souls of his ancestors at the intervals specified. His executors were charged to arrange for 'a thousand priests to say a thousand *Placebo* and *Dirige*, with 1000 masses . . and every priest therefore to have sixpence', and alms were to be distributed at Windsor when he was buried, at Sulby in Northamptonshire (the family mausoleum) and among poor people in five counties to ensure they remembered him with affection in their prayers. This was an age which believed fervently that intercession by the living could shorten the time which the deceased spent in purgatory, and it must have grieved Elizabeth that she was unable to make similar financial provision for the well-being of her own soul. It was perhaps some consolation that those who gazed at her portraits in the windows of Canterbury Cathedral and Little Malvern Priory would at least remember her; but she could do nothing to ensure their thoughts would be kind.

Elizabeth died at Bermondsey Abbey nearly two months after making her will, on Friday 8 June 1492. Her body was conveyed by boat to Windsor on Whit Sunday, 10 June, the twenty-seventh anniversary of her coronation, accompanied by Prior Ingilby, Dr Brent, Edward Haute, her second cousin, and two gentlewomen, one of them her husband's illegitimate daughter, Grace. The wooden coffin was taken 'prevely' (privately or secretly) from the Thames to the Castle and was received there at eleven at night by a single priest and a clerk. There was no ringing of bells nor formal reception by the dean and canons of St George's Chapel, and she seems to have been interred almost immediately without any form of ceremony. The Marquess of Dorset, his half-sisters Anne, Catherine and Bridget, Edmund de la Pole (the slain Earl of Lincoln's brother) and other relatives reached Windsor on Tuesday, and that evening the Bishop of Rochester conducted the services of dirige and requiem mass. The Queen was prevented from attending by her impending confinement; but the King, and the other senior peers and churchmen were all conspicuous by their absence, and one of the heralds present was shocked by the general modesty of the proceedings. His comment that 'ther was nothyng doon solemply for her savyng a low herse suche as they use for the comyn peple with iiij wooden candilstikks abowte hit' and that there was 'ther never a new torche, but old torches, nor poure man in blacke gowne nor hoods, but upon a dozeyn dyvers olde men holdyng old torches and torches endes'[59] requires no elaboration, and it is unclear why the Dean of Windsor, who was present, played no part in the services himself. It is sometimes suggested that Elizabeth had requested a simple and inexpensive funeral out of a deep sense of piety and that was accordingly what she was given:[60] but she would have been aware that a deceased's estate normally bore these expenses, and that queenly obsequies were beyond her means. Elizabeth may have thought of piety in terms of poverty, although few great noblewomen would have chosen austerity or thought money and their faith incompatible. Margaret Beaufort, who was as pious as she was powerful, used her great wealth to found chantries and university colleges and to support numerous religious 'good causes', and when she died in June 1509 her total assets, in plate, jewels and rich materials still amounted to £14,724.[61] Her elaborate funeral, which cost £1,021, was a far cry from Elizabeth's impoverished burial when, it seems, Dorset paid the 40*s* in alms which was distributed after mass out of his own pocket.[62] Requests for a modest funeral were a mark of humility, largely ignored by contemporaries who felt that the deceased should be buried in accordance with his or her rank in society, and it is difficult to believe that she who had once been Queen of England had insisted upon this dismal and unqueenly ending. Be that as it may, in the course of her life Elizabeth had mourned the deaths of all five of her brothers, all but one of her seven sisters, four of her five sons and two of her daughters, and she may have felt that there was little to detain her in this world when her own time came.

9

Elizabeth's Reputation

There can be no doubt that Elizabeth Woodville is one of the most maligned characters of the Yorkist period and indeed of the entire Middle Ages. The traditional portrait of the haughty Queen and her grasping relatives has become as much a part of the story of the Wars of the Roses as Richard III's alleged villainy, but no Society has arisen to re-interpret her actions or take a more favourable view of her character. It is a story that has been repeated so often, both in serious works and novels, that it is sometimes difficult to believe that it could ever have been otherwise. The fact remains, however, that there were a number of contemporaries who admired Elizabeth, and the purpose of this chapter is to see how the *legend* of Elizabeth Woodville developed, and how opinions of her have varied over the years.

One of the most interesting contemporary views of Elizabeth is that of the Croyland continuator, in a passage which forms part of his description of the situation in the capital in the aftermath of King Edward's death. Lord Hastings, he says, had threatened to retire to Calais if Edward V and his uncle Lord Rivers marched on London with a large force of soldiers, and 'the benevolent queen, desirous of extinguishing every spark of murmuring and unrest'[1] sought to appease him by instructing her brother to limit the boy-king's escort to 2,000 men. It would be unwise to make too much of this comment in isolation – Henry T. Riley restricts it to that moment in time by translating it as 'the queen most beneficently tried to extinguish every spark of murmuring and disturbance'[2] and if John Gunthorpe, Elizabeth's former secretary, was the author it can hardly be regarded as impartial.[3] But it is broadly supported by other writers who respected her, not least a Londoner who wrote a poem celebrating Edward IV's recovery of his throne in 1471 and who devoted three verses to Elizabeth in which he expressed both his approval of her conduct during her husband's exile and the hope that she would use her influence to pacify differences and 'helpe every man to have justice'. His sentiments are very close to those of the continuator, although it is improbable there is any connection between them; they simply shared a common admiration for Elizabeth, which they (and presumably many others) had felt for much of her reign:

O quene Elizabeth, o blessid creature,
　O glorius God, what payne had sche?
What langowr and angwiche did sche endure?
　When hir lorde and sovereyn was in adversité.
　To here of hir wepyng it was grett peté,
When sche remembirde the kynge, she was woo.
Thus in every thynge the wille of God is doo.

Here aftir, good lady, in your felicité,
　Remembir olde trowblis and thynges paste,
And thyncke that Cryste hym selfe is hee
　That is kynge of kynges, and ever shall laste.
　Knytt it in youre herte suerly and faste,
And thyncke he hath delyveryd you owte of woo;
Hertly thoncke hym, hit plesith hym so to doo.

And ever, good lady, for the love of Jhesu,
　And his blessid modir in any wise,
Remembir suche personus as have be trewe,
　Helpe every man to have justice.
　And thes that wille othir maner maters device,
Thay love not the kynge, I dar say soo,
Besechyng ever God that his wille be doo.[4]

A similar compliment was paid Elizabeth when her eldest son visited Coventry in April 1474. The pageant staged for the Prince's entertainment included 'three Kings of Cologne' played by local inhabitants, who stressed the antiquity of the House of Luxembourg in these terms:

128

O splendent Creator! In all oure speculacion,
　　More bryghter then Phebus, excedent all lyzt!
We thre kyngs beseche the, with meke mediacion,
　　Specially to preserue this nobull prynce, thi knyght,
　　Wich by Influens of thy grace procedeth a-right.
Of on of us thre lynnyally, we fynde,
His Nobull Moder, quene Elizabeth, ys comyn of that kynde.[5]

Reference to the descent of the Luxembourg family from the Emperor Charlemagne (who died in 814) was probably used to counter the allegation that Elizabeth was a parvenu, or upstart, on many occasions; and though the citizens would hardly have said as much to the young Prince and those accompanying him, it may be significant that their words were pure praise.

While Elizabeth was clearly not liked by everyone these comments show that she succeeded in winning the admiration of at least some of her subjects. There is no evidence that those who expressed misgivings when she married King Edward remained resolutely antagonistic towards her, but she could not avoid the ill-feeling which marked the deteriorating relationship between the Earl of Warwick and other members of her family. 'Robin of Redesdale's' complaints were directed against Earl Rivers, his wife and sons, and other lords who were using their influence with the King 'to their singuler lucor and enricheyng of hem selfe and their blood as wele in grete possessiones as in goodis';[6] and although Elizabeth was not accused personally it was apparent that none of this could, or would, have happened without her. The moment passed but the aspersions lingered. The deaths of her father and mother and the successes of Edward's last years effectively stymied further criticism, but the events of 1483 allowed Richard of Gloucester to disinter the old charges of sorcery and transfer to Elizabeth the suspicions that had once threatened her mother Jacquetta. The dramatic scene described by Thomas More and Polydore Vergil – when Gloucester bared his withered arm and accused her of using witchcraft to 'dissolve' it – must hark back to the propaganda of the period and to the stories that influenced Dominic Mancini. Mancini was an Italian cleric whom Angelo Cato, Louis XI's physician and councillor, apparently dispatched to England in the summer of 1483 to assess the prevailing situation. He seems to have lacked well-placed informants (except, perhaps, for Edward V's doctor, John

Argentine) and had an unfortunate tendency (although perhaps he had little alternative) to assume that current hearsay provided an accurate picture of the immediate past. There is no independent, contemporary evidence that Elizabeth and the Woodvilles had 'alone managed the public and private businesses of the crown' and 'ruled the very king himself', or that Gloucester had complained 'of the insult done him by the ignoble family of the queen' and had resided in the north partly to avoid her 'jealousy';[7] but his account indicates what at least some people (mainly Londoners) were thinking and saying and their natural propensity to believe the worst.

Mancini's account, which was unknown to historians until C.A.J. Armstrong re-discovered it in the Bibliothèque Municipale at Lille in 1936, confirmed that neither Gloucester's character assassination of the Queen (and her family) nor the popular suspicions of his motives were later inventions. He clearly had a poor opinion of both of them, and differs from many later writers who thought the sins of one vindicated the other. Tudor critics of the Protector tended to be more favourably disposed towards Elizabeth, while his seventeenth-century defenders alleged that she was ultimately responsible for his more extreme actions. Edward Hall's *The Union of the Two Noble and Illustrious Families of Lancaster and York*, completed probably shortly before his death in 1547, described her as 'a woman more of formal countenaunce than of excellent beautie, but yet of suche beautie & favor that with her sober demeanure, lovely lokyng, and femynyne, smylyng (neither to wanton nor to humble) besyde (besides) her toungue so eloquent, and her wit so pregnant'.[8] We have already noticed how Hall sympathised with her predicament when she surrendered her daughters to the newly crowned King Richard, and William Shakespeare was no less understanding. Elizabeth features in both *King Henry VI* Part 3 and *The Tragedy of King Richard III* (the play which created the legend of the hunchbacked monster clawing his way to power), but the characterisation never hints at ambition or malevolence. She is portrayed as the innocent victim of circumstance during the disturbances of 1469–70 ('Till then, fair hope must hinder life's decay/ And I the rather wean me from despair . . . And bear with mildness my misfortune's cross'), and is still an object of pity in 1483 when she laments her situation with the words 'Ah, who shall hinder me to wail and weep,/ To chide my fortune, and torment myself? . . . All springs reduce their currents to mine eyes/ That I, being govern'd by the watery moon,/ May send forth plenteous tears to drown the world!'[9] It was Richard's earliest apologists, most notably Horace Walpole (1717–97), who, faced with the task of excusing the inexcusable, made her a scapegoat for their hero's misdemeanours. Walpole alleged that the force which accompanied the young Edward V to London (which Elizabeth had insisted should be limited to 2,000 men and which was easily brushed aside at Stony Stratford) was 'likely to strike, as it did strike, the Duke of Gloucester and the ancient nobility with a jealousy, that the queen intended to exclude them from the administration'. 'All her conduct' (he says) 'intimated designs of governing by force in the name of her son', and 'gave the first provocation to Richard and the princes of the blood to assert their rights.'[10] Walpole differs from his predecessors inasmuch as these are not the old charges of bewitching the King and promoting her family, but rather an assumption that her wickedness did not end with the death of her husband. If Elizabeth had sought to dominate the government and advance her family at the expense of those with a better right to be the King's counsellors in Edward's lifetime, how much more likely was it that she would continue to do so now that her position was genuinely threatened. This, of course, assumes that she and Gloucester *were* at loggerheads, something which modern historians, citing his apparently cordial relationship with her brother Anthony, have called into question. Rivers had asked Gloucester to arbitrate in a dispute between himself and a neighbour in Norfolk as recently as 25 March 1483, and the cordiality of their meeting in Northamptonshire just before he was arrested shows plainly that he suspected nothing.[11] It is probable that Elizabeth's fear of the Protector – and her subsequent animosity towards him – was a direct consequence of the events of 29–30 April rather than a positive dislike extending over decades; but this did not suit Walpole's version of the tale.

These were the opinions of writers who, it could be argued, tended to see history in terms of heroes and villains and who failed to appreciate that those they praised were not perfect nor those they denigrated without redeeming qualities. We might expect modern historians to avoid such essentially black and white classifications, but with one or two very recent exceptions the majority have remained wedded to the old traditions. Agnes

Strickland, whose *Lives of the Queens of England* was published in 1840, readily appreciated her subject's difficulties, but considered that 'there never was a woman who contrived to make more personal enemies'. 'Elizabeth', she writes, 'from first to last, certainly held potent sway' (over the mind of King Edward) – 'an influence most dangerous in the hands of a woman who possessed more cunning than firmness, more skill in concocting a diplomatic intrigue than power to form a rational resolve. She was ever successful in carrying her own purposes, but she had seldom a wise or good end in view; the advancement of her own relatives, and the depreciation of her husband's friends and family, were her chief objects. Elizabeth gained her own way with her husband by an assumption of the deepest humility; her words were soft and caressing, her glances timid.'[12]

The fiction of the last sentence is matched only by the bias of the assumptions which precede it, and Miss Strickland's many errors of fact do not inspire confidence in her conclusions. She says in one place (for example) that Elizabeth, Lady Scales, Anthony Woodville's first wife, was 'the richest heiress in the kingdom, whom the duchess of York designed for her son Clarence' (what about Warwick's daughters?), and implies that Elizabeth was still angling for a marriage between Anthony and Mary of Burgundy three years after Mary had married Maximilian![13] A more accurate – and more balanced – portrait might be expected from Cora L. Scofield, the next authoress to deal with the subject, in her monumental *Life and Reign of Edward the Fourth*, published in 1923. Miss Scofield was a careful, painstaking researcher whose work, although biased towards foreign policy, is still admired by modern historians, but even she could not disentangle herself from the lush growth of legend which surrounded Elizabeth. 'Even wise heads', she claimed, 'have been known to be turned by a sudden elevation in rank, and Elizabeth Woodville's head, which was not wise, had evidently been badly turned. Worse still, love seemed to have turned her husband's head as well. For, not content with the folly of having married this "widow of England", there was no end to the favours Edward was ready to shower on her undeserving family.' Warwick, she added, 'seemed to be forgotten and set aside – set aside not merely for Lord Herbert, who . . . had fought for the house of York, but set aside for the Woodvilles, who were no better than upstarts and who had clung to the house of Lancaster till the last moment'.[14] The same is true of James Gairdner, recently described (quite correctly) as 'a colossus of Victorian historians of the Wars of the Roses',[15] whose biography of Richard III first appeared in 1878 and was re-issued with revisions twenty years later. Gairdner engaged in a public debate with Sir Clements Markham (Richard's most ardent defender) in the columns of the *English Historical Review*, but his sceptical view of the King's motives did not prevent him from criticising Elizabeth: 'At the licentious court of the late king', (he remarks), 'although the queen's influence was great with Edward himself, she was scarcely regarded with more respect by the nobility than the courtesans by whom she was dishonoured. To the last she and her family were regarded as upstarts, and their interference in public affairs was generally resented.'[16] The Elizabeth who emerges from these pages – parvenu, diehard Lancastrian, selfish, cunning, ambitious, undeserving and the butt of sly humour on the part of both the nobility and court prostitutes – is unrecognisable as the Queen whose life-story we have been following. All three writers, the one an amateur and the others concerned primarily with other subjects, surely accepted a tradition which they had not seriously examined for themselves.

This brings us to David MacGibbon, Elizabeth's 1938 biographer, who certainly studied her career in detail, but whose work is disappointingly lacking in both accuracy and originality. He begins by quoting in full two letters which the Duke of York and the Earl of Warwick addressed to a Dame Elizabeth Wodehill at the beginning of the 1450s asking her to consider taking Sir Hugh John, one of their partisans, as her husband. MacGibbon accepted that Dame Wodehill was Elizabeth Woodville, notwithstanding that the former was clearly able to give her own hand in marriage (the Duke and Earl would obviously have sought the consent of Lord Rivers if his daughter had been the object of their solicitations), and the fact that George Smith, the editor of *The Coronation of Elizabeth Woodville*, had already questioned the identification. He repeats, uncritically, the old stories that Elizabeth procured the execution of the Earl of Desmond and ruthlessly persecuted Sir Thomas Cook, and confuses the various charges of sorcery by alleging that Clarence accused Elizabeth of witchcraft in 1478. He consistently supports his statements with multiple references (although, in many cases, there is no likelihood of these being called into question), and implies that an opinion expressed by Bishop Stubbs (for example) is somehow vindicated if it is repeated by Pauli, Ramsay, Oman, Markham, Stratford, and Miss Scofield.[17] He follows his sources very closely, sometimes borrowing phrases and passages from them without acknowledgement, and it is this adherence which leads him to portray Elizabeth as both the plucky but pitiful queen of Hall and Shakespeare and as 'a person of a cool calculating decision of character, without any deep affection, but of steady dislikes and revengeful disposition'.[18] He may, possibly, have held a more favourable personal view of her in reality, but his respect for the opinions of earlier historians (and his corresponding reluctance to challenge them) has resulted in his work being couched essentially in their terms.

The old tradition is also found in the writings of Professor Paul Murray Kendall, whose 1955 biography of Richard III includes a good deal of informed (and sometimes not so well informed) guesswork, but which is unlikely to be surpassed as a popular and readable life of the King. Kendall's Richard is as moral and just as his Elizabeth Woodville is unprincipled and vindictive, and their mutual mistrust can, he suggests, be traced back to the mid-1460s when 'the Queen, beautiful and rapacious, would know how to show her haughtiness to the undersized lad from Yorkshire with the awkward torso and the solemn face'. Elizabeth is still blamed for the executions of the Earl of Desmond and the Duke of Clarence 'done to death, all believed, by the insatiable Queen whom he had dared to scorn', and is elsewhere described as the 'impelling spirit', the 'greediest and the most wilful' of the Woodville family.[19] There is (as we have already noted) no evidence of any ill-feeling between Richard and Elizabeth before the dramatic events of the summer of 1483, and the allegations that she was widely blamed for Clarence's downfall and was the chief promoter of her family's excesses are based on the assumption that the motives he attributes to her on this occasion can be applied to the whole of her married life. Similarly, there is nothing to support his assertion that she was not named as one of the executors of her husband's final will because, he implies, Edward had lost confidence in her. The will has disappeared, but it is most unlikely that Elizabeth would have been excluded from it and she did not attend the meeting called to discuss the costs of the late King's funeral on 7 May (the probable source of Kendall's conjecture) because she was by then in the Westminster sanctuary.[20] Kendall's opinion is obviously highly speculative, and such speculations (in the hands of an engaging and widely read author) have an unfortunate tendency to become 'facts'.

It is only within the last quarter of a century or so that scholarly opinion has begun to turn in Elizabeth's favour, and even then the process has been decidedly hesitant. Professor Charles Ross, whose biography of Edward IV was published in 1974, finally exonerated her from any involvement in the execution of Desmond and made it clear that King Edward (whatever his reasons) was alone responsible for Clarence's downfall. But he remained critical of the provision made for her brothers and sisters in Edward's first reign and for her children (particularly the children of her first marriage) in his second, and took the view that 'her rather cold beauty was not offset by any warmth or generosity of temperament. She was to prove a woman of designing character, grasping and ambitious for her family's interests, quick to take offence and reluctant to forgive.'[21] Dr Rosemary Horrox points out that equipping Sir Edward Woodville's fleet in April 1483 absorbed all Edward IV's cash reserves (there was no Woodville 'raid' on the Treasury as described by Mancini and no evidence that Elizabeth received any money), and Dr Anne Sutton and Ms Livia Visser-Fuchs have demonstrated that, far from joining her relatives in penalising Sir Thomas Cook, she probably rescinded her entitlement to 'Queen's Gold'.[22] These authors take a rather pragmatic view of Elizabeth – it is perhaps an oversimplification to say that 'there is no evidence for her actions' (in the years 1483–87) 'and no indication that she had any freedom to manoeuvre in a political world of male decisions made without reference to her wishes',[23] – but their work is a major contribution to the debate surrounding her, and counters the assumption that only King Richard's reputation can be favourably re-assessed.

There are, however, a number of other allegations against Elizabeth which are still regularly taken at face value and deserve to be questioned. By the standards of the day her parents were an ill-matched couple and had indisputably supported the House of Lancaster; but Richard Woodville, created a baron in 1448 and Knight of the Garter three years later, was scarcely more parvenu than the Kingmaker who had been granted his title (after his marriage to the heiress of the last Beauchamp Earl of Warwick) as recently as 1449. Warwick's father, another Richard Neville, the eldest son of the then Earl of Westmoreland's second marriage, owed his comital status to his union with the Montacute heiress to the earldom of Salisbury, and both had claimed to be King Henry's loyal subjects throughout the conflicts of the 1450s. They might point the finger at Rivers and his son Anthony at Calais; but none of them were strangers to opportunism and it is a pity that William Paston does not tell us how the Woodvilles responded to the Yorkist lords' tongue-lashing, and whether it was essentially in kind! Elizabeth's own alleged haughtiness owed more to the demands of court protocol than to delusions of grandeur (it is unlikely that a higher born queen would have been accused of such overbearing behaviour), and if the King was obliged to make suitable provision for her brothers and sisters it was hardly her fault that so many of them (perhaps all of them) had survived infancy. She was expected to intercede with her husband on behalf of their subjects (it has yet to be shown that her influence over him was undue or unacceptable), and in fairness she can hardly be blamed for wanting to crown Prince Edward, whose right to the throne was undisputed until ten weeks after his father's death. The charge that she attempted to dominate the political situation during his minority is challenged by Mancini (no friend of the Woodvilles) who tells us that although the Council resolved to deny Gloucester a full protectorship they agreed that 'the government should be carried on by many persons among whom the duke, far from being excluded, should be accounted the chief'.[24] The disinterment of the old allegation of witchcraft shows that it was, in fact, Gloucester who was seeking to damage Elizabeth, and the Woodvilles, instead of being on their guard against him and seeking to harm him, were completely wrong-footed by the turn of events.

The real problem is perhaps that Elizabeth's critics have failed to imagine themselves in her position, and to pause for a moment to consider how they might have responded to it. Do they really think that she could have left her brothers and sisters in relative penury while she sat on the throne? And if they were not to be married to members of the nobility, then to whom? We do not know if she actually revelled in her new-found wealth and fortune, but she would have been no less criticised if she had displayed an unacceptable degree of humility. Similarly, although her relations with her ambitious brothers-in-law were bound to be tinged with apprehension, there is no evidence that she tried to harm either of them, notwithstanding Clarence's involvement in the death of her father. She may have breathed a sigh of relief at the Duke's demise at the hands of her husband, but her undoing in 1483 was not that she sought to pre-empt Gloucester but rather that she placed too much confidence in him. It is difficult to avoid the conclusion that his allegations formalised the slurs and innuendos of the previous two decades, and that, overall, she was more sinned against than sinning. But they are at least one inasmuch as their reputations were besmirched by both contemporaries and later generations of historians, and it has taken five centuries to present a more reasoned case.

Epilogue: A House of Queens

Elizabeth Woodville is not unusual in that her grandson, Henry VIII, became King of England, but it is remarkable how many of her immediate descendants became queens regnant or queens consort. Her daughter Elizabeth of York married King Henry VII; her granddaughters Margaret and Mary (Henry VIII's sisters) married King James IV of Scotland and King Louis XII of France respectively; her great-granddaughters, Queens Mary I and Elizabeth I, dominated the latter half of the sixteenth century; and her great-great-granddaughters, Mary, Queen of Scots and Lady Jane Grey, the 'nine days queen' were sent to the block.

Elizabeth of York is an enigma. Nancy Lenz Harvey, her 1973 biographer, portrayed her as a determined personality who sustained her faltering mother in the Westminster sanctuary, but there is nothing to suggest that she was ever the dominant female member of the family.[1] She only emerges from the shadows occasionally, perhaps most notably in February 1485 when, as we have already noticed, she wrote to the Duke of Norfolk expressing the hope that Queen Anne's illness would soon prove fatal and that she would then marry her uncle King Richard. Her letter, of which Sir George Buck (1560–1622) had seen 'the autograph or original d[raft] under her [own] hand' in the cabinet of the Earl of Arundel (Norfolk's descendant) is no longer extant and some writers have questioned its authenticity; but there is no reason to doubt the view of Arthur Noel Kincaid, Buck's modern editor, that it once existed, and may still exist among the scattered and inaccessible Norfolk papers.[2] It is surely significant that the King was afterwards compelled to deny, both before the Council and publicly, that the idea of marrying his niece had ever occurred to him, although the Croyland writer remarks that 'there were some persons, however, present at that same council, who very well knew the contrary'.[3] The 'problem' is that the letter is so fulsome that it is difficult to believe that

Elizabeth was writing to the man who, less than two years earlier, had executed her uncle and deposed her brother. Was he really 'her only joy and maker in [this] world' and was she 'his in heart and in thoughts, in [body,] and in all',[4] or were the words dictated by her mother, who knew that Richard needed her daughter to win over disaffected Yorkists as much as the Woodvilles, regretfully, needed him? There is, unfortunately, no answer, but it is possible to discern Elizabeth Woodville's hand at work in this matter as on other occasions when her family's fortunes were at stake.

The marriage between Elizabeth of York and Henry VII was a formal political union in striking contrast to her parents' love match. Elizabeth had probably never seen him until she was brought from Sheriff Hutton castle after Bosworth (it is unlikely they met during the 're-adeption' when Henry attended his uncle Henry VI's court and she was in sanctuary), and she may have resented his treatment of her mother after 1487. They continued to have children, however; four survived infancy and five others died early, and there is even evidence of a growing warmth in their relationship by the time Arthur, their eldest son, died in 1502. 'When his grace understood that sorrowful heavy tidings' (wrote a contemporary), 'he sent for the Queen, saying that he and his Queen would take the painful sorrows together. After that she was come and saw the King her lord, and that natural and painful sorrow, as I have heard say, she, with full great and constant comfortable words besought his Grace that he would first after God remember the weal of his own noble person, the comfort of his realm, and of her. She then said, that my lady, his mother, had never no more children but him only, and that God by his grace had ever preserved him, and brought him where that he was. Over that, how that God had left him yet a fair prince, two fair princesses; and that God is where he was, and we are both young enough; and that the prudence and wisdom of his Grace sprung (was known) over all Christendom, so that it should please him to take this according thereunto. Then the King thanked her of her good comfort. After that she was departed and come to her own chamber, natural and motherly remembrance of that great loss smote her so sorrowful to the heart, that those who were about her were fain to send for the King to comfort her. Then his Grace, of true, gentle, and faithful love, in good haste came and relieved her, and showed her how wise counsel she had given him before; and he, for his part, would thank God for his son, and would she should do in like wise.'[5]

Elizabeth of York lived quietly in the shadow of others. There is nothing to suggest she was able to influence Henry politically: indeed, Lady Margaret Beaufort, who survived her, occupied that special place in her son's affections which his wife might otherwise have taken. Polydore Vergil's final compliment to her was that 'she was a woman of such a character that it would be hard to judge whether she displayed more of majesty and dignity in her life than wisdom and moderation'.[6]

A more public and turbulent role awaited Elizabeth's daughter Margaret, who was married to James IV, King of Scots, at the age of fourteen in 1503. James was more than twice her age and had a number of illegitimate children by various ladies; but she accepted that her 'exile' was part of her responsibility to serve England's interests as well as she could. She bore James five children (although only one, the future James V, survived infancy), and was left suddenly and dramatically widowed when he disregarded her pleas not to engage in war with England and fell at Flodden in 1513. Thereafter she struggled to preserve the two things which mattered most to her – her son's birthright and her brother Henry VIII's friendship – by intriguing against the ambitions of the Scottish nobles and trying to frustrate an alliance between her adopted country and England's other traditional enemy, France. She re-married twice, but neither union was universally popular (shades of Elizabeth, her grandmother), and neither brought her lasting personal happiness. She lived apart from Archibald Douglas, Earl of Angus, the father of her daughter Margaret (Lord Darnley's mother) for eight years before divorcing him in 1527 (Henry VIII, still the Pope's loyal subject, expressed shock and indignation although he was similarly seeking to end his own marriage to Catherine of Aragon), and her long-time lover and third husband, Harry Stuart (whom James V created Earl of Methven) eventually deserted her for Lord Atholl's daughter Janet, who bore him a son. By the time she died in October 1541 her son (now aged twenty-nine) had long since assumed responsibility for Scottish policy, and was only a little more than a year away from his own death in the aftermath of his defeat at Solway Moss. Her life, like her grandmother's, had been long and often difficult, and both women shared a dedication to a calling which was not entirely of their own choosing. But Margaret was not allowed to rest quietly. She had avoided the dangers of the Reformation in her lifetime, but in 1559 the royal tombs in Perth's Carthusian Abbey were attacked by Calvinists and her remains were burned.

Mary, her sister, born in March 1496, was as beautiful and vivacious as Margaret was plain and unremarkable, but her destiny – marriage to an older, foreign ruler – was very similar. While she was for many years betrothed to Prince Charles of Castile (the future Emperor Charles V), the shifting alliances of continental politics led, ultimately, to her union with Louis XII of France, a man three times her age, in October 1514. Louis died a mere eighty-two days after the wedding, and the roles of the two sisters diverged dramatically. There was no prince to keep Mary in her adopted country, and she had been careful to extract a promise from her royal brother that he would allow her to choose her next husband for herself. The result was that she risked his anger (and made it infinitely more difficult for him to arrange another foreign marriage for her) by marrying her long-time admirer, Charles Brandon, Duke of Suffolk (the son of Henry VII's standard-bearer on Bosworth Field) before she returned to England.[7] Henry feigned anger, for Suffolk had promised that he would not seek to marry Mary before leaving for the Continent; but in reality they were great friends, and the recovery of most of her dowry allowed the King to forgive them and arrange for them to be publicly remarried in England on 13 May 1515. Mary bore Suffolk three children, and they shared an almost idyllic life in London and East Anglia until the matter of Henry's divorce from Queen Catherine came between them. Suffolk, who owed everything to Henry, supported his master unequivocally, but Mary sympathised with Catherine's predicament and expressed a hearty dislike for Anne Boleyn. The result was that she came to court less frequently than formerly, and a short, unexplained, illness prevented her from attending Anne's coronation (at which her husband acted as Lord High Steward) on 1 June 1533. She died twenty-five days later, and was buried in Bury St Edmunds Abbey with the ceremony that befitted the King's sister and a dowager queen of France.

Margaret had probably derived something of her stoicism and dedication to duty from her grandmother, just as Mary had inherited her beauty, and perhaps it was as well that their gifts were apportioned in this manner since the former was obliged to spend many years manoeuvring for position in Scotland while the latter was surrounded by ease and privilege all her life. Mary's eldest daughter, Frances, married Henry Grey, the first Marquess of Dorset's grandson, and their daughters, Jane, Katherine, and Mary, were thus directly descended from Elizabeth Woodville on both sides. It was Jane – Lady Jane Grey as she is known to history – who became the figurehead, and ultimately the victim, of the Duke of Northumberland's bid to preserve the Protestant reformation in England after Edward VI's premature death in 1554.[8] Jane was malleable because she breathed the rarefied air of a young intellectual who found it difficult to believe she was ever wrong or that others did not share her opinions; and it was her conviction that God meant her to be Queen (if he had not, he would not have placed her in this situation) which led her to become a willing, and to some extent active, participant in Northumberland's plans. In the end it was Henry VIII's daughter, Mary, who commanded a popularity which Jane had neither sought nor comprehended, who triumphed, but even then Jane would have kept her head if her father had not become involved in Thomas Wyatt's rebellion against the new Queen's proposed marriage with Philip of Spain. Guildford, her husband, Northumberland's youngest son, shared her fate (his elder brothers, including Robert, Queen Elizabeth I's future favourite, were, fortunately for them, married before the conspiracy was mooted), and it is characteristic of Jane that she blamed no one for her dramatic reversal of fortune.[9] Her last letter to her father, who had hoped to gain so much by her elevation, contains no hint of recrimination, and she went to the block, at still only sixteen, fortified by the intense Protestantism which had ruled her short life. Queen Mary burned religious opponents; Queen Jane might well have resorted to similar methods to convince Catholics of the error of their ways.

Her two sisters were scarcely more fortunate. Queen Elizabeth was determined to ensure they remained unmarried and produced no legitimate heirs or potential claimants, but both contrived to thwart her. Katherine secretly married Edward Seymour, Earl of Hertford, eight years after Jane's execution, but their union could not be concealed when she became pregnant with their son Edward and both of them were sent to the Tower. Elizabeth ordered that they were not to be allowed to meet in any circumstances, and, when a second son was born eighteen months later, fined Hertford £15,000. Katherine was thereafter lodged with a succession of trusted courtiers (who ensured that she did not see her husband) until she died in 1566 aged twenty-seven, and Hertford was not able to establish the legitimacy of his marriage until after James I succeeded in 1603. Mary, the youngest and least attractive of the sisters (she has been described as dwarf-like), covertly married Martin Keyes, a royal sergeant porter, who was a large man physically and a widower with several children. They doubtless hoped that Elizabeth would not regard them as a threat to her position, but Mary was similarly confined to a succession of country houses when the union was discovered and only released from supervision after her husband's death. In 1577, the year before she died, she compiled a memoir of the troubles that had beset her family, which was eventually published as *The Tablette Booke of Ladye Mary Keyes*. This provides a fascinating insight into her life at Bradgate (and the strict manner in which she, Jane and Katherine were brought up there), and is a unique, personal source of information for Jane's last days in the Tower. Only Frances, the girls' mother, who had been careful to commit no treason herself and who had perhaps been too close to the throne for too long to be treated over-harshly, was able to re-build her life in the aftermath of her husband's and daughter's executions. She was allowed to keep Groby and other properties in Leicestershire, and promptly married Adrian Stokes, her handsome master of the horse, who was fifteen years her junior. This misalliance troubled contemporary society as much as those of her great-great-grandparents Richard and Jacquetta Woodville and her great-grandparents Edward IV and his Elizabeth, but critics again had no choice but to accept what was a *fait accompli* and Frances was buried in Westminster Abbey with full royal honours when she died in 1559. Of all these ladies, perhaps only Mary of Suffolk found much pleasure in the role which fate had assigned her, and it is curious to reflect how queenship (or an aspiration to it) troubled Elizabeth Woodville's descendants in so many different ways.

Appendix 1

Memorials of Queen Elizabeth and the Woodville Family

1. QUEEN ELIZABETH

Queen Elizabeth was buried with Edward IV, her second husband, in the first bay of the north choir aisle of St George's Chapel, Windsor. The grave was disturbed when a new pavement was laid in 1789, and Elizabeth's skeleton was observed lying within her decayed wooden coffin which had been placed on top of her husband's leaden sarcophagus. It has not, so far as is known, been seen since that time, and Hanoverian souvenir hunters and the passing of more than two centuries have probably ensured that relatively little now remains.

A number of contemporary or near contemporary likenesses of the Queen have survived and may be summarised as follows:

i. An early sixteenth-century copy of a panel portrait measuring 37.5 x 26.4 cm in the Royal Collection at Windsor. This is the prototype of the likenesses in Queens' College, Cambridge, the Ashmolean Museum, Oxford, and others at Longleat House, Ripon Cathedral Deanery, and Dunham Massey Hall, Altrincham. David MacGibbon suggested in 1937 that the true exemplar was a panel dated 1463, which was then in the possession of Dr William Shaw of the Public Record Office and which he assumed had been painted by the King's painter, John Stratford; but Frederick Hepburn believes that the year was added later and that it is 'further removed' from the original than some of the works mentioned above.[1]

ii. Representations in stained glass in the windows of the north cross or martyrdom chapel of Canterbury Cathedral, and the east window of Little Malvern Priory Church (Worcestershire) The magnificent Canterbury portrait, which has been dated to 1482 and may be the work of John Prudde, the King's glazier at Westminster, has survived the vicissitudes of the centuries; but the upper section of the contemporary figure of the Queen at Little Malvern (which formed part of a similar series of portrayals of members of the Yorkist royal family sponsored by the loyal Bishop Alcock) has unfortunately been lost.

iii. Pictures in books, in the *Illuminated Book of the Fraternity of Our Lady's Assumption* of the Skinners' Company (where she is portrayed in her robes of estate and regalia against a background of red and white gillyflowers entangled with red and white roses); in a copy of the *Dictes and Sayings of the Philosophers* preserved in Lambeth Palace Library [MS. 265, f.lv], (this shows Anthony, Earl Rivers, presenting the work to the King, Queen and Prince Edward, but is an illuminated miniature rather that a true portrait); and in the *Luton Guild Book*, (where she is shown kneeling before the Trinity with King Edward, Bishop Rotherham and her mother-in-law Cecily Neville). There is a comparable illustration in green and brown in a genealogical roll written by Thomas Haseldon soon after Edward and Elizabeth's marriage, showing them again kneeling (this time with St George) before God and Christ crucified praying for a fruitful union (now Jesus College, Oxford MS. 114 fo. 34). The drawing of Edward is poor, but Elizabeth's features are quite striking and she is beautiful in a somewhat gaunt way.[2]

Elizabeth is particularly associated with a number of places and properties, especially Grafton, in Northamptonshire. The family manor house passed to the Crown in Henry VIII's reign when the second Marquess of Dorset exchanged it for other properties, and it became an occasional royal residence until it was severely damaged in the Civil War. There is a belief that the existing house preserves fragments of the original structure, but H.M. Colvin is adamant that 'it incorporates no recognisable portion of its fabric'.[3] The Hermitage, which once housed a small religious community sometimes patronised by the Woodvilles and which would also have been familiar to the Queen, has likewise vanished (the discovery of alternating Woodville and Yorkist floor tiles in the chapel during the 1964–65 excavation led to speculation that this might have been the secret place where she married King Edward); but the village church is still much as she would have known it and preserves an incised slab of about 1415 depicting Sir John Woodville who, the inscription tells us, completed the tower. The 'Queen's Oak' at nearby Potterspury, severely damaged by fire in 1995, is too young to have been the tree beneath which Elizabeth first met King Edward, but the tradition was continued when the Prince of Wales planted a new tree at Grafton on 4 September 2000.

Elizabeth and Sir John Grey may have resided at the now much altered and ruinous castle at Astley (Warwickshire), but she would certainly have known, and perhaps spent part of her childhood at Groby Old Hall in Leicestershire, the home of her husband's parents, Sir Edward Grey and Elizabeth, Lady Ferrers, and would have been familiar with their estate at Bradgate, now a public park. While the present building at Groby has evolved over the centuries, it incorporates stone which Pevsner thinks may have been part of the outer walls of Groby Castle, and the south tower (with the Ferrers arms set in blue bricks against a red background) is clearly late fifteenth-century work. The Queen is also particularly associated with other buildings: with Queens' College, Cambridge which she re-founded in 1465; with the Great Hall at Eltham with its magnificent fifteenth century oak roof; and with the Palace of Sheen, granted to her by Edward IV. This last was rebuilt and renamed Richmond by Henry VII, but a few remains, including one of the gateways, still exist between Richmond Green and the Thames.

2. ELIZABETH'S BROTHERS AND SONS

The Queen's eldest brother, Anthony, second Earl Rivers, and Lord Richard Grey, her second son by her first marriage, were executed at Pontefract Castle on Wednesday 25 June 1483 in much the same circumstances as her father, the first Earl, and next brother, Sir John, had suffered outside Coventry on 12 August 1469. Their places of burial are unknown; and there is no indication that memorials were provided for any of them when the tide of politics again turned in the family's favour. Sir

Edward Woodville died abroad, as did Bishop Lionel, although a canopied tomb at the intersection of the north-west transept and the north choir aisle in Salisbury Cathedral may have been built by the latter. Richard, Elizabeth's last surviving brother, asked in his will to be buried in the abbey of St James in Northampton, which has entirely disappeared.[4] He is usually described in family pedigrees as Elizabeth's youngest brother, but the fact that he received the earldom in 1485 proves that he was older than Edward and perhaps also Lionel.[5] The Marquess of Dorset was almost certainly buried with other members of the Grey family in St Mary's at Astley (Warwickshire); but the former collegiate church has lost much of its glory (severe damage was caused by the collapse of the spire in the seventeenth century) and the only effigies which survive are those of Sir Edward Grey (Elizabeth's father-in-law by her first marriage), Elizabeth Talbot, Viscountess Lisle (her sister-in-law), and Dorset's second wife, Cecilia Bonville, who bore him fifteen children. Of Elizabeth's three sons by King Edward, George, who died young, was buried in St George's Chapel, Windsor, in 1479 (no memorial), and the bones discovered in the Tower in 1674 and placed in an urn in Westminster Abbey may be those of Edward V and Richard, Duke of York. The remains were examined by specialists in 1933 but the results were unsatisfactory (the investigators found, to some extent, what they were looking for), and although a new investigation, using genetic fingerprinting and other more modern techniques, would be of great interest, the Richard III Society rightly takes the view that the tomb should not be disturbed to produce another potentially inconclusive result when scientific advances promise greater certainty in a few years' time.

3. ELIZABETH'S SISTERS AND DAUGHTERS

There is a brass of Elizabeth's sister Jacquetta (d. 1481), her husband John, Lord Strange of Knockyn and their daughter Joan in the church of St John the Baptist, Hillingdon (Middlesex), but the inscription (now lost) indicated that Jacquetta was buried elsewhere. The likenesses of two of her brothers-in-law, Thomas Fitzalan, Earl of Arundel (the former Lord Maltravers), and Sir Anthony Grey, son and heir of Edmund Grey, Earl of Kent, who married her sisters Margaret (d. before 1491) and Joan (d. 1491), remain in St Nicholas's Church, Arundel and St Albans Cathedral; but Grey died many years before his wife and Fitzalan many years after and there is no proof that they were buried together. Anne, Countess of Kent, who married, secondly, George Grey, Joan's husband's younger brother, was buried at Warden, in Bedfordshire, when she died in 1489 but has no surviving memorial, and the same is true of her three remaining sisters, Catherine, Duchess of Buckingham (who took Sir Richard Wingfield as her third husband and died in 1513), Mary, Countess of Huntingdon (her widower married Richard III's illegitimate daughter Katherine after her death in 1481), and Martha, who married Sir John Bromley of Bartomley and Hextall (Shropshire), and whose date of death is unknown.

Two of the Queen's daughters, Margaret and Mary, died young, the former shortly after her birth in 1472 and the latter aged fourteen in May, 1482. Mary was buried in St George's Chapel and an account of her funeral survives in College of Arms MS I. 11, f. 21r-v and British Library MS Stowe 1047, f. 219r-v.[6] Elizabeth of York, her eldest daughter, who died in 1503, lies with her husband Henry VII in his chapel in Westminster Abbey, and is represented by a magnificent bronze effigy sculpted by the Florentine Torrigiano. The *Complete Peerage* states that Princess Cecily, who married successively Ralph Scrope of Upsall (Yorks), John, Viscount Welles and Thomas Kyme of Friskney (Lincs), lived on the Isle of Wight with her third husband and when she died in 1507 was buried in Quarr Abbey; but it is possible that a tomb which the seventeenth-century antiquary Thomas Dingley apparently saw in the church of St Alkmund at Whitchurch, in Shropshire (which collapsed into ruin in 1711) and which he described as 'of white marble . . . of one Lady Scroop Daughter of K. Edward' may have been hers.[7] Princess Anne, who died in 1512, married Thomas Howard, Earl of Surrey and afterwards Duke of Norfolk (the grandson of the Duke who had died fighting for Richard III at Bosworth), but it is Howard's second wife, Elizabeth Stafford, daughter of the third and last Duke of Buckingham, who lies beside him on his fine tomb in St Michael's Church, Framlingham (Norfolk). Princess Catherine, Elizabeth's second youngest and longest-lived daughter, became the wife of Sir William Courteney, the only son of the Earl of Devon, and was buried in the Courteney Chapel in St Peter's Church, Tiverton (Devon) when she died in 1527. The Chapel has suffered many vicissitudes over the centuries, and W.E. Hampton's suggestion that her tomb 'must have been placed more or less where now stands the tomb-chest of John Waldron (d. 1579)' has recently been taken up by local historian Michael Martyn who, at the time of writing, is proposing to use ground-penetrating radar to see if any trace of an earlier burial or structure remains beneath.[8] Princess Bridget, the least known of the Queen's daughters to reach maturity, became a nun at Dartford and died in about 1517.

There are few enough reminders of Elizabeth and her immediate family left to us: let us be diligent in preserving those remembrances which still remain.

Appendix 2

The Woodvilles and Witchcraft

Witchcraft seems to have fulfilled two purposes in the later Middle Ages. Firstly, it allowed intelligent but unsophisticated minds to explain the inexplicable, and secondly, it gave them the means to bring potentially damning charges against opponents and enemies. Accusers had to show that the individual or individuals concerned had been inquiring into, and had sought to influence, the future; but it would be virtually impossible for them to prove that their 'necromancy' was without malice, and a court might take a decidedly jaundiced view. H.A. Kelly has asserted that 'every sovereign from Edward III to Elizabeth I was affected by witchcraft'; it was therefore likely that the Yorkist royal family and the Woodvilles would face problems of this nature in their turn.[1]

The most famous witchcraft trial of the fifteenth century – one which would have been well remembered in the Woodvilles' heyday – was that of Eleanor Cobham, who had married Humphrey, Duke of Gloucester, Henry V's youngest brother and Henry VI's uncle and heir apparent, in 1431. She was arrested ten years later and accused of using potions supplied by Margery Jourdemayne (who lived at Eye-next-Westminster and was known as the 'Witch of Eye') to make Gloucester fall in love with and marry her, and of subsequently arranging for Margery and two priests who dabbled in the black arts, Roger Bolingbroke and Thomas Southwell, to cast the King's horoscope to discover if her husband would succeed him. This may have amounted to no more than innocent, idle curiosity; but it was clearly capable of a more sinister interpretation, and was music to the ears of the Duke's enemies who regarded his belligerence as the main obstacle to peace with France. The three magicians had apparently made a wax image which the prosecution alleged was of the King and designed to procure his death (by melting it), but which Eleanor said represented a baby and was intended only to help her bear a child. Such arguments were, as we have already noted, incapable of proof or disproof, and in this case the court decided to take no chances. Southwell died in prison, Bolingbroke was hanged, drawn and quartered, Margery Jourdemayne was burnt at Smithfield, and Eleanor's marriage was formally dissolved (by no less a person than the Archbishop of Canterbury sitting with two cardinals, the three bishops who had conducted the trial 'and divers doctors and masters of divinity') on the premise that, by using witchcraft, she had interfered with Duke Humphrey's freedom of choice. She was sentenced to do public penance through the streets of London on three separate occasions (walking barefoot and bareheaded and carrying a candle weighing two pounds, much as Jane Shore was to be punished in Richard III's reign), and then to life imprisonment, which she served first at Chester and then at Peel Castle on the Isle of Man.[2] Her real offence may have been no more than foolishness, but in the ideological climate of the mid-fifteenth century not even her husband's high birth and position could rescue her from her fate.[3]

It was thus almost inevitable that, in an age when the king and his greatest subjects nearly always married to gain some advantage for their kingdom or families (and love was a bonus), some would find in witchcraft an explanation – perhaps the only feasible explanation – of why Edward IV had turned his back on the political and financial benefits of a foreign marriage to wed Elizabeth Woodville. The Cobham case had shown how such allegations, if proven, could result in the dissolution of a union, and those who regretted or resented Edward's decision would not have been slow to seize an opportunity which held out some prospect of retrieving the situation. It is surely no coincidence that no sooner had the King been detained by the Earl of Warwick after the Battle of Edgecote than Jacquetta, Elizabeth's mother, was accused by Thomas Wake of Blisworth, a supporter of the Nevilles and a near neighbour in Northamptonshire, of using sorcery to procure his union with her daughter. Wake produced a leaden figure of a man at arms, broken in the middle and fastened with wire, which, he claimed, Jacquetta had made for this purpose, and called upon John Dauger, the parish clerk of nearby Stoke Bruerne, to bear witness that she had also fashioned two others representing the King and Queen. There seems little doubt that Warwick, who had just arbitrarily executed Earl Rivers and John Woodville, was now bent on the destruction of the rest of the family, and that Jacquetta would have shared the fate of Eleanor Cobham if the political situation had not again altered by the time she was tried in January 1470. By then Edward IV had regained his freedom, Dauger, prudently, declined to give the required evidence, and the King and a group of his councillors (including Warwick, who again had to contain his anger) dismissed the case.[4] Edward might have been sympathetic even if Jacquetta had not been his mother-in-law since it was afterwards said that he was assisted in the recovery of his kingdom by Friar Bungay, 'astronomer and necromancer', who supposedly used his enchantments to prevent Queen Margaret from crossing to England and impeded the Lancastrian forces with mists at the Battle of Barnet in 1471.[5]

Jacquetta's death in 1472 meant that this was the end of the matter for her personally, but it was again resurrected, this time implicating Elizabeth, when Richard III seized power in 1483. Polydore Vergil records that when Hastings was arrested Richard began the proceedings by declaring that 'by the space of a few days by past nether nyght nor day can I rest, drynk, nor eat, wherfor my blood by lyttle and lyttle decreaseth, my force fayleth, my breath shorteneth, and all the partes of my body do above measure, as you se (and with that he showed them his arme) faule away; which mischief veryly procedeth in me from that sorceress Elizabeth the quene, who with hir witchcraft hath so enchantyd me that by thannoyance thereof I am dissolvyd'.[6] Thomas More comments that the assembled lords were well aware that the claim was spurious – Richard's arm was 'ever such since his birth' and 'wel thei wist that the quene was to wise to go aboute any such folye (folly)'; but this did not prevent him from returning to the theme in the *Titulus Regis* which declared that the 'ungracious pretensed marriage' (between Elizabeth and King Edward) 'was made . . . by sorcerie and witchcrafte, committed by the said Elizabeth and her moder, Jaquett Duchess of Bedford, as the common opinion of the people and the publique voice and fame is through all this land; and hereafter, if and as the case shall require, shall bee proved suffyciently in tyme and place convenient'.[7] It is usually assumed that Richard's case was based firmly on the pre-contract and that the old allegation of sorcery and the objection to the secrecy of the marriage were essentially sideshows; but W.E. Hampton has suggested that the witchcraft charge was not as fanciful as might be supposed. He points out that 30 April, the date on which Edward traditionally halted at Stony Stratford before riding over to Grafton to marry Elizabeth early the next morning, was St Walpurga's eve, one of the four Grand Sabbaths of the Witches' Year. The 'coarsely orgiastic' rituals practised on these occasions lasted from about midnight to cockcrow, and although they might, occasionally, be held in a large private house, a preferred location (which may find an echo in the traditional version of the story) was 'an open waste beneath some blasted oak'. Could Edward, he wonders, have made his lone journey to Grafton in the very early hours of 1 May, when local people would have bolted their doors for fear of the witches, and was his marriage to Elizabeth made, as the *Titulus Regis* claims, by witchcraft, in a 'profane place', and not 'aftre the lawe of Godds churche'? It would at least explain why the athletic young King was so inexplicably exhausted when he rejoined his followers at Stony Stratford (partly, perhaps, as a result of the after-effects of the aphrodisiacs and stimulants known to have been used on such occasions), and why he immediately retired to bed.[8]

The possibility that the King and the Woodvilles were involved in activities of this nature is intriguing and potentially plausible, but there are some difficulties, or objections which cannot be disregarded. Edward could hardly have slipped past his own sentries, still less have risked his disappearance being suddenly discovered by his army; nor could his journey have been secret in the sense that even his closest attendants were unaware of his intentions. It has been suggested that William, Lord Hastings, the King's dear friend and fellow-voluptuary, knew of his infatuation and helped him; but the evidence of Hastings's own recent dealings with Elizabeth – the hard terms of the agreement by which she had obtained his help in her dispute with her mother-in-law – makes this somewhat improbable, and it is more likely that his senior guards and body servants were told of his destination and the likely duration of his absence if not the precise reasons for it. Secondly, there is no tangible evidence against Elizabeth and Jacquetta. Only their enemies pointed the finger at them, and then only with regard to the King's marriage. Elizabeth was not accused of using witchcraft to change the course of events in 1470–71 or 1483 (except for King Richard's alleged outburst), possibly because these situations were clearly resolved by war and negotiation and no magical explanation was necessary. It is true that Richard offered to prove, before an ecclesiastical court, that dark forces had been used to procure his brother's marriage, something he did not do with regard to the pre-contract; but it is possible that the only pieces of evidence he proposed to bring forward were the old charges against Jacquetta that had been stymied in 1470. It is not improbable that Jacquetta, who knew that the King desired her daughter, had sought out those who professed the ability to foresee the outcome; but whether she had then asked them to facilitate the union (or had herself been one of the facilitators) is less certain. It was easy for a King to claim he had been bewitched (as Henry VIII was to claim Anne Boleyn had bewitched him, for example), but Edward had probably only lost his heart to a pretty face.

Appendix 3

Elizabeth Woodville's 'Diary'

A journal, or diary, said to have been kept by Elizabeth Woodville when she was in her youth and again living in her parents' house at Grafton, is first mentioned by T.R. Potter in his *History and Antiquities of Charnwood Forest*, published in 1842. He gives an extract from the journal in a footnote, and this is confirmed, and to some extent augmented, by an undated newspaper cutting pasted into a copy of Thomas Kay's *The Story of the 'Grafton' portrait of William Shakespeare* (1914) held at the Northamptonshire Record Office.[1] Potter does not, unfortunately, mention the source of his information, but the 'cutting' says that the original is 'locked up in Drummond Castle' referring, apparently, to Grimsthorpe and Drummond Castle in Lincolnshire rather than to the estate near Perth. Enquiries at Grimsthorpe have failed to locate it, however, and it is not included in the calendar of the Earl of Ancaster's papers published by the Historical Manuscripts Commission. It must, therefore, be judged on the basis of the following compilation taken principally from Potter, with additions from the 'cutting' in italics (minor differences in phraseology have been ignored):

Thursday (*Monday*) Morning (May 10 1451). – Rose at four o'clock, and helped Katherine to milk the cows: Rachael, the other dairy-maid, having scalded one of her hands in a very sad manner last night. Made a poultice for Rachael and gave Robin a penny to get her something comfortable from the apothecary's. Six o'clock. – Breakfasted. The buttock of beef rather too much boiled, and the ale (*beer*) a little the stalest. Memorandum to tell the cook about the first fault, and to mend the second myself, by tapping a fresh barrel directly.

Seven o'clock. – Went out with the Lady Duchess, my mother, into the court-yard; fed five and thirty (*twenty*) men and women; chid Roger very severely for expressing some dissatisfaction in attending us with the broken meat. Eight o'clock. – Went into the paddock behind the house with my maiden Dorothy: caught Stump (*Thump*), the little black pony, myself, and rode a matter of six miles, without either saddle or bridle. Ten o'clock. – Went to dinner. John Grey one of our visitants – a most comely youth – but what's that to me? A virtuous maiden should be entirely under the direction of her parents. John ate very little – stole a great many tender looks at me – said a woman never could be handsome, in his opinion, who was not good-tempered. I hope my temper is not intolerable; nobody finds fault with it but Roger, and Roger is the most disorderly serving man in our family. John Grey likes white teeth – my teeth are of a pretty good colour, I think, and my hair is as black as jet, though I say it – and John, if I mistake not, is of the same opinion. Eleven o'clock. – Rose from table, the company all desirous of walking in the fields. John Grey would lift me over every stile, and twice he squeezed my hand with great vehemence. I cannot say I should have any aversion to John Grey: he plays prison-bars as well as any gentleman in the country, is remarkably dutiful to his parents, *my lord and lady*, and never misses church of a Sunday. Three o'clock. – Poor farmer Robinson's house burnt down by an accidental fire. John Grey proposed a subscription among the company *for the relief of the farmer*, and gave a matter of no less than five (*four*) pound himself to this benevolent intention. Mem. Never saw him look so comely as at that moment. Four o'clock. – Went to prayers, *after which my weekly meeting with farmers wives and maids. The spirit of Brotherhood makes labour but a joy. Mem., To speak at my next meeting on how love lightens labour and softens pain. Women well combined maketh for knowledge and giveth strength to the nation.* Six o'clock. – Fed the poultry and hogs. Seven o'clock. – Supper at the table; delayed *until that hour* on account of farmer Robinson's fire and misfortune. *Mem.*, The goose pie too much baked, and the loin of pork almost roasted to rags. Nine o'clock. – The company almost all asleep. These late hours are very disagreeable. Said my prayers a second time, John Grey disturbing my thoughts too much the first. Fell asleep about ten, and dreamt that John had come to demand me of my father.

Recent writers have tended to dismiss the diary as an obvious forgery. Agnes Strickland refers to this 'well-known and amusing paper' (which) 'is a palpable fabrication', and David MacGibbon calls it 'pure imagination'.[2] P.W. Hammond has drawn attention to a comparable piece entitled 'Elizabeth Woodville: an Autographic Sketch of the 15th Century' by Miss (Elizabeth) Benger which appeared in *The Literary Souvenir* in 1827, the year of her death. This purports to be a letter written by a 'bosom friend and kinswoman' of the Queen to a noble lady in France, and describes episodes in her life including the uncorroborated statement that she had three children by Sir John Grey. Miss Benger wrote both novels and more serious works, and Mr Hammond is probably correct in his assumption that 'she allowed herself to mix the two forms'.[3]

There is no doubt that both transcripts, as they stand, express 'the language and sentiments of the late eighteenth or early nineteenth century',[4] but we would perhaps be guilty of throwing the baby out with the bathwater if we dismissed the 'Diary' out of hand. The idiom is certainly modern, but it is not an obvious forgery written by someone who plainly had little or no knowledge of life at the end of the Middle Ages. Medieval people did, as the journal indicates, eat three meals a day: breakfast at a very early hour, dinner (the main meal of the day) at between nine and eleven, and supper before darkness, perhaps at three in the winter but later in summer. Elizabeth may well have breakfasted at six, had dinner at ten, and a (delayed) supper at seven on a May evening, and the food she is said to have eaten – beef, pork, and goose pie – could all have been consumed in this period. Monday (Potter is incorrect in saying that 10 May 1451 was a Thursday) was, like Sunday, Tuesday and Thursday, a flesh day in most households (the fish days were Wednesday, Friday and Saturday), and there is a note of authenticity in the comment that the ale served at breakfast was going stale. Ale did not keep as well as other drinks, and a quantity sufficient for the needs of the establishment was brewed about once a week. It is also likely that the Woodvilles displayed their *largesse* by feeding a number of poor people with the surplus left over from their own meals, and there can be no doubt that Elizabeth, like nearly all medieval gentlewomen, was able to ride a horse well. Prison Bars (or Base, or Bars or Prisoner's Bars) was a game of hot pursuit in which individual members of a team ran after opponents in an effort to touch or 'tick' them. It was popular among children (the earliest reference to it dates from Edward III's reign), and John Grey and Elizabeth could well have played it in their youth.[5]

So far, so good, but there are other aspects of the document which are rather more questionable. The various contemporary or near-contemporary portraits of Elizabeth leave little doubt that she had fair, not black, hair (Miss Benger's 'letter' also made this error); and the four or five pounds which John Grey donated to help the unfortunate farmer seems a very large sum. H.L. Grey has calculated that in 1436 a squire's lands yielded an average income of £24 per annum and that a gentleman (someone on the lowest rung of the aristocratic ladder) would have received between £5 and £20 yearly.[6] John Grey, as the son of a knight and a minor baroness, probably fell into one of these categories, and five *shillings* would have been a generous gift. No Robinsons are known to have lived in the village in earlier centuries in any case,[7] and it is uncertain whether Elizabeth would have used an expression like 'roasted to rags'. Similarly, her remark that 'a virtuous maiden should be entirely under the direction of her parents' appears superfluous given that daughters (and sons also) remained rigidly under parental authority even when adults. The *Paston Letters* contain examples of a daughter being beaten for refusing to marry the elderly but wealthy husband her mother had chosen for her, and of the eldest son of the family being effectively banished for some misdemeanour until he had made his peace with his father.[8] The future queen also seems to have been preoccupied with tasks which would have been very much part of the life of a farmer's daughter – milking the cows, feeding the animals, and tapping a new barrel of ale – but there is no mention of reading, sewing or the other 'polite' pastimes which filled the leisure hours of ladies in her social position. It is possible to argue that these were too mundane to warrant mention in an everyday journal, but so too were some of the activities which are recorded and it seems likely that someone as intelligent and cultured as Elizabeth would have enjoyed them from an early age.

The conclusion then must be that some parts of the diary may be authentic, others less so. It is to be hoped that Elizabeth was not as insufferable as the homily on the merits of hard work (which the 'cutting' says she delivered to the servants) implies she was, and it may well have been added to the original manuscript. It is just – but only just – possible that the mangled and 'improved' text we now have was derived from a fuller, genuine journal, one which may be re-discovered someday.

Appendix 4

Elizabeth Woodville and Jocelyn of Hardwick

In 1845 Henry Coore JP, DL, published at Halifax a pamphlet entitled *The Story of Queen Elizabeth Woodville*. It was the substance of a paper he had earlier read 'before an assemblage of West Riding antiquaries in Leeds', and although intended only for private circulation proved sufficiently popular to warrant reprinting. A copy of the reprint (perhaps 'second edition' would be a more accurate description) in the British Library has handwritten corrections and emendations made by J.M. Berkeley Blount in 1899, in which he particularly notes that 'for some unexplained reason, the editor [probably Coore himself] has omitted from this reprint a quantity of material included in the original pamphlet relating to the attempt of Richard Neville, Earl of Warwick, to promote a marriage between Elizabeth Woodville and Sir Hugh St (sic) John and shewing the St John lineage'.[1] The work consists mainly of a telescoped and not always accurate account of the Wars of the Roses in which Elizabeth makes occasional appearances, and its only real interest lies in the space given to the Hardwycke (or Hardwicke) family of Hardwick Hall in Derbyshire, who were related to the Greys. Roger de Hardwycke was cousin to Lady Ferrers, Sir John Grey's mother, and Coore recounts a tradition that a relationship developed between the newly widowed Elizabeth and Roger's nephew Jocelyn, the son of Sir John de Hardwycke of Bolsover, in the autumn of 1461. Elizabeth, he says, visited Hardwick Hall and was betrothed to Jocelyn 'who had for a long time ardently admired her', but does not indicate why they were not subsequently married. David MacGibbon suggests that the liaison may have been kept secret to avoid further antagonising the Earl of

Warwick (whom he supposes Elizabeth had earlier alienated by refusing to marry Sir Hugh John), but we learn only that she afterwards returned to Grafton and remained a widow until she married the King. Jocelyn, says Coore, shared Edward IV's exile in 1470–71 'having sworn never to marry, but to devote his whole life to the service of his Queen, whom he continued to adore as much as ever',[2] and was subsequently killed fighting for Henry Tudor (seeking to rescue his heroine from Richard III's clutches) on Bosworth Field. He lived 'just long enough to witness the death of the usurper, and the triumph of his old love the Dowager Queen'.[3]

There is a story that Elizabeth went hunting with Jocelyn, his relative Roger de Hardwycke of Pattingham, and one of the Vernon family of Haddon, and were intrigued by some gipsies they found camping near Hardwick park.[4] 'The quartet being young and full of hilarity', says Coore, 'desired a withered old hag to tell their fortunes, which she did after the usual preliminaries of crossing the palm with money. Holding the hands of the three young men together, she repeated the following lines:

> A royal prince, fair lady, shalt thou wed,
> But troubles dire shall fall upon thine head,
> Bone of thy bone shall by future fate,
> With blend of these three houses surely mate.[5]

Elizabeth, of course, subsequently married the handsome young King, 'and within a few years of her daughter's marriage with Henry VII, the "Stags of Hardwycke"[6] were united in marriage to the Vernons of Haddon Hall, and a daughter of this union was afterwards married to one of the Hardwyckes of Pattingham, the result being a blend of the three families in the person of a son.' The prophecy is said to have been fulfilled in 1763 when William Hardwicke of Burcote Hall, 'the descendant of the blend of the three houses' married Mary Perton, who could trace her ancestry back to Elizabeth Woodville through Mary, a daughter of Thomas Grey, Marquess of Dorset, who had married Walter Devereaux, Viscount Hereford.[7]

The problem with this intriguing romantic story is that it is impossible to trace its origins or verify it by reference to contemporary documents. The author of *The Old halls, Manors, and families of Derbyshire* could find scarcely any mention of the Hardwicke family in his sources ('who were these Hardwicks?', he asks plaintively) and notes only five generations settled at Old Hardwick Hall, William, whose son John married Elizabeth Blackwell; 'whose son John mated with Elizabeth Pinchbeck; whose son John espoused Elizabeth Leake; whose son John had Elizabeth Draycott, and died without issue, leaving his sister Elizabeth (the famous Bess) his heiress'.[8] It is likely that the John who married Elizabeth Pinchbeck and who died late in 1507 (a writ of *diem clasusit extremum* was sent to the escheator for Derbyshire on 20 November)[9] was Jocelyn's cousin; but Jocelyn himself is conspicuous only by his absence. There is no Hardwicke among the knights of the Yorkist period, nor were any of them returned to Parliament or even appointed Commissioners of the Peace or of array. Joseph Tilley's comment that 'any family desirous of being shorn of their memorabilia, or of losing identity, had only to settle (during the Middle Ages) in this county and they became fleeced of their lineage, honours, and traditions absolutely, or ignored' is obviously exaggerated;[10] but the Derbyshire Hardwickes seem to have had little influence locally (even an authoritative modern work such as Susan M. Wright's *The Derbyshire Gentry in the Fifteenth Century* makes no further reference to them) and the vast probability is that the story recounted by Coore is a later tradition. It may, possibly, owe something to the much married Bess (another Elizabeth), sometime wife of the Earl of Shrewsbury (Mary, Queen of Scots' jailer) and the builder of 'new' Hardwick Hall, but this is only to heap speculation upon speculation without offering a solution. All we can say is that Coore's version (which is repeated by David MacGibbon) is not demonstrably a real episode in the life of Elizabeth Woodville, and is perhaps more apocryphal than the 'Diary' considered in Appendix 3.

Appendix 5

Was John Gunthorpe, Elizabeth's Secretary, the Author of the 'Second Continuation' of the Croyland Chronicle?

The so-called 'second continuation' of the Croyland Chronicle has been cited in this book more often than any other contemporary authority, principally because the anonymous writer, unlike Thomas More and Dominic Mancini, was intimately connected with many of the events he described in his narrative, and because there is some evidence that he was particularly close to Elizabeth. All that is known for certain is that he visited Croyland (modern Crowland), a minor Benedictine abbey in the Lincolnshire fen country, in the first year of Henry VII's reign, and offered, or was invited, to add to the chronicle the monks had themselves concocted, or copied, shortly before 1470. This he did in spectacular fashion, not merely taking up his pen where the previous writer had laid his down, but intruding a uniquely well-informed history beginning with the Battle of Ludford Bridge in October 1459 and ending with King Henry's marriage to Elizabeth of York in January 1486.

The debate which has surrounded the identity of the mysterious individual who wrote the Continuation has turned upon the extent to which the leading candidates, John Russell, Bishop of Lincoln, Henry Sharp, Protonotary of Chancery, Richard Lavender, Archdeacon of Leicester, and Piers Curtis, Keeper of the Great Wardrobe, satisfy a number of criteria, suggested by internal evidence, which may be applied to the author. He was, apparently, a senior but somewhat worldly churchman whose main religious concern was the iniquity of clerical taxation;[1] he was a doctor of canon law and a Yorkist civil servant cum counsellor who, in the summer of 1471, was sent on a mission to the Duke of Burgundy;[2] he was a southerner, apprehensive of the north and northerners, who was familiar with London;[3] he (obviously) had occasion to stay at Croyland and to comment favourably on the abbey's hospitality;[4] and although he continued to serve Richard III after the Usurpation of 1483 he was less in favour with him – and markedly less well disposed towards him – than with Edward IV.[5] The problem is that none of the preferred authors fulfil all the criteria: in particular, Russell's elevation to the chancellorship in May 1483 is incompatible with the corresponding decline in the quality of the continuator's information; Lavender was not employed as an ambassador; Curtis (who was not a clergyman) passed Richard's reign in obscurity; and Sharp was a doctor of civil, rather than of canon, law.

Commentators have tried to supplement the little that is known about the continuator by, for example, deducing something of his interests and background from asides in the chronicle, and by noting the occasions when he betrays his presence by speaking in eyewitness terms. Usually (as, for instance, when he describes the trial of the Duke of Clarence or the grief of King Richard and Queen Anne when the news of their only son's death reached them at Nottingham)[6] the persons who were – or who might have been – watching are too numerous for the 'clue' to be genuinely helpful; but there is one scenario, Edward IV's 1475 French Expedition, where we have a situation in which the continuator was himself present and the names of many and perhaps nearly all, of the principal participants are known. The writer peppers his account of the campaign with personal pronouns ('you might have seen some of our people rejoicing', 'and he [the Duke of Burgundy] said these very words in public', 'an enemy proposal reached us', 'our men had used up all their wages' etc.),[7] and it is probable that he is among the King's followers who are noticed in one or both of the two fullest records, College of Arms MS. 2. M. 16, and the Tellers' Rolls.[8] These documents refer specifically to those principals who were paid to accompany the great enterprise, but it is noteworthy that of the popular candidates only the unlikely Piers Curtis appears among the Household and other officials – Lavender and Sharp are absent as indeed is Russell who, as a member of the Council, would have had particular responsibilities in England while Edward was overseas.[9]

The likelihood, then, is that the author of the 'Second Continuation' was a member of the 1475 Expedition who has not previously been associated with the Chronicle, and a candidate who satisfies most (and possibly all) of the criteria is Elizabeth's secretary, John Gunthorpe, afterwards Keeper of the Privy Seal and Dean of Wells. Gunthorpe was a humanist scholar and bibliophile who distinguished himself at Cambridge in the 1450s and passed the first years of Edward IV's reign at Ferrara, the Studio of Padua, and Rome. The Italian universities were magnets for disciples of the New Learning, and Gunthorpe's contemporaries at Padua included the cultured but brutal John Tiptoft and Piers Courteney, the future Bishop of Exeter described as 'the venerable . . . the flower of the knighthood of his county' in one of the few compliments the continuator bestowed.[10] His talents secured him a place in King Edward's Household on his return to England, and he progressed from royal chaplain (by August 1466) to King's Almoner (from 1468 to 1476) to Dean of the Chapel of the King's Household (from 1476 to, probably, May 1483) and doubled as the Queen's secretary for some ten years from 1467 to 1477. These offices were complemented by his role in the embassies sent to Castile in 1466 and 1470, and in 1468 he accompanied Margaret, the King's sister, to her marriage in Burgundy where he delivered several Latin speeches before Charles the Bold. He was formally appointed Keeper of the Privy Seal (in succession to Russell) by Richard III on 27 June 1483 and continued to be employed as an ambassador,[11] but his relationship with the new King (like that of the Continuator) was unmistakably cooler. There was, as Dr Horrox has noted, nothing of the lavish generosity which characterised Richard's relationship with a more junior official, his secretary, John Kendall, and whereas Gunthorpe's services to Edward had been rewarded with a succession of ecclesiastical dignities in London and the south of England (culminating in 1472 in the gift of the Deanery of Wells and the Archdeaconry of Essex) he now 'received few signs of royal favour beyond a gift of swans'.[12] Richard naturally wished to retain the allegiance of his brother's officials, but it is possible that Gunthorpe's 'promotion' effectively removed him from the Household and from sources of intelligence nearest the King.

The evidence, then, is that both Gunthorpe and the continuator were senior clerics who were familiar with London, both were royal servants employed on embassies to Burgundy, both participated in the 1475 French expedition, and both were apparently disappointed with King Richard and less intimate with government after the changes of 1483. But these coincidences do not account for all the known criteria, and against them must be weighed the objections that Gunthorpe, as Dean of Wells, had no discernible links with Croyland Abbey (unless, perhaps, his appointment as Prebendary of Banbury (Oxon) in 1471 had permitted him to establish a relationship with another part of the Diocese of Lincoln),[13] and he may not have been a doctor of canon law. Nothing is known of his origins, but it is not without interest that of four English villages called Gunthorpe one (near Peterborough) is less than six miles from Croyland and the others (in Rutland, Norfolk and Nottinghamshire) are within easy distance.[14] Members of his family may have resided in one or more of these places, and although the local manor belonged to Peterborough Abbey,[15] Croyland's great rival, John, may have preferred to stay at the lesser establishment on his occasional visits 'home'. The University of Cambridge awarded him the degree of Master of Arts in or before 1452 (to which was added a baccalaureate in theology in 1468) and he is often styled 'master' in official documents; but the designation was applied indifferently to some who were certainly doctors and very probably to others unknown.[16] It is, therefore, entirely possible that the author of *The Narrative of the Marriage of Richard Duke of York with Anne of Norfolk 1477*, who described how 'Doctour Gunthrope, Deane of the Kings Chappell, shewed an ample bull of authority, that they might proceede to the contracte and matrimony before rehersed'[17] has preserved a fuller record of his qualifications than other authorities. The precise nature of his doctorate (if we may suppose the title to be more than mere courtesy) is not recorded, but there is ostensibly no reason why such a diligent and accomplished scholar[18] should not have spent some of his years of obscurity in a detailed study of canon law. The chronicler's reference to Elizabeth as 'the benevolent queen' may also be significant. She was not, as we have seen, universally admired by her contemporaries, but Gunthorpe, her former secretary, would almost certainly have liked and respected her.[19] The comment that she agreed to let her younger son join his brother in the Tower 'assenting with many thanks to this proposal'[20] suggests that he was attempting to portray her as a somewhat naive but well-meaning woman out of her depths in politics, someone clearly more sinned against than sinning and in no sense malign.

It would require much space to compare Gunthorpe's candidacy with those of his main rivals, but the latters' compliance with the known criteria may be ascertained from the detailed studies pertaining to them[21] and the whole tentatively summarised by the following chart:

	Russell	Sharp	Lavender	Curtis	Gunthorpe
Senior Churchman	x		x		x
Doctor of Canon Law	x		x		
Royal Official (both reigns)	x	x			x
Ambassador to Burgundy	x		x	x	x
Southerner/Londoner	x	x	x	x	x
Visited Croyland	x				
On 1475 expedition				x	x
Diminished relationship with Richard III		x		x	x
Total	6	4	3	4	6

'x' indicates that an individual satisfies the criteria; questionable and negative responses have been left blank. It may be observed that six is probably Russell's maximum (he is the only candidate known to have visited Croyland at the right period) whereas Gunthorpe *could* merit a higher score.

John Gunthorpe took no discernible part in the events of April to August 1485 and continued to serve the Crown as an ambassador into the first years of Henry VII's reign before retiring to his deanery, where he died in 1498.[22] It is, of course, unlikely that he, or any of his contemporaries, will ever be positively identified as the 'Second Continuator', but the evidence suggests that his candidacy is at least equal to, and in most cases better than, the alternatives put forward thus far.

Appendix 6

The Fate of the Princes in the Tower

In Chapter 7 we tried to deduce from Elizabeth Woodville's actions what she knew, or supposed, had happened to her sons by King Edward, and concluded that she would not have countenanced the possibility of her daughter Elizabeth marrying either Richard III or Henry Tudor if she had thought that even one of them was still living. There is, of course, no definitive proof that the boys were murdered, but Elizabeth would have been more concerned than anyone to discover what had become of them and it is difficult to avoid the conclusion that she had learned the worst.

The notoriety of the Princes' disappearance has led, inevitably, to a number of alleged 'sightings' of them, both in contemporary documents and in the flesh. It has been suggested that they were among the high-born children mentioned in the ordinances regulating the conduct of the King's northern household at Sheriff Hutton castle in July 1484; and that one of them was the 'lord Bastard' who received an allowance of clothing the following March.[1] But there is no evidence that they were ever at Sheriff Hutton, and the 'lord Bastard' may have been John of Gloucester, King Richard's own illegitimate son. In her book *The Mystery of the Princes*, Audrey Williamson has drawn attention to a 'pre-eighteenth century tradition' that the Princes and their mother lived at Sir James Tyrell's house, Gipping Hall, near Stowmarket (Suffolk) 'by permission of the uncle',[2] and Jack Leslau, a retired London jeweller, has suggested that they can be identified by rebuses (hidden clues with double meanings) in two portraits attributed to Holbein.[3] He believes that the Tudors allowed them to adopt new identities, Edward V becoming Sir Edward Guildford and his younger brother Dr John Clement

(Thomas More's son-in-law), and that the mystery would be solved if their remains, and those of their 'parents', Edward IV and Queen Elizabeth, could be compared using genetic technology. Mr Leslau stresses that Elizabeth never (as far as is known) claimed that her sons were missing, but he does not allow the probability that this was because she knew they had already been killed.

Another possible Prince Richard was Perkin Warbeck, or Osbeck, who troubled Henry VII from his first appearance in Ireland in 1491 until he was captured six years later. Warbeck is a plausible candidate inasmuch as he clearly resembled Edward IV, his alleged father, and never, apparently, betrayed himself by his words or actions. But he always refused to give a detailed and verifiable account of how he escaped when his elder brother was murdered because, he said, 'it is fit it should pass in silence, or, at least, in a more secret relation, for that it may concern some alive and the memory of some that are dead'.[4] It is curious that King Henry failed to confront him with his 'sister' Elizabeth of York and also declined assistance from others who had known Prince Richard. But whether this was because he was afraid to do so or because he was already convinced that Warbeck was an impostor is unclear.

We might suppose that authors who were writing at the time, or within a few years of the Princes' disappearance, would be able to enlighten us, but their comments are often little more than hearsay. Dominic Mancini, who left England at the time of Richard III's coronation and wrote his account in December 1483, reported that 'after Hastings was removed, all the attendants who had waited upon the king were debarred access to him. He and his brother were withdrawn into the inner apartments of the Tower proper, and day by day began to be seen more rarely behind the bars and windows, till at length they ceased to appear altogether. The physician Argentine, the last of his attendants whose services the king enjoyed, reported that the young king, like a victim prepared for sacrifice, sought remission of his sins by daily confession and penance, because he believed that death was facing him . . . I have seen many men burst forth into tears and lamentations when mention was made of him after his removal from men's sight; and already there was a suspicion that he had been done away with. Whether, however, he has been done away with, and by what manner of death, so far I have not at all discovered.'[5] The Croyland continuator wrote in April 1486 that at the time of Buckingham's rebellion (autumn 1483) 'a rumour was spread that the sons of King Edward had died a violent death but it was uncertain how'; but he nowhere else mentions the Princes, nor accuses King Richard, nor indicates whether he himself believed the story.[6] The Act of Attainder passed in November 1485 against Richard (and other Yorkists who had fought at Bosworth) accused him of the 'shedding of infants blood', but curiously, did not say whom he had allegedly harmed or killed.[7]

The popular story of the Princes' murder begins with the report of *The Great Chronicle of London* (*c*. 1496) that after Easter 1484 (when Richard's own son died) 'much whysperyng was among the people that the kyng hadd put the childyr of kyng Edward to deth',[8] a death which, the writer suggests, may have been procured by drowning in malmsey wine (left over, presumably, from the execution of their uncle George of Clarence), poisoning, or smothering 'atwene ij ffethyr beddis'.[9] It is this last possibility which re-appears in the fine circumstantial story which Sir Thomas More recounted in his *History of King Richard III* (1513), and which, via Holinshed and Shakespeare, has become the 'traditional' version of the tale. This need not long detain us, but briefly More's story is that Richard first ordered Sir Robert Brackenbury, the governor of the Tower, to kill them, and when he refused turned instead to Sir James Tyrell, who was given the keys of the prison for one night. Tyrell, we are told, employed Miles Forest 'a felowe fleshed in murther before time' and John Dighton, his own horsekeeper, 'a big brode square strong knave' and these two stole upon the sleeping Princes and 'sodainly lapped them up among the clothes, so bewrapped them and entangled them, keping down by force the fetherbed and pillowes hard unto their mouthes, that within a while smored and stifled, theyr breath failing, thei gave up to God their innocent soules into the joyes of heaven, leaving to the tormentors their bodyes dead in the bed'. Tyrell had them buried 'at the stayre foote, metely depe in the grounde under a great heape of stones', but one of Brackenbury's priests subsequently disinterred them and 'secretelye entered them in such place, as by the occasion of his deathe, whiche onely knew it, could never synce come to light'.[10]

More's source was an alleged confession made by Tyrell shortly before he was executed on other charges in 1502. But curiously, the admission was never published (Henry VII, it is assumed, simply mentioned it an uncertain time afterwards), and if it so neatly explained everything it is hard to understand More's caution when he wrote 'I shall rehearse you the dolorous end of those babes, not after every way that I have heard, but after that way that I have so heard by suche men and by such meanes, as me thinketh it wer hard but it should be true'.[11] The story was probably an official attempt to close the file on the Princes by 'proving' they had been murdered, but it won little support among contemporaries. Even Polydore Vergil, the Tudors' official historian, who was completing his account of Richard's reign in about 1517–18, says simply that 'with what kinde of death these sely (innocent) chyldren wer executyd yt is not certanely known'.[12]

The only piece of evidence which might appear to lend some credence to More's story is the discovery, in 1674, of a wooden chest containing the skeletons of two children when a stone staircase leading to the chapel in the White Tower was being demolished. The bones were scientifically examined in 1933 and the ages of the individuals estimated at between twelve and thirteen and about ten respectively; and since Edward V was born in November 1470 and his brother in August 1473 these would have been their approximate ages when they disappeared in the late summer of 1483. This identification, if admitted (and some modern scientists would argue that differences in bone development make precise estimates of age very difficult) would absolve Henry Tudor from any involvement in the boys' murder, and it is likely that his marriage to their sister and his dependence on the support of the Woodville faction would have prevented him from harming them even if he had found them alive in England in August 1485. But if they were killed in Richard's reign (as the timing of their disappearance suggests), why do knowledgeable contemporaries either fail to accuse him or only do so in an obviously tortuous way? A possible answer could be that although the princes died in Richard's lifetime the King was not himself directly responsible, and this would explain both Elizabeth Woodville's willingness to be reconciled to him (even to the extent of urging her eldest son Dorset to desert Henry) and why Sir Robert Brackenbury, who must also have known the truth of the matter, was still willing to die for him on Bosworth Field. Who, then, was the real culprit? John Howard, Duke of Norfolk has been accused, chiefly because he had acquired the inheritance which King Edward had reserved for Prince Richard, and because of an order he gave for quicklime to be delivered to the Tower on 21 May 1483. But the boy was no threat to Howard while Richard remaincd King of England, the lime may have been required for nothing more sinister than whitewash or fertiliser, and in December Howard was granted (retrospectively perhaps?) a London dwelling called 'The Tower'![13] A more likely candidate is Henry Stafford, Duke of Buckingham, the man who, more than any other, had helped to make Richard king but who rebelled against him in October 1483. Buckingham was, as we have noted, a shallow individual who had never been entrusted with high office but whose descent from Edward III's youngest son, Thomas of Woodstock, made him a candidate for the succession in his own right. He may have decided to remove the Princes as a preliminary to his own rebellion, and there are, in fact, five contemporaries, the Frenchmen Jacques de Molinet and Philip de Commines, the unknown authors of the fragments known as 'The Historical Notes of a London Citizen' and *MS. Ashmole 1448.60*, and the Dutch *Divisie Chronicle*, who state that he was responsible for, or was at least implicated in, the crime. The foreign writers had heard a variety of stories – the *Divisie Chronicle*, composed about 1500, mentions a rumour that the boys had been starved to death, adding 'some others will say that the Duke of Buckingham killed these children hoping to become king himself'[14] – but the English commentators are more certain. The Ashmolean document says that Richard killed the Princes 'at the prompting of the Duke of Buckingham'[15] and this is broadly supported by the author of the 'Historical Notes' (College of Arms MS. 2M6) who does not implicate Richard but states that 'this yer (1483) King Edward the Vth, late callyd Preince Walys, and Richard duke of Yourke hys brother . . . wer put to deyth in the Towur of London be the vise (by the devising of, or on the advice of) the duke of Buckingham.'[16] But Buckingham could hardly have killed the boys unless he thought he had at least the King's tacit approval, and it is possible to imagine him convincing a reluctant Richard that their survival posed a real threat to his authority. This would have added to Richard's rage when he heard that Buckingham had rebelled against him (and understood the true reason why the Duke wanted to be rid of them);[17] and although he presumably explained the situation to Elizabeth Woodville he could not excuse himself more publicly without implying that he was not his own man. Similarly, Henry Tudor's reluctance to inquire into the matter – and end the speculation once and for all – could have stemmed from the fact that although the Duke had committed the crime to further his own ambitions the revised object of 'Buckingham's Rebellion' had been to depose Richard in favour of Henry. A formal investigation would have found it difficult to avoid the conclusion that Buckingham had killed the boys on behalf of Henry (and therefore, presumably with his agreement), and so Henry, like Richard, preferred to say as little about the matter as possible. Perhaps Edward V and his brother were, to some extent, victims of the ambitions of all of them. In the words of Paul Murray Kendall, 'a deposed monarch has nowhere to fall but into the grave'.[18]

Appendix 7

The End of the Hastings–Grey/Woodville Quarrel

The differences between William, Lord Hastings and Elizabeth Woodville, and the rivalries between Hastings and the second Earl Rivers and the Marquess of Dorset, did not end with the deaths of the main protagonists. Instead, they continued into the next generation, and although later disputes were more localised there seems little doubt that each family came to regard the other as its traditional enemy. The Woodvilles were extinct in the male line by 1491 and there is no evidence of conflict between Thomas Grey, Marquess of Dorset and Hastings's son, Lord Edward, who died in 1501 and 1506 respectively: but the quarrel was taken up by their successors, the second Marquess of Dorset (Queen Elizabeth's grandson) and Edward Hastings's son George, created Earl of Huntingdon in 1529. These men did not allow their differences to disturb Henry VIII's court as their predecessors had threatened the peace of Edward IV's; instead their feuding was confined to their Leicestershire heartland where their interests were represented by Dorset's brothers and Hastings's mother, Lady Mary Hungerford, and her second husband Sir Richard Sacheverell. Sacheverell, who had been Edward Hastings's Receiver-General, had married his former mistress by 1511, and it was his pride in his new status (and his arrogance towards the Grey family) which now exacerbated the former ill-feeling which, if it had been in abeyance, had clearly not been forgotten by those concerned.

The disputants' main bone of contention, and, in a sense, their principal testing-ground, was the forest, the conglomeration of woodlands, pastures and closes which formed part of the

Honour of Leicester and which had been customarily administered by the Hastings family from the beginning of King Edward's first reign. The Master Forestership was one of the offices for which Lord George had paid the King 4,000 marks on 23 August 1507, but the Greys, too, had ambitions in the baliwick, and his influence diminished in the next decade. There is no record of the incidents, or processes, which produced this change in the balance of authority, but by 1519 the dispute was having such deleterious effects on the royal vert and venison that Chancellor Wolsey was moved to intervene. He imposed an interim settlement, to last until such time as the parties should appear before him, which required Dorset's sister and her husband to vacate Bird's Nest Lodge (the moated house in the forest which in William Hastings's time had been occupied by Roger Bowlett, his steward), enjoined Lady Mary and Sacheverell to leave Newark College (of which more presently), and bound both interests to discharge the armed servants which had doubtless been used to promote the feud. Dorset protested that his sister and brother-in-law were ready to comply with the ruling, but alleged that Lady Mary had remained in the College on the pretext of illness and that Sacheverell had shown his contempt for the agreement by behaving in a provocative and intimidatory manner. He was said to have ridden to the Lodge with twenty-four followers armed with bows and arrows on the pretext that he 'only came to thank her (Dorset's sister) for the good cheer she made him at Bradgate' but had then departed 'shooting up and down to the further side of the Frith towards the forest, and broke down the pale so that a great number of the deer were destroyed and slain'.[1] The Hastings faction continued to express their dissatisfaction by, among other things, 'braking down' Dorset's arms in the church at Desford because 'mine arms stood higher than Lord Hastyngs' as the Marquess later complained to his brother Leonard;[2] but Wolsey was hardly an impartial arbiter and may indeed have secretly favoured the Greys.[3]

There is little evidence to illuminate the progress of the contest in the early 1520s, but the surviving fragments are unanimous in that matters remained substantially unamended and ambitions were only marginally restrained. A survey of the forest commissioned by the Chancellor of the Duchy of Lancaster in 1523 reported that the King's woods were 'all decayed and wasted'[4] and although Wolsey had subsequently tried to reduce the areas of conflict by instructing both parties to refrain from attending the local assizes and sessions with their retinues, it was duly reported (admittedly, by one favourable to Dorset) that Sacheverell 'followed the commandment by the space of two years or thereabouts' since when he had attended regularly, sometimes with more than 100 followers, so that he (the informant) 'thinketh it clearly that at all times when the said Sir Richard was absent there was much better order and quiet at sessions and assizes than since the coming of the same Sir Richard again'.[5] There is no reason to doubt the substance of these testimonies, but they must be weighed against the certainty that the Greys were no less active in advancing their own position in the same period, most notably by encroaching on certain forest offices which the Hastings affinity would formerly have held. By 1525, when the evidence again becomes more plentiful, Dorset had become keeper of the 'reserved part' of Heathley ward,[6] and his brother Leonard controlled the rounding-up of cattle and insisted that Hastings's men observed the same rules as commoners in the Frith. Thomas Dunham testified before the Star Chamber that on 8 September in that year Lord Leonard had sent him to attach himself to Sacheverell and his party of 'seven score horsemen' at Kirby Muxloe and to observe their 'demeanour' as they rode through the forest, a ploy designed to monitor their respect for royal (and, more specifically, Grey) interests with a view to discrediting them in the eyes of the King. Sacheverell's men were irked by Dunham's attention and by his lack of respect for their master, but they contented themselves with bringing him before Sir Richard at the point of a crossbow and compelling him to raise his cap. They were clearly aware that he purposed more than his claim to 'walk as a keeper', but it is instructive that their retribution was limited to Martin a Lee's 'Knave, and ever thou come in Leicester thou shalt have thy head broken' and other, similar, threats.[7]

Lee's remark suggests that although the Greys had by this time made significant inroads into the jurisdiction of the forest the Hastings faction still held the upper hand in the town of Leicester, and this is borne out by an incident which had taken place there a few weeks earlier in July. Dorset's servant John Gladwyn told the court that this arose out of a fracas between his master's cook and one Bradshaw, a servant of Hastings's kinsman Thomas Brooksby, in which Bradshaw was worsted by several of the cook's fellows and obliged to seek refuge in a nearby house.

The town, in which Lord Hastings appears to have been genuinely popular, was soon in uproar, and sixteen or seventeen of Dorset's followers, fearing reprisals, banded together at the 'George' in the Swinesmarket (the present High Street) while more than sixty of Lady Mary's servants (together with some 200–300 of the populace) gathered menacingly at the nearby High Cross. Henry Gillett, the mayor, tried to defuse the crisis by offering to convey Dorset's men to safety 'on the backside of the said sign of the George and down the back lanes' as the testimony has it, but Gladwyn replied that 'they had rather be slain than it should be said in Leicester that they should steal forth on the backside, for it should be dishonor to their master and shame to them'.[8] The situation was saved by the arrival of a more senior retainer, Anthony Buggegood, who ordered them to disperse quietly 'as they would avoid my lord Marquis's displeasure', and this might have been the end of the matter had Gladwyn not then remembered that he had left his horse tethered in the High Street (modern High Cross Street) 'at the sign of the Rose'.[9] Buggegood told him that if he hoped to recover it he must 'take his adventure', a warning fully justified when, as he approached the tavern, he was noticed by some of the multitude assembled at the High Cross. He recounted how 'many of my lady Hungerford's and Mr Sacheverell's servants . . . came running down with swords and bucklers in their hands, and the wife of the sign of the Rose shut the door of the same house till they were passed the door . . . and this deponent (Gladwyn), seeing that, got on his horse and put his spurs to his horse and ran down a back lane in Leicester from thence over a hedge and ditch in Saint Margaret's parish of Leicester and so escaped them'.[10]

The rivalry between the two families within the town centred, inevitably, upon Newarke College and Hospital where Lady Mary and Sacheverell sometimes resided and where Lord George Grey (another son of the first Marquess of Dorset) had been some years established as Dean. The College of the Annunciation of St Mary in the Newark was an enlargement of the Hospital founded in 1330 by Henry, Earl of Lancaster and Leicester, 'in honour of God and the glorious Virgin and All Saints and in special reverence of Our Lady' and maintained an establishment of 100 poor men and women together with the clergy and others who ministered to their needs. The more recent benefactors had included William, Lord Hastings,[11] but it was probably the

Lancastrian antecedents of the foundation rather than her father-in-law's generosity which led Lady Mary to give of her patronage and to mark it for her own burial-place.[12] The Dean found her presence – and that of Sacheverell and their servants – irksome, and lodged an unspecified complaint with the Privy Council; but the evidence given in London did not produce a settlement and the matter was passed to Bishop Longland of Lincoln, who visited the College in November 1525.[13] The principal 'witnesses' at the hearings before the Bishop were the twelve canons of the establishment who gave answers to thirty-nine interrogatories, or questions, posed by Sacheverell and Lady Mary, and to eighteen presented by the Dean. They were designed to elicit answers which would either extol the questioner's virtues or confirm the misdemeanours committed by the opposing faction, but the canons' replies were invariably taciturn and can have given little comfort to either side. The clergy found the Dean haughty and overbearing (he had called certain of them names such as 'false perjured priest' and 'lewd priest' and 'shewed them a forbidding countenance'), but at the same time they felt that the presence of Lady Mary, Sacheverell, and their servants was (as Grey alleged) both unnecessary and a source of friction and would have preferred them to have resided without. Neither Richard Brooksby, who had been presented to the sixth prebendal stall by his kinsman George Hastings, nor his fellow canon John Whetwode, who owed his appointment to Dorset, supported their respective benefactors and their parties wholeheartedly, and it may be supposed that the picture which emerges from the testimonies is accurately, if cautiously, drawn.[14] The Dean complained that he and his servants had suffered a series of threats, insubordinations, and physical abuses committed by members of the Hastings faction: there had been jostling and 'hubbing' by the holy-water stoup; Lady Mary's serving men had 'faced and braced' him in the choir; some of them had made as though they would pick the lock of the stocks in which he had set one of the clerks of the College; Chauncy, his servant, had been struck by one of Sacheverell's followers and showed 'a plump on his head as much as a walnut'; and Syndall, another of his fee'd-men, had been threatened with a sword by one of the opposing party and had run away for fear of his life. Lady Mary and her husband were personally accused of holding bear-baitings, May-games, and 'common spectacles' in the

College, and were said to have allowed their 'dogs, hawks and hounds' to roam freely in the Church while the priest was officiating, 'to the great annoyance of the same'.[15] The canons agreed that there was much truth in these allegations, but there was often difficulty in reconciling the details remembered by different witnesses[16] and no little doubt as to whether some of the incidents, or misdemeanours, could properly be attributed to the feud. The precincts of the College were not infrequently the scene of disorder – Whetwode had on one occasion flung beer over Canon Gillot while Brooksby had punched a clerk after dragging him out of the cloister – and the alleged incidents almost certainly owed something to personal, as opposed to factional, rivalries, and to the generally violent tenor of the times. As for the rest, it was said in mitigation that it was customary to allow pageants within the College (these being for the benefit of the parish churches), and that the Dean's own hounds were, if anything, a worse nuisance than Sacheverell's because the latter's were at least kept out of the choir!

Lady Mary and Sacheverell countered these allegations with charges that the Dean had exceeded his authority and had even made off with the common money-bag,[17] but there are hints in the canons' statements that they had tried to restrain the excesses of their followers and were prepared to exchange confrontation for peace. Sir Richard had committed two of his men to Leicester prison for fighting within the College precincts, and another, Lane, had been warned not to meddle with the Dean's servants 'for to do so would cost him his place'. Anthony Harcott, who served Lady Mary, complained that he and his fellows had been forbidden to retaliate when the Dean's followers allowed their swords to rap them on the shins as they walked together in procession; but some of the aggrieved found more subtle ways of raising Grey's hackles and must have been delighted with the results. It was said that at evensong on Relic Sunday (9 July 1525)[18] a group of Sacheverell's servants, led by Thomas Cawardyn, had stood within sight of the Dean's stall 'about the door of the choir screen' and had menacingly fingered their swords and daggers while pretending to join in the prayers. Grey rose to the bait and ordered them away from the entrance; but no sooner were they gone than their places were taken by a gentleman named John Haryngton and others of the same group. Lady Mary was worshipping in a side chapel, and the Dean appealed to her to remonstrate with her followers; but the good matron told him bluntly that it was no crime for men to say their prayers in the choir porch 'as well may they do this as you to be from service hunting and come home at midnight', and drew comparisons with the misbehaviour of his brother Dorset's servants who caused her great inconvenience in the Frith. Lady Mary could, like the Dean and her husband, be haughty and impervious to criticism, and however much she might desire an end to the conflict she could barely conceal her contempt.

Bishop Longland adjourned his visitation on 28 November, but before he left he arranged a *modus vivendi* between the Dean and Canons whereby they made peace in his presence and forgave each other their offences of word and deed. He subsequently issued them with a long series of injunctions for the better ordering of the College, and although these contained no direct reference to the dispute between the Dean and Lady Mary and Sacheverell it would appear that the visitation, and the mutual desires of the parties, brought this phase of the quarrel to a close. Cardinal Wolsey and others prepared draft proposals for the better administration of – and the division of authority within – the Honour of Leicester, and in May 1526 these were formally approved by King Henry 'for the quiet and rest of the shire'.[19] Dorset and Hastings were bound in a bond of £1,000 to preserve the accommodation,[20] and when, on 25 September 1528, Longland's chancellor and commissary, Dr John Rayne, visited Newarke College, there was no mention of the rivalries of three years before.

It would, perhaps, be unrealistic to suggest that all this stemmed from Elizabeth's dealings with William Hastings in the early 1460s, but there seems little doubt that each phase or 'incident' contributed to a growing fund of ill-feeling between their respective families. The marriages which had established kinship between them, particularly that between the first Marquess of Dorset and Hastings's step-daughter Cecily Bonville, had signally failed to engender cordiality, but it is significant that in this second phase of the quarrel the principals stood increasingly aloof. The rivalry between William Hastings and the elder Thomas Grey had been personal and dangerously divisive; but Henry VIII did not find it necessary to reconcile the heads of the two families on *his* deathbed, and it is instructive that when selecting men to accompany him to France in 1520 he chose from Leicestershire not only George Hastings and Richard

Sacheverell but also Lord Leonard and his brothers John and Richard Grey.[21] Sir William Skevington told the Star Chamber that 'he hath heard divers times my lord marquess say that he would have been glad to have had my lord Hastings' and the said Sir Richard's goodwill and favour' and that 'he often times hath moved my lord marquess to the same because of the nighness of blood between them, wherein he always found him conformable':[22] but it must be supposed that, this notwithstanding, a private reconciliation could have been accomplished only on Dorset's own (unacceptable) terms. Thomas Dunham alleged that 'some lewd knaves bore words betwixt them and made it worse between them than it would be'[23] but the servants of both factions were merely the tools of their masters' differences, and it may be noted that the Greys, like Lady Mary and Sacheverell in Newarke College, remained firmly entrenched at Bird's Nest Lodge. The second Marquess of Dorset appears, indeed, a more determined adversary than his father; but his pursuit of his Leicestershire interests (and George Hastings's response to his aggression) was a local matter directed from a safe distance, and courtly unity was not threatened as such.

Notes and References

Abbreviations

The following abbreviations are used in the notes that follow. Other works and sources are cited in full on first reference to them in each set of notes and in a shortened form thereafter. The place of publication is London except where otherwise stated.

Croyland Chronicle	*Ingulph's Chronicle of the Abbey of Croyland*, translated with notes by Henry T. Riley (1854).
MacGibbon	David MacGibbon, *Elizabeth Woodville* (1937).
Mancini	Dominic Mancini, *The Usurpation of Richard III*, translated and with an introduction by C.A.J Armstrong (2nd edition, Oxford 1969, reprinted Gloucester 1984).
More	More's *History of King Richard III*, edited by J. Rawson Lumby D.D. (Cambridge 1883).
Paston Letters	*The Paston Letters, AD 1422–1509*, edited by James Gairdner, 6 vols. (1904).
Ross, *Edward IV*	Charles Ross, *Edward IV* (1974).
Scofield	Cora L. Scofield, *The Life and Reign of Edward IV*, 2 vols. (1923, reprinted 1967).

Chapter One

1. Her date of birth is unknown, but a portrait dated 1463 indicates that she was then twenty-six.
2. Most commentators assume that it was Richard's father who occupied Grafton when Thomas, his half-brother, died, but it is distinctly possible that he remained at the Mote and that it was his son, who had already distinguished himself in royal service, who took up residence and served as Sheriff of Northamptonshire in 1438.
3. She was descended from Guy de Montfort, third son of the Earl killed at the Battle of Evesham in 1265 (see Table 4), and gave precedence only to Katherine of Valois, Henry V's widow, in England. (The child-king Henry VI was unmarried and Bedford was his eldest surviving uncle.)

4. The Woodvilles resided at Grafton, but the abbey of Grestain in Normandy held the lordship of the manor. The abbot sold it to a merchant named Tidemann de Lymbergh to help ransom his patron after the Battle of Crecy. De Lymbergh sold it to the de la Pole family, who retained their interest until the Duke of Suffolk relinquished it to Richard Woodville, Elizabeth's father, in 1440.

5. *Rotuli Parliamentorum* (Rolls of Parliament), ed. J. Strachey *et al.*, 6 vols. (1767–77) iv, p. 498.

6. Her misalliance invites comparison with the clandestine union between Katherine of Valois and her squire Owen Tudor, and it is possible that one may have influenced the other. Professor Griffiths suggests, probably rightly, that the public remained unaware of Katherine's second marriage until after she died on 3 January 1437 (R.A. Griffiths, *The Reign of Henry VI* (1981), pp. 60–1); but she had four children by Owen in the 1430s, and it is reasonable to suppose that Jacquetta, her kinswoman, knew of the arrangement and was emboldened to marry for love herself.

7. These particulars are taken from the articles in the *Dictionary of National Biography*, ed. L. Stephen and S. Lee, 63 vols. (1885–1900), lxii, pp. 414–5, and G.E.C. *et al.*, *The Complete Peerage*, 12 vols. (1910–59), xi, pp. 19–22.

8. David MacGibbon prints two letters from the Duke of York and the Earl of Warwick addressed to 'Dame Elizabeth Wodehill' (whom he mistakenly identifies with Elizabeth) asking her to look favourably on their client, Sir Hugh John, who wished to marry her (see Chapter 9). The best reason he could give for including them was that 'the name of Woodville is known to have been written in no less than six different ways'. MacGibbon, pp. 15–17.

9. More, pp. 58–9, MacGibbon, pp. 17–18. George Smith suggests that the Isabella and Elizabeth who served Margaret may have been one and the same person. *The Coronation of Elizabeth Wydeville* (1935, reprinted Gloucester 1975), p. 27. Elizabeth was the widow of Sir Ralph Grey of Heaton (Ethel Seaton, *Sir Richard Roos, Lancastrian Poet* (1961), pp. 64, 302).

10. See M.A. Hicks, 'The Changing Role of the Wydevilles in Yorkist Politics to 1483', in *Patronage, Pedigree and Power in Later Medieval England*, ed. C. Ross (Gloucester, 1979), pp. 62–3.

11. *Complete Peerage*, v, p. 362.

12. See M.K. Jones and M.G. Underwood, *The King's Mother* (Cambridge 1992), pp. 39–40.

13. Margaret was physically ejected from the disputed manor of Gresham in 1450 and contested Drayton with the Duke of Suffolk in the mid-1460s. See H.S. Bennett, *The Pastons and their England* (Cambridge, 1922), pp. 63–6.

14. *Paston Letters*, iii, p. 204 (spelling and punctuation modernised).

15. Scofield, i, pp. 177–8. Anthony Woodville married Elizabeth, Baroness Scales in her own right, between 25 July 1460 (when her father died) and 29 March 1461. He was recognised as Lord Scales *jure uxoris*, and summoned to Parliament under this title from 22 December 1462.

16. Public Record Office, *Early Chancery Proceedings*, Bundle 27, nos. 268, 269, 271, cited by MacGibbon, pp. 29–30.

17. K.B. McFarlane has noted the case of Maud Burnell, a wealthy heiress whose first husband, John, Lord Lovel, was killed at Bannockburn in 1314. She subsequently married John Hadlow, and entailed much of her inheritance upon herself and Hadlow in jointure with remainder to the heirs male of their two bodies and only a reversion, them failing, to her eldest son by Lovel. The result was that the Lovels were denied the Burnell inheritance until the last Hadlow heir died in 1420. K.B. McFarlane, *The Nobility of Later Medieval England* (Oxford 1973), p. 67. These arrangements needed royal approval of course, but Bourchier was a junior member of the new royal family and was likely to be given his way.

18. Historical Manuscripts Commission, 78, *Report on the Manuscripts of R.R. Hastings*, 4 vols. (1928–47), i, pp. 301–2. A further complication was that Anne, Hastings's sister, was the wife of Sir Thomas Ferrers of Tamworth, Elizabeth's mother-in-law's cousin!

19. J.R. Lander, *Government and Community* (1980), pp. 237–8, note 4.

20. MacGibbon, pp. 32, 33.

21. C. Fahy, 'The Marriage of Edward IV and Elizabeth Woodville. A New Italian Source', *English Historical Review*, lxxvi (1961), pp. 660–7.

22. Robert Fabyan, *The New Chronicles of England and France*, ed. Sir H. Ellis, (1811), p. 654. A short chronicle known as *Hearne's Fragment*, written by a royal servant close to the Duke of Norfolk, claims that Edward married Elizabeth in 1463 'on the first day of May in the beginning of his third year'. The fact that Edward's third regnal year extended from 4 March 1463 to 3 March 1464 confirms that 1463 was not a slip of the pen, but it is contradicted by all other evidence. The writer compounds his error by stating that Elizabeth was crowned in 1464 rather than 1465, but adds the interesting detail that 'the priest that wedded them lieth buried at the Minories by London before the high Altar, whose name was * * * *' (blank in manuscript). *The Chronicles of the White Rose of York*, ed. J.A. Giles (1845), p. 16.

23. It is possible that it was Edward who initially referred Elizabeth's suit to Hastings before there were any close feelings between them. David MacGibbon suggests that he asked Hastings to help only after he became infatuated with her – but at such a high price? MacGibbon, pp. 31–2. Elizabeth's father had been restored to the Council in 1463, but there is no evidence that he used whatever influence he now possessed on his daughter's behalf.

24. Ross, *Edward IV*, p. 86.

25. Other brides proposed for Edward (perhaps with varying degrees of seriousness) included a member of the ducal house of Burgundy, the Scottish regent, Mary of Guelders (a lady whose age was as doubtful as her reputation), and Isabella, the future Queen of Castile, who (as she informed Richard III twenty years afterwards) 'was turned in hur hart fro England in tyme past for the unkyndeness the which she toke against the king last decessed, whom God pardon, for his refusing of her and taking to his wiff a wedowe of England'. *Letters and Papers*

Illustrative of the Reigns of Richard III and Henry VII, ed. J. Gairdner, 2 vols. (1861–3), i, p. 32.

26. It was perhaps to counter the innuendo that there was something lacking in her queenship that Elizabeth adopted a deep red gillyflower, a bloom associated with the purity of the Virgin and symbolising virtuous love and marriage, as her personal device. See Anne F. Sutton and Livia Visser-Fuchs, 'The Device of Queen Elizabeth Woodville: A Gillyflower or Pink', *The Ricardian*, xi (1997), pp. 17–22.

27. Jean de Waurin, *Anchiennes Cronicques d'Engleterre*, ed. E. Dupont, 3 vols. (Paris, 1858–63), ii, pp. 327–8, quoted in translation in Ross, *Edward IV*, p. 89.

28. For a fuller disscussion of this point see Joanna L. Chamberlayne, 'Crowns and Virgins: Queenmaking During the Wars of the Roses', in *Young Medieval Women*, ed. K.J. Lewis, N.J. Menuge and K.M. Phillips (Thrupp, 2001), pp. 47–68.

29. Ross, *Edward IV*, p. 90.

30. In the event, the Black Prince predeceased his father; but there is no doubt that, had he succeeded, Joan would have been accepted as his queen.

31. *Calendar of State Papers and Manuscripts Relating to English Affairs Existing in the Archives and Collections of Venice, and in other Libraries in Northern Italy*, i, 1202–1509, ed. R. Brown (1864), p. 114. *The Household Books of John Howard, Duke of Norfolk, 1462–1471, 1483–1485*, introduced by A. Crawford (Stroud, 1992), i, pp. 196–7. B. Botfield, the original 1841 editor, commented that 'there can be little doubt that this letter refers to the marriage of the King with Elizabeth Wydeville; its date may, therefore, be assigned either to 1464 or 1465: it has every appearance of having been addressed to Richard, Lord Rivers, her father'; p. 197, note 1.

32. J.L. Chamberlayne (Laynesmith), *English Queenship 1445–1503*. (Unpublished University of York D.Phil thesis, 1999), p. 56. (To be published by Oxford University Press).

33. Ross, *Edward IV*, p. 92, quoting Waurin, *Anchiennes Cronicques*, ii, pp. 326–7.

34. *Calendar of the Patent Rolls, Edward IV, 1461–1467* (1898), p. 433 & p. 525.

35. Scofield, i, p. 375.

36. Smith, *Coronation of Elizabeth Wydeville*, p. 7.

37. *Acts of Court of the Mercers' Company 1453–1527*, ed. L. Lyell and F.D. Watney (Cambridge, 1936), p. 281. Court held 9 May 1465 (not 1466 as printed).

38. These included Elizabeth's younger brothers, Richard and Edward Woodville.

39. Chamberlayne, *English Queenship*, pp. 80–1.

40. The quotations are taken from Smith, *Coronation of Elizabeth Wydeville*. They are indicative of how the highest in society 'enjoyed' the least privacy at the time.

Chapter Two

1. G.E.C. *et al.*, *The Complete Peerage*, 12 vols. (1910–59), xii, part i, p. 356 and references, says that Jacquetta was married *c.* 1450, but it seems highly improbable that a younger sister would have been married to a member of the nobility this early. Similarly, Catherine's marriage is said to have taken place in 1466, but the contemporary account of her sister's coronation describes her as 'Duchess of Buckingham' in May 1465.

2. See, for example, K.B. McFarlane, 'Had Edward I a "Policy" towards the Earls?', *The Nobility* (Oxford, 1973), pp. 248–67.

3. J.R. Lander, 'Marriage and Politics in the Fifteenth Century: the Nevilles and the Wydvilles', *Crown and Nobility 1450–1509* (1976), p. 110.

4. *Ibid.*, p. 113.

5. M.A. Hicks, 'The Changing Role of the Wydevilles in Yorkist Politics to 1483', ed. C. Ross, pp. 66–9.

6. Scofield, i, p. 374, quoting *Excerpta Historica*, ed. S. Bentley (1833), pp. 176–212.

7. Ross, *Edward IV*, p. 95.

8. *The Great Chronicle of London*, ed. A.H. Thomas and I.D. Thornley (1938, reprinted Gloucester, 1983), p. 204.

9. Olivier de la Marche, *Memoirs*, ed. H. Beaune and J. d'Arbaumont, 4 vols. (Paris, 1883–88), iii, p. 154, quoted in Scofield, i, p. 419.

10. J. Leland. *De Rebus Britannicis Collectanea*, ed. T. Hearne, 6 vols. (1770), iv, p. 249. These particulars are taken from an account of the ceremony performed for Elizabeth of York in 1486, but the details would have varied little from birth to birth or from queen to queen.

11. *Calendar of the Patent Rolls, Edward IV, 1467–1477* (1900), p. 154.

12. Scofield, i, p. 393.

13. *The Travels of Leo of Rozmital*, ed. and trans. M. Letts (Hakluyt Society, Cambridge 1957), pp. 45–8. I am grateful to the Society and to David Higham Associates for permission to reproduce this text.

14. This was probably Warwick – the King was prevented by convention from presiding himself.

15. Kings had collected such relics since Anglo-Saxon times, and did not doubt their authenticity and efficacy, even when there were more of them in circulation than could possibly be genuine. They took the view that such artefacts could be legitimately multiplied (perhaps in a process akin to the miraculous mass feedings mentioned in the New Testament), and were all acceptable as such.

16. Quoted by John Twigg, *A History of Queens' College, Cambridge 1448–1986* (Woodbridge, 1987), p. 9.

17. Ross, *Edward IV*, p. 269.

18. *Paston Letters*, v., pp. 14, 24. The Pastons also sought the assistance of Lord Rivers, Lord Scales and Sir John Woodville, but apparently received little comfort from the father and only fair words from his sons, pp. 30–33.

19. British Library Harleian Manuscript 433, ed. R. Horrox and P.W.

Hammond, 4 vols. (1979–1983), iii, p. 108. Paul Murray Kendall took the view that Richard's comparison confirmed Elizabeth's involvement (*Richard the Third* [1955], p. 444, note 8), but, as Anne Sutton and Livia Visser-Fuchs observe, there is no reason to suppose he meant more than he said. 'A "Most Benevolent Queen", Queen Elizabeth Woodville's Reputation, her Piety and her Books', *The Ricardian*, x (1995), p. 218.

20. See Scofield, i, pp. 436–8. Ross, *Edward IV*, pp. 101 (note 2), 203–4.
21. This and the following quotations are taken from *The Great Chronicle of London*, pp. 204–8.
22. Fabyan thought that Rivers and Jacquetta were so angry that Cook had escaped more serious punishment that they secured Chief Justice Markham's dismissal: but Anne Sutton has found evidence in the Public Record Office (in C81/1381/26) that he asked to resign, on account of 'his grete age and debilite', at the end of this year or the beginning of the next. See Anne F. Sutton, 'Sir Thomas Cook and his "troubles": an investigation', *Guildhall Studies in London History*, iii (1978), pp. 89–90, and *The Politics of Fifteenth Century England: John Vale's Book*, ed. M.L. Kekewich *et al.* (Stroud, 1995), pp. 88–91.
23. *Croyland Chronicle*, p. 457.
24. See, for example, the deferential tone adopted in his letter to Edward, probably datable to October 1463, printed in *John Vale's Book*, pp. 171–2.
25. *The Great Chronicle of London*, p. 208.

Chapter Three

1. These are summarised by Ross, *Edward IV*, pp. 124–5 on which the following is based.
2. John Warkworth, *A Chronicle of the First Thirteen Years of the Reign of King Edward the Fourth*, ed. J.O. Halliwell (Camden Society, 1839), pp. 47–51.
3. *Paston Letters*, v, p. 30.
4. *Ibid.*, p. 34.
5. See H. Harrod, 'Queen Elizabeth Woodville's visit to Norwich in 1469', from the Chamberlains' Accounts for the ninth and tenth years of King Edward IV, *Norfolk Archaeology*, v (1859), pp. 32–7.
6. The charges brought against Jacquetta are discussed in Appendix 2.
7. These quotations are taken from 'Chronicle of the Rebellion in Lincolnshire in 1470', ed. J.G. Nichols, *The Camden Miscellany*, vol. 1 (Camden Society, 1847), pp. 6, 11, 12.
8. Ross, *Edward IV*, p. 144.
9. R.R. Sharpe, *London and the Kingdom*, 3 vols. (1894–5), iii, pp. 385–6, quoting some minutes of the proceedings of the common council of the city.
10. *The Politics of Fifteenth-Century England: John Vale's Book*, ed. M.L. Kekewich *et al.* (Stroud, 1995), pp. 220–2. See also Cora L. Scofield, 'Elizabeth Wydevile in the Sanctuary at Westminster, 1470', *English*

Historical Review, xxiv (1909), pp. 90–1.

11. *Paston Letters*, v, p. 85.

12. MacGibbon, p. 96, quoting BL, Add. MSS 4614, f. 222.

13. A. Strickland, *Lives of the Queens of England*, 8 vols. (revised edition, 1857), ii, p. 341. Miss Strickland notes that its strength was such that 'the workmen employed in its demolition, in the last (eighteenth) century, almost despaired of ever being able to level it'.

14. *Historie of the Arrivall of Edward IV in England and the Finall Recouerye of his Kingdomes from Henry VI. A.D. M.CCCC. LXXI*, ed. J. Bruce (Camden Society, 1838), p. 163. A contemporary verse printed in *Political Poems and Songs relating to English History*, ed. T. Wright, 2 vols. (1859–61), ii, p. 274, expresses the same sentiments:

    'The kyng comfortid the quene, and other ladyes eke;
    His swete babis full tendurly he did kys;
    The yonge priynce he behelde, and in his armys did bere.
    Thus his bale turnyd hym to blis;
    Aftur sorow joy, the course of the worlde is.
    The site of his babis relesid parte of his woo;
    Thus the wille of God in every thyng is doo'

15. *The Great Chronicle of London*, ed. A.H. Thomas and I.D. Thornley (1938, reprinted Gloucester 1983), p. 217.

16. *Arrivall of Edward IV*, p. 31.

17. More, p. 2; Mancini, p. 65.

18. *Arrivall of Edward IV*, p. 34.

19. The Yorkist writer recorded that he died from 'pure displeasure and melencoly' (*Arrivall of Edward IV*, p. 38) but the Lancastrians were in no doubt that he had been murdered. His skull was found to be unusually thin when his tomb was opened in 1910 and a third possibility is that he may have fainted on hearing the news of Tewkesbury and fatally struck his head on the stone floor.

20. MacGibbon, p. 109, quoting BL, Add. MSS 6113, f. 100b. This was in 1472.

21. On this point see Colin Richmond and Margaret Lucille Kekewich in *John Vale's Book*, p. 47, where it is argued that Edward successfully 'pinned' responsibility for the Lincolnshire rebellion on Warwick and Clarence in order to be rid of them.

22. Ross, *Edward IV*, p. 176.

Chapter Four

1. He was in custody until 20 May 1475, after which he appears to have been released and allowed, or ordered, to join the King's expedition to France in July. He was drowned on the return journey, between Calais and Dover, in September 1475. G.E.C. *et al.*, *The Complete Peerage*, 12 vols. (1910–59), v, pp. 214–5.

2. A. Strickland, *Lives of the Queens*, ii, p. 307.

3. BL, Add. MSS 4614, ff. 340–1, 222–3, quoted by MacGibbon, p. 109, note 3.

4. C.L. Kingsford, *English Historical Literature in the Fifteenth Century* (Oxford, 1913), pp. 386–7. The name of the individual who held the office of Bluemantle Pursuivant is unknown.

5. *Paston Letters*, v, p. 112.

6. Kingsford, *English Historical Literature*, p. 379.

7. *Calendar of the Patent Rolls, Edward IV, 1467–77*, (1900), p. 283.

8. The household accounts make it clear she was present at the birth of Elizabeth's second daughter, Princess Mary, and this probably formed part of a regular pattern. See MacGibbon, p. 67.

9. See Appendix 2, 'The Woodvilles and Witchcraft'.

10. H.T. Evans, *Wales and the Wars of the Roses* (Cambridge 1915, reprinted 1998), p. 116.

11. See, for example, M.A. Hicks, 'The Changing Role of the Wydevilles in Yorkist Politics to 1483', in *Patronage*, ed. C. Ross, pp. 76–7.

12. D.E. Lowe points out that Rivers was not only a capable warrior but also a hard-headed businessman typical of his class and period. These, and his cultural interests, made him an ideal choice to oversee the young Prince's upbringing. 'Patronage and Politics: Edward IV, the Wydevilles, and the Council of the Prince of Wales, 1471–83', *Bulletin of the Board of Celtic Studies*, xxix (1981), p. 553.

13. Lowe argues that nearly all those appointed to the enlarged Council who became active working members were in some way associated with the Woodvilles, although some of the relationships he cites are very distant. He admits that they were not 'in themselves strong enough necessarily to have predetermined political attitudes and political actions' but considers that 'together they form a sufficiently coherent pattern to suggest a least a predisposition in the council to accept Wydeville leadership'. Conversely, he considers Bishop Alcock one of the few genuinely independent members of the establishment, although Alcock and Rivers obviously worked closely and amicably together and were mutually devoted to Prince Edward. There is, admittedly, no evidence to connect Alcock to the Woodvilles before 1472, but his appointment as President and keyholder would have been unthinkable if they had not already been on good terms. *Ibid*, pp. 558–9.

14. Professor Hicks points out that, far from seeking to establish a permanent power base, Rivers proposed to divide his estates between his two surviving brothers, neither of whom was married and likely to found a dynasty. 'The Changing Role of the Wydevilles in Yorkist Politics', p. 74.

15. Although the King credited the amount against Hastings's debts to the Crown leaving Elizabeth free to take the profits. Hicks, 'The Changing Role of the Wydevilles in Yorkist Politics', in *Patronage*, ed. C. Ross, p. 73.

16. More, p. 50.

17. *Ibid.*, p. 9.

18. Mancini, p. 69.

19. See E.W. Ives, 'Andrew Dymock and the Papers of Antony, Earl Rivers 1482–3', *Bulletin of the Institute of Historical Research*, xli (1968), p.

221. Edwards's confession has been printed by James Gairdner, *History of the Life and Reign of Richard III* (Cambridge, 1898), p. 339.

20. *Calendar of the Close Rolls Edward IV – Edward V – Richard III, 1476–1485* (1954), p. 221. The settlement was dated 12 October 1479.

21. J. Anstis, *Register of the Most Noble Order of the Garter*, 2 vols. (1724), ii, pp. 194–6. They were nominated for membership early in 1476.

22. A.R. Myers, 'The Household of Queen Elizabeth Woodville, 1466–7', *Bulletin of the John Rylands Library*, 1 (1968), pp. 451–2. Anne Hastings received £6 13s 4d, and Elizabeth Donne £10.

23. Mancini, p. 69.

24. *Croyland Chronicle*, p. 485.

25. *Paston Letters*, v, pp. 135–6.

26. M.A. Hicks, *False, Fleeting, Perjur'd Clarence* (Gloucester, 1980), p. 116.

27. Although historians differ. Professor Hicks thinks that 'Clarence's anger at Gloucester's attempt to disturb the settlement was perfectly understandable' (Hicks, *Clarence*, p. 114), while Professor Ross is of the opinion that 'Duke Richard . . . showed considerable moderation throughout', *Edward IV*, p. 189.

28. *Paston Letters*, v, pp. 188–9.

29. *Ibid.*, p. 195.

30. Contemporaries expected the Earl of Warwick and his brother to be attainted after Barnet, and common law proceedings, which were often a preliminary to parliamentary sentences of attainder and could take effect without them, were instituted before special commissions in Hertfordshire and Middlesex in May 1472. Clarence and Gloucester first received the Warwick inheritance in the form of grants of forfeited lands from the Crown; but such grants were subject to royal Acts of Resumption, and the preamble to the Act debarring George Neville makes it clear that they had pressured the King to stay the formal proceedings in Parliament (and then nullified the claims of George and the Countess of Warwick) in order to allow them – or, more precisely, their wives – to inherit at law. They were at least united in wanting their titles to be secure!

31. *Calendar of State Papers and Manuscripts existing in the Archives and Collections of Milan, I 1385–1618*, ed. A.B. Hinds (1913), pp. 197–8.

32. *Edward IV's French Expedition of 1475*, ed. F.P. Barnard (1925, reprinted Gloucester 1975), f. 2R. The only other member of the family so engaged was the Marquess of Dorset, who was to receive ten shillings a day as opposed to Rivers's six shillings and eightpence, but the size of his contingent (if any) is unknown.

33. *British Library Cottonian Manuscript Vespasian C XIV*, f. 244, quoted by Scofield, ii, p. 125, n. 2.

34. These quotations are taken from the transcription of Edward's will printed in *Excerpta Historica*, ed. S. Bentley (1833), pp. 366–79.

35. The Count of St Pol, his duplicity at St Quentin notwithstanding, also pleaded with Edward not to come to terms with Louis, but was reduced to calling him a poor, dishonourable, cowardly monarch who

would soon discover that the French had hoodwinked him. He expected Duke Charles to shield him from the anger of both kings, but Charles handed him over to Louis, who beheaded him at the end of the year.

36. Edward was lucky in that if his allies had supported him, and territory had been captured, he would have been obliged to incur the expense of defending it, possibly for years. A fuller account of the French expedition may be found in Ross, *Edward IV*, pp. 205–38.

Chapter Five

1. Mancini, pp. 60–1; More, p. 59.
2. F. Hepburn, *Portraits of the Later Plantagenets* (1986), pp. 54–60.
3. See Chapter 2.
4. Elizabeth's clerk referred to Margaret's 1452–3 account as a precedent on several occasions, suggesting that, for whatever reason, it was the only record of its kind to survive from the recent Lancastrian period, even by 1466–7.
5. See A.R. Myers, 'The Household of Queen Elizabeth Woodville 1466–7', *Bulletin of the John Rylands Library*, l (1967–8), pp. 207–35, 443–81.
6. A.R. Myers, *The Household of Edward IV* (Manchester, 1959), p. 92.
7. Myers, 'Household of Queen Elizabeth Woodville', pp. 210–11, and 'The Household of Queen Margaret of Anjou, 1452–3', *Bulletin of the John Rylands Library*, xl (1957–8). There was one occasion when Edward IV, having exempted the Bishop of Durham from paying £70 to Elizabeth in respect of Queen's Gold, borrowed money to reimburse her, an expedient which can have done little to improve its credibility as a source of wealth. Public Record Office, E404, 75/2, f. 38.
8. Myers, 'The Household of Queen Elizabeth Woodville 1466–7', p. 215. Elizabeth of York followed her husband Henry VII's practice of initialling accounts to indicate that she had seen them and found them satisfactory, but it would be dangerous to assume that Edward IV's and Elizabeth Woodville's failure to do so is evidence of a lack of concern.
9. Elizabeth had instructed her master forester of Blackmore to present Stonor with a buck only a year earlier. *The Stonor Letters and Papers*, ed. C.L. Kingsford, 2 vols. (1919), ii, pp. 127–8.
10. *Ibid.*, pp. 150–1. The places mentioned are Barnwood Chace and Eggshill Common, both in Gloucestershire. This letter, and the above instruction, have been preserved because Stonor's correspondence was seized by the government to search for evidence of treason when he joined in Buckingham's Rebellion late in 1483.
11. R. Horrox, *Richard III: A Study in Service* (Cambridge, 1989), p. 80.
12. Anne Crawford suggests that it was Sir John Howard (later Duke of Norfolk), who afterwards retained Bliaunt who persuaded Elizabeth to intervene. See *Letters of the Queens of England 1100–1547* (Stroud, 1994), pp. 135–6.
13. *Paston Letters*, vi, pp. 105–6, and correction, i, p. 340.

14. *The Coventry Leet Book*, ed. M.D. Harris, 4 parts (Early English Text Society, 1907–13), pp. 391–4, 405–6, 407–8.

15. *Stonor Letters and Papers*, i, pp. 122–3. C.L. Kingsford places the letter between 1470 and 1473.

16. Ross, *Edward IV*, Appendix 2, p. 436.

17. S. Thurley, *The Royal Palaces of Tudor England* (New Haven, 1993), pp. 19–20.

18. H.M. Colvin *et al.*, *The History of the King's Works*, 6 vols. (1963–82) i , p. 537.

19. Eight of Elizabeth's children were born in the three palaces mentioned, Elizabeth, Mary, Cecily and Anne at Westminster, Margaret and George at Windsor, and Catherine and Bridget, the two youngest, at Eltham. The only exceptions were Edward, born in the Westminster sanctuary, and Richard, born at Shrewsbury.

20. This and what follows is based on the seminal work of Anne Sutton and Livia Visser-Fuchs, 'A "Most Benevolent Queen". Queen Elizabeth Woodville's Reputation, her Piety and her Books', *The Ricardian*, x (1995), pp. 230–1, and 'The Cult of Angels in Late Fifteenth-Century England: An Hours of the Guardian Angel presented to Queen Elizabeth Woodville', in *Women and the Book*, ed. L. Smith and J.H.M. Taylor (1996).

21. Elizabeth and Cecily of York could not, strictly speaking, have described themselves as the King's daughters after this date. It has been alleged that the Queen owned two other books in the Royal collection, a thirteenth-century missal and a *Life of Our Lady* by John Lydgate, but the evidence for these is rejected by Sutton and Visser-Fuchs in 'A Most Benevolent Queen', pp. 231–2. She purchased one book in the year covered by her surviving account (for £10) but it is unfortunately not named.

22. The only legal difference between Queen Elizabeth and other noblewomen was that she, unlike them, could acquire land independently of her husband, and had the right to plead in her own name.

23. See, for example, *Paston Letters*, v, p. 112.

24. These particulars are taken from 'A Most Benevolent Queen', and the sources there cited.

25. *Acts of Court of the Mercers Company*, ed. L. Lyell and F.D. Watney (1936), pp. 123–7.

26. N.H. Nicolas, *Privy Purse Expenses of Elizabeth of York: Wardrobe Accounts of Edward IV* (1830, reprinted 1972), pp. 4, 14, 23, 37, 53.

Chapter Six

1. Anne Sutton and Livia Visser-Fuchs suggest that the reglazing of the nave at Fotheringhay, which was probably not completed until 1475, may also be a reason for the delay. P.W. Hammond, A.F. Sutton and L. Visser-Fuchs, 'The Reburial of Richard, Duke of York, 21–30 July, 1476', *The Ricardian*, x (1994), p. 124.

2. The carriage was a four-wheeled vehicle surmounted by a framework of hoops supported by horizontal bars, probably similar to the structure surrounding the famous effigy of Richard Beauchamp (d. 1439) in St Mary's Church, Warwick. It would have been partly covered with material, but the Duke's features would have been clearly visible to the onlookers.

3. Convention presumably prevented Elizabeth from participating directly in the formal reception of the cortège, although she was clearly present. Earl Rivers and the Marquis of Dorset were among those who did.

4. From a contemporary description of the scene copied by a Chester Herald (original in French). 'The Reburial of Richard, Duke of York', pp. 130–8.

5. *Ibid*, p. 138.

6. Scofield, ii, p. 185.

7. Professor Hicks supposes that Margaret and Clarence would have lived in England, but his position would still have been potentially ambiguous in the event of a future war with Scotland. Clearly, Edward's 'excuse' allowed him to diplomatically reject any 'unsuitable' bride. M.A. Hicks, *Clarence*, p. 133.

8. Miss Scofield thought that Burdet's execution was intended to punish Clarence for treating Twynho and Thursby 'as though he had used a king's power', but there is no evidence that the two cases were linked. Scofield, ii, pp. 187–9.

9. *Croyland Chronicle*, p. 479.

10. *Ibid.*, p. 478.

11. Mancini, p. 63.

12. Hicks, *Clarence*, pp. 150, 150–7.

13. The same reasoning could be applied to Elizabeth's brother-in-law Henry Stafford, Duke of Buckingham, who afterwards helped Richard of Gloucester destroy the power of the Woodville family.

14. Hicks, *Clarence*, p. 151.

15. It may be thought sinister that William Alyngton who, as Commons' Speaker, formally requested Clarence's execution, was also the Prince of Wales's chancellor, but there is no evidence that he was using (or misusing) his position in Parliament to further Elizabeth's interests in a manner that was inconsistent with royal policy as a whole.

16. *Paston Letters*, v, pp. 257–8. Sir John Paston to his mother, 21 March 1476.

17. B.A. Pocquet du Haut-Jusse, *Francois II, Duc de Bretagne, et l'Angleterre* (Paris, 1929), quoted by Ross, *Edward IV*, p. 247.

18. 'Narrative of the Marriage of Richard Duke of York with Anne of Norfolk: the Matrimonial Feast and the Grand Jousting', *Illustrations of Ancient State and Chivalry from manuscripts preserved in the Ashmolean Museum*, ed. W.H. Black (Roxburghe Club, 1840), pp. 28–31. The original has 'my *Lord* of Richmond', but Henry Tudor was in exile so *Lady* (Margaret Beaufort, Countess of Richmond) must be meant.

19. Ross, *Edward IV*, p. 249.

20. F. Madden, *The Gentleman's Magazine* (January 1831), p. 25.

21. See Muriel St Clare Byrne, *The Lisle Letters*, 6 vols. (1981). Tradition

has it that he was born before Edward's marriage, probably between 1461 and 1464. Little is known of his earlier years, but he obtained a succession of positions at court after 1501, and was particularly favoured by Henry VIII, who created him Viscount Lisle in 1523. His *Letters* date from the period 1533–40 when he was Lord Deputy of Calais, and have survived because they were seized to search for evidence of treason when he fell foul of his suspicious master. He died on 3 March 1542 (he was by then nearly eighty), possibly of a stroke brought on by the news that he was to be released!

22. *The Historical Collections of a London Citizen*, ed. J. Gairdner (Camden Society, 1876), p. 226.
23. More, p. 2; Mancini, p. 67; *The Memoirs of Philip de Commines*, ed. A.R. Scoble, 2 vols. (1855–6), i, p. 276.
24. A. Wood, *History of the University of Oxford*, ed. J. Gutch, 2 vols. (Oxford, 1792–6), i, pp. 637–8.
25. The chronicler says that 'the sleeves of the robes were very full and hanging, greatly resembling a monk's frock, and so lined within with most costly furs, and rolled over the shoulders'. *Croyland Chronicle*, pp. 481–2.
26. *Ibid*, p. 482.
27. More, pp. 9–12.
28. Scofield, ii, p. 365.
29. He may, of course, merely have added codicils to his earlier will.
30. It is likely that his confidence in Gloucester had increased over the years, and there was no longer the difficulty which naming him over the head of Clarence would doubtless have created in 1475.

Chapter Seven

1. Mancini says that Gloucester 'avoided the jealousy of the queen from whom he lived far separated' (Mancini, p. 65), but this may only reflect his own prejudices based on the fact that Duke Richard had been absent in northern England, acting as his brother's viceroy, for much of the previous decade.
2. In the two most recent cases, Richard II had begun to exercise power by 1384 when he was seventeen, and Henry VI was declared of age on 12 November 1437 when he was only fifteen.
3. This was again in keeping with the precedents of 1377 and 1429, when Richard II and Henry VI had been crowned at the ages of ten and seven respectively.
4. *Croyland Chronicle*, p. 485.
5. Thomas More says that Elizabeth and her enlarged family did not go to the sanctuary building itself (as they presumably had in 1470) but to 'the abbottes place' or apartments, where they would have enjoyed the same degree of moral, if not physical, protection (More, p. 19). Miss Strickland conjectures that 'the noble hall, now used as a dining-room for the students of Westminster school was, doubtless, the place where Elizabeth seated herself "alow on the rushes" in her despair'. A.

Strickland, *Lives of the Queens of England*, 8 vols. (revised edition, 1857), ii, pp. 357–8.

6. More, pp. 19–20.

7. *The Stonor Letters and Papers 1290–1483*, ed. C.L. Kingsford, 2 vols. (1919), ii, pp. 159–60. Mancini, pp. 124–5.

8. Both surviving letters may be conveniently found in P.W. Hammond and A.F. Sutton, *Richard III. The Road to Bosworth Field* (1985), pp. 103–4.

9. David MacGibbon, following the Tudor writer Polydore Vergil, suggests that it was Hastings who began to suspect Gloucester's intentions and sought the Queen's assistance, but it seems more likely that it was Elizabeth who first suspected the Protector and approached Hastings. Hastings would perhaps not have thought of enlisting the support of the scattered and defeated Woodvilles, but Elizabeth had already turned to him in another crisis in 1464. MacGibbon, p. 149. Jane Shore's involvement is conjectural, and More says that Elizabeth hated her 'as that concubine whom the king her husband had most loved' (p. 47); but she had all the right contacts and Gloucester's subsequent treatment of her seems particularly severe. C. Ross, *Richard III* (1981), p. 137.

10. More, pp. 32–41 passim.

11. *Rotuli Parliamentorum*, ed. J Strachey *et al.*, 6 vols. (1767–77), vi, pp. 240–2. She was a daughter of John Talbot, Earl of Shrewsbury who had been killed at Castillon in 1453. Sir Thomas Butler, her first husband, died in 1461, so her liaison with the King presumably occurred at some time between then and the early months of 1464. See John Ashdown-Hill, 'Edward IV's Uncrowned Queen: The Lady Eleanor Talbot, Lady Butler', *The Ricardian*, xi (1997), pp. 166–90.

12. See R.H. Helmholz, 'The Sons of Edward IV: A Canonical Assessment of the Claim that they were Illegitimate', in *Richard III: Loyalty, Lordship and Law*, ed. P.W. Hammond (1986), and H.A. Kelly, 'The Case Against Edward IV's Marriage and Offspring: Secrecy; Witchcraft; Secrecy; Precontract', *The Ricardian*, xi (1998), pp. 326–35. Kelly points out that 'precontract means *previous marriage* when alleged as a challenge to a subsequent marriage . . the word does not mean "preliminary contract" or "betrothal". A betrothal to one person did not invalidate a subsequent marriage to another person' p. 327.

13. The weapons had been assembled for a campaign against the Scots, and King Edward's 'treasure' was, as Professor Hicks points out, insufficient to pay his funeral expenses! *Richard III: The Man Behind the Myth* (1991), p. 103.

14. Mancini, p. 79; *Croyland Chronicle*, p. 487.

15. Mancini, pp. 77–9.

16. Mancini, p. 93. Mancini had personal information that Gloucester had dismissed the young King's personal servants, and the dangers facing a deposed monarch (Edward II and Richard II had been killed within a short time of being imprisoned and Henry VI had been allowed to survive only as long as his son would have inherited his title) were only too plain.

17. *Croyland Chronicle*, p. 491.
18. *Ibid*. The Tudor chronicler Edward Hall's description of the Queen's reaction to the news perhaps owes as much to the imagination as some of Thomas More's purple passages, but may still preserve the gist of something he had heard from a near contemporary or copied from a source now lost. Elizabeth, he writes, fainted, and then 'wept and sobbed and with pitiful screeches she replenished the whole mansion, her breast she punched, her fair hair she tore and pulled in pieces and being overcome with sorrow . . . rather desired death than life'. Edward Halle, *The Union of the Two Noble Families of Lancaster and York*, 1550 [Hall's Chronicle] (reprinted Menston, 1970), 'King Richard the III', f. iv, (spelling & punctuation modernised).
19. *Three Books of Polydore Vergil's English History*, ed. Sir H. Ellis (1844), pp. 195–7.
20. *Rotuli Parliamentorum*, vi, p. 244.
21. *Croyland Chronicle*, p. 496.
22. Ross, *Richard III*, p. 101.
23. BL, Harl. MS 433, ed. R. Horrox and P.W. Hammond, 4 vols. (1979–83), iii, p. 190. (I am grateful to Peter Hammond and the Richard III Society for permission to quote this text.)
24. It is possible to make out a case against Buckingham who, allegedly, killed the Princes to assist Henry Tudor, but who planned to seize the throne when the rebellion succeeded. See Appendix 6.
25. Ross, *Richard III*, p. 101.
26. John Nesfield had commanded the guard which Richard had placed on the Westminster sanctuary, and the statement that Elizabeth's annuity was to be paid to him implies some continuing authority.
27. BL, Harl. MS 433, iii, p. 114.
28. *Croyland Chronicle*, p. 498.
29. Sir George Buck, *The History of King Richard the Third (1619)*, ed. A.N. Kincaid (Gloucester, 1979), p. 191.
30. Some writers suggest that Richard compelled Elizabeth to write to Dorset, but there can be little doubt that, if this was the case, she would have found ways and means to warn her son that he was walking into danger. The fact that Dorset did try (unsuccessfully) to slip away from Henry Tudor indicates that he was convinced he was safe.
31. *Croyland Chronicle*, pp. 499–500.
32. The crucial factors are that Richard had placed the Princes in a position in which they were likely to be killed (see n. 15), and that many of his subjects believed him responsible for their deaths.
33. No English king had been killed in battle since Harold in 1066 (and before that since Osberht of Northumbria in 867), and a defeated Richard would have been expected to survive and attempt to recover his throne later – hence the caution of many present on Bosworth Field.

Chapter Eight

1. *Rotuli Parliamentorum*, ed. J. Strachey *et al.*, 6 vols. (1767–77), vi, pp. 288–9. For the grants see *Materials for a History of the Reign of Henry VII*, ed. W. Campbell, 2 vols. (1873–7), i, pp. 347–50.
2. Historical Manuscripts Commission, *12th Report, Rutland Manuscripts*, 4 vols. (1888–1905), i, p. 8.
3. The King, in fact, allowed the arrays to be suspended a few days afterwards. *Tudor Royal Proclamations*, ed. P.L. Hughes and J.F. Larkin, 3 vols. (New Haven, 1964), i, p. 5.
4. See the report of Sir Hugh Conway's conversation with Sir Richard Nanfan and Sir Sampson Norton in *Letters and Papers Illustrative of the Reigns of Richard III and Henry VII*, ed. J. Gairdner, 2 vols. (1861–3), i, pp. 234–5.
5. Although the Croyland Chronicler suggests that some of the rebels persisted with their purpose, and almost succeeded in capturing the King at York. *Croyland Chronicle*, pp. 513–4.
6. J. Leland, *De Rebus Britannicis Collectanea*, ed. T. Hearne, 6 vols. (1770), iv, pp. 204–7.
7. Dr Bennett raises the possibility that a name as remarkably uncommon as Lambert Simnel was itself a pseudonym (the lad is called 'John' in the account of an unnamed herald who accompanied the Tudor army), and suggests that there may have been two priests called Simons, a William, who at the beginning of 1487 confessed in convocation that he had taken Simnel to Ireland, and a Richard who was captured with his protégé after the Battle of Stoke. Michael Bennett, *Lambert Simnel and the Battle of Stoke* (Gloucester, 1987), pp. 43, 44–45, 48–49.
8. *The Anglica Historia of Polydore Vergil AD 1485–1537*, ed. D. Hay (Camden Society, 1950), pp. 13–15.
9. Henry informed the receivers that 'of late by thadvise of the lords and other nobles of our counsaill for diuers consideracions vs and theym moeuyng (we) have seased into our hands all honors, castelles, manoirs, (etc) late assigned vnto Queene Elizabeth, late wif to the full noble prince of famous memorye Edward the Fourth and . . . haue assigned (them) vnto our derrest wif the quene'. Campbell, *Materials*, ii, p. 148. I have assumed that 'seased' means seized, but it might, possibly, mean 'seised'.
10. Hall's *Chronicle*, 'The Politique Governaunce of Kyng Henry VII', f. viii.
11. Francis Bacon, *The History of the Reign of King Henry the Seventh*, ed. R. Lockyer (1971), p. 55. Bacon is, of course, a secondary authority who did not always adhere to his own high precepts of scholarship. But he clearly knew something of the stories, or traditions, of an earlier generation, and I have cited him when he offers seemingly authentic particulars, or insights, which would otherwise be lost to view.
12. Bacon, *Henry VII*, p. 60.
13. See M.K. Jones and M.G. Underwood, *The King's Mother* (Cambridge, 1992), p. 108.
14. M.K. Jones, 'Collyweston – An Early Tudor Palace', in *England in the Fifteenth Century*, ed. D. Williams (Woodbridge, 1987), pp. 137–41.

15. These details are taken from Jones and Underwood, *The King's Mother*, pp. 71, 73, 75, 86.

16. Leland, *Collectanea*, iv, p. 235. It is sometimes suggested that the Scottish marriage negotiations prove that Elizabeth was still in favour and her absence from her daughter's coronation can (therefore) only be explained by illness; but if she was too ill to attend such an important ceremony she was (presumably) too ill to be married to King James as well.

17. Vergil, *Anglica Historia*, ed. D. Hay, pp. 16–19. Anne Sutton and Livia Visser-Fuchs argue that because Vergil did not specifically state that Elizabeth was involved in the Simnel conspiracy in the revised, printed, version of his book written between 1521 and 1524 (when, perhaps, he could have spoken more plainly) the excuse that she had incurred Henry's displeasure by surrendering her daughters to King Richard must be accepted. But Vergil probably still felt a sense of loyalty towards his late patron and could hardly admit that he had set out to deliberately mislead his public without damaging his own reputation. 'The "Retirement" of Elizabeth Woodville, and her Sons', *The Ricardian*, xi (1999), pp. 561–4.

18. Campbell, *Materials*, ii, p. 555.

19. Leland, *Collectanea*, iv, p. 249.

20. *Rotuli Scotiae*, ed. D. Macpherson *et al.*, 2 vols. (1814–19), ii, pp. 475–7.

21. King James was murdered after the Battle of Sauchieburn (11 June 1488), so the fiction did not have to be maintained for long.

22. The examples of Lady Margaret's influence are drawn from the period after the Simnel rebellion, but Henry's reliance on her might, if anything, have been greater in the first two years of his reign.

23. Vergil, *Anglica Historia*, ed. D. Hay, pp. 14–15.

24. *Rotuli Parliamentorum*, vi, p. 436. Sante's alleged treason in January 1487 is dismissed in half a sentence, whereas his part in a less serious plot to free the Earl of Warwick in December 1490 is rehearsed at considerable length.

25. *The Registers of Robert Stillington, Bishop of Bath and Wells, 1466–1491, and Richard Fox, Bishop of Bath and Wells 1492–1494*, ed. Sir H.C. Maxwell-Lyte, Somerset Record Society, lii (1937), pp. xii–xiii. Again, we can only conjecture that Stillington's 'conspirares' were concerned with the Simnel rebellion, but his downfall coincided with Elizabeth's and must reflect Henry's concern with the revival of Yorkist aspirations in the early months of 1487.

26. Bacon, *Henry VII*, p. 61. Henry says as much in his letter to Sir Gilbert Talbot (*Original Letters Illustrative of English History*, ed. Sir H. Ellis, 1st series [1824], i, pp. 19–20), although his efforts to blame the whole enterprise on Duchess Margaret must be taken with a pinch of salt.

27. Lincoln was attainted with effect from 9 March 1487, although the indictment noted that he did not leave England until the 19th (*Rotuli Parliamentorum*, vi, pp. 397–8). But James Taite, who had stabled the Earl's horse at York the previous summer, recognised it at Doncaster on Lady Day (25 March 1487), and it is possible that Lincoln did not take

ship until he had first sounded out dissidents in the north. See Robert Davies, 'Original Documents Relating to Lambert Symnell's Rebellion in the Second Year of King Henry VII', *Proceedings of the Archaeological Institute: 1846* (1848), pp. 2–6, 9. Lovel left England in the latter part of January (*Paston Letters*, vi, p. 95).

28. Bacon, *Henry VII*, p. 64.
29. Dr Bennett suggests that a proclamation which Henry issued on 5 June declaring his intention to march northwards shows that he was already aware of the rebels' landing, but the most stalwart horseman could not have covered the near 200 miles from Furness to Kenilworth in less than three to four days. Bennett, *Lambert Simnel*, p. 75.
30. Edward Grey, Viscount Lisle, supported Richard III in the summer of 1483 but successfully transferred his allegiance to Henry Tudor two years later. He never seems to have sided with his former sister-in-law and her second family.
31. See Leland, *Collectanea*, iv, pp. 210, 214–5; *Paston Letters*, vi, pp. 101–2, 187. An analysis of the known domiciles of these and of an additional 53 of Henry's supporters whose names are recorded by Polydore Vergil (*Anglica Historia*, ed. D. Hay, pp. 22–3, n. 15) reveals a goodly response from the Midlands and East Anglia, a more restrained approach by those who resided in the southern counties and the West Country, and (apart from Stanleyan Cheshire) the failure of all but a handful to join him from the North.
32. Leland, *Collectanea*, p. 212.
33. *The Great Chronicle of London*, ed. A.H. Thomas and I.D. Thornley (1938, reprinted Gloucester 1983), p. 241.
34. Leland, *Collectanea*, iv, p. 212.
35. *Great Chronicle*, p. 241.
36. Bacon, *Henry VII*, p. 68.
37. *Chroniques de Jean Molinet (1474–1506)*, ed. G. Doutrepont and O. Jodogne, 3 vols. (Brussels, 1935–7), i. pp. 563–4.
38. Leland, *Collectanea*, iv, p. 212.
39. *Ibid.*
40. *Ibid.*, p. 213.
41. *Ibid.*
42. *Rotuli Parliamentorum*, vi, pp. 397, 502.
43. Bacon, *Henry VII*, p. 66.
44. Leland, *Collectanea*, iv, p. 214.
45. Vergil, *Anglica Historia*, ed. D. Hay, p. 25.
46. Hall's *Chronicle*, Henry VII, f. ix
47. *Ibid.*, f. x.
48. One is reminded of the manner in which Commines dismissed the Frenchmen who accompanied Henry Tudor to Bosworth as 'the loosest and most profligate persons in all that country' (*The Memoirs of Philip de Commines*, ed. A.R. Scoble, 2 vols. [1856], ii, p. 64), a stricture which their conduct in the battle effectively belied.
49. Lovel's disappearance is examined more fully in my article 'What Happened to Lord Lovel?', *The Ricardian*, vii (1985), pp. 56–65. It has since been noticed that his name was included in a Scottish letter of

safe-conduct a year after the battle, but there is no evidence that this was ever used. Sheilah O'Connor, 'Francis Lovel and the Rebels of Furness Fells', *The Ricardian*, vii (1987), pp. 366–9.

50. Vergil, *Anglica Historia*, ed. D. Hay, p. 23. Bacon, *Henry VII*, p. 63.
51. Campbell, *Materials*, ii, pp. 319–20 (30 May 1488); *Calendar of the Patent Rolls. Henry VII, 1485–1494* (1914), p. 302.
52. MacGibbon, quoting BL, Harl. MS 231, f. 37b.
53. David MacGibbon thinks that Bermondsey was chosen as Elizabeth's place of residence for this reason (see MacGibbon pp. 197–8), but Katherine of Valois, who had no connection with the Clares, had been sent there in 1436, perhaps, as Professor Griffiths suggests, when her clandestine marriage to Owen Tudor was discovered (R.A. Griffiths, *The Reign of Henry VI*, [1981], p. 61). It seems likely that the Abbey, which had been built in a secluded position on a Thames islet, came to be regarded as a semi-secure place of residence for disgraced royalty, and that its long-standing obligations were only part of the story.
54. MacGibbon, p. 221.
55. G. Baker, *History of Northamptonshire*, 2 vols. (1822–41), ii, pp. 165–6.
56. On this point see K.B. MacFarlane, *The Nobility*, pp. 148–9.
57. MacGibbon, pp. 199–200.
58. J. Nichols, *The History and Antiquities of the County of Leicester*, 4 vols. (1795–1811), iii, part 2, pp. 569–71. Nichols omits repetitive words and phrases which add nothing to what has already been said.
59. *British Library Arundel Manuscript 26*, ff. 29v–30, printed in A.F. Sutton and L. Visser-Fuchs, 'The Royal Burials of the House of York at Windsor', *The Ricardian*, xi (1999), pp. 456–7.
60. See (for example) MacGibbon, p. 200; Sutton and Visser-Fuchs, *The Ricardian*, xi, p. 453.
61. Jones and Underwood, *The King's Mother*, p. 239.
62. *Ibid.*, p. 237, n. 26. Sutton and Visser-Fuchs, *The Ricardian*, xi, p. 457.

Chapter Nine

1. *The Crowland Chronicle Continuations 1459–1486*, ed. N. Pronay and J. Cox (1986), p. 155.
2. *Croyland Chronicle*, (ed. Riley), p. 485.
3. See Appendix 5.
4. *Political Poems and Songs Relating to English History*, ed. T. Wright, 2 vols., (1859–61), ii, pp. 281–2.
5. *The Coventry Leet Book*, ed. M.D. Harris, 4 parts (1907–13), p. 393.
6. *The Politics of Fifteenth Century England: John Vale's Book*, ed. M.L. Kekewich *et al.* (Stroud, 1995), p. 213.
7. Mancini, pp. 65, 75.
8. Edward Halle, *The Union of the Two Noble and Illustrious Families of Lancaster and York 1550*, [Hall's Chronicle] (reprinted, Menston, 1970), 'the fourth year of Edward IV', f. v.

9. William Shakespeare, *The Third Part of King Henry the Sixth*, IV. iv, *King Richard the Third*, II. ii.

10. Horace Walpole, *Historic Doubts on the Life and Reign of King Richard III*, ed. P.M. Kendall (1965), pp. 171, 174. The first edition was published in 1768.

11. C.E. Moreton, 'A Local Dispute and the Politics of 1483: Roger Townshend, Earl Rivers and the Duke of Gloucester', *The Ricardian*, viii (1989), pp. 305–7. See also M. Hicks, *Richard III, The Man Behind the Myth* (1991) pp. 96–9.

12. A. Strickland, *Lives of the Queens*, ii, pp. 331, 367.

13. *Ibid.*, pp. 332 & 352.

14. Scofield, pp. 397–8.

15. By Keith Dockray in *The Ricardian*, xi (1999), pp. 426–45.

16. J. Gairdner, *History of the Life and Reign of Richard the Third* (Cambridge, 1898), p.70.

17. See, for example, his long note dealing with the precise manner in which Edward, the Lancastrian Prince of Wales, met his death at the Battle of Tewkesbury, pp. 106–7. The same is true of Dr Gairdner's belief that Richard was responsible for the Princes' murder, a view which is no more reliable just because it is shared by Ramsay, Lingard, Oman and Pauli (p. 170, note 3). MacGibbon did not (apparently) subscribe to the opinion that 'historians repeat each other'!

18. *Ibid.*, p. 41.

19. P.M. Kendall, *Richard the Third* (1955), pp. 61, 71, 160, 165

20. *Ibid.*, p. 160. Kendall's phrase is that Elizabeth had been 'dropped' from the list of executors. He even suggests that the Woodvilles destroyed the will to prevent Edward's designation of Gloucester as Protector from becoming known, p. 461, note 9.

21. Ross, *Edward IV*, pp. 87–8, 97, 336–7.

22. R. Horrox, *Richard III: A Study in Service* (Cambridge, 1989), p. 91. A. Sutton and L. Visser-Fuchs, 'A "Most Benevolent Queen"', pp. 216–7.

23. *Ibid.*, p. 222.

24. Mancini, p. 71. This was similar to the restricted authority which the Council had allowed Humphrey, Duke of Gloucester (contrary to his late brother, Henry V's, wishes) during the minority of Henry VI.

Epilogue

1. N.L. Harvey, *Elizabeth of York: Tudor Queen* (1973).

2. Generations of historians have cast doubts on Buck's assessment of the letter, but without, it seems to me, seriously denting his credibility. See Sir George Buck, *The History of King Richard the Third*, ed. A.N. Kincaid (Gloucester, 1979), pp. xc–xciv; A. Hanham, 'Sir George Buck and Princess Elizabeth's Letter: A Problem in Detection', *The Ricardian*, vii (1987), pp. 398–400; and A. Kincaid, 'Buck and the Elizabeth of York Letter: A Reply to Dr Hanham', *The Ricardian*, viii (1988), pp. 46–9.

3. *Croyland Chronicle*, p. 499. The writer was in no doubt that some of Richard's northern supporters forced the abandonment of the project because they feared for themselves if the Woodvilles recovered their authority (pp. 499–500).

4. Buck, *Richard III*, p. 191.

5. J. Leland, *De Rebus Britannicis Collectanea*, ed. T. Hearne, 6 vols. (1770), v, p. 373.

6. *The Anglica Historia of Polydore Vergil AD 1485–1537*, ed. D. Hay (Camden Society, 1950), p. 133.

7. Brandon is a model of what was feasible in an age when divorce was all but impossible in that he had already been married three times and two of his wives were still living. He married for a fifth time after Mary's death.

8. Margaret's granddaughter, Mary, Queen of Scots, had been excluded from the succession by the terms of Henry VIII's will, and Mary's heiress Frances was apparently persuaded to allow her daughter to take her place.

9. Jane attributed her downfall to the offence she had caused God 'in that I have followed over–much the lust of mine own flesh, and the pleasures of this wretched world'. N.H. Nicolas, *The Literary Remains of Lady Jane Grey with a Memoir* (1825), p. 52.

Appendix 1

1. F. Hepburn, *Portraits of the Later Plantagenets* (1986), p. 58, n. 16. See generally pp. 54–60.

2. I am indebted to Geoffrey Wheeler and Jonathan Hughes for information relating to this portrait. The work also contains an interesting coloured sketch of a 'debauched and cruel-looking' Prince Edward of Lancaster, Henry VI's son.

3. H.M. Colvin *et al.*, *The History of the Kings Works*, 6 vols. (1963–82), iv, p. 96.

4. Although recent excavations unearthed more than 200 skeletons on the site.

5. George Smith suggests that Richard was older than both John and Edward: but John was already a knight and married when his two brothers were created knights of the Bath at the Queen's coronation in 1465. *The Coronation of Elizabeth Wydeville* (1935, reprinted Gloucester 1975), p. 51.

6. See A. Sutton and L. Visser-Fuchs, 'The Royal Burials of the House of York at Windsor', *The Ricardian*, xi (1999), pp. 446–51.

7. G.E.C. *et al.*, *The Complete Peerage*, 12 vols. (1910–59), xii, part 2, p. 450. See P.S. Routh, 'Lady Scroop Daughter of K. Edward: an Enquiry', *The Ricardian*, ix (1993), pp. 410–16.

8. W.E. Hampton, *Memorials of the Wars of the Roses* (Upminster, 1979), p. 44. See *The Sunday Express*, 21 January 2001, p. 42; 28 January 2001, p. 5.

Appendix 2

1. H.A. Kelly, 'English Kings and the Fear of Sorcery', *Mediaeval Studies*, xxxix (1977), pp. 206–38.
2. Professor Ralph Griffiths has suggested that Richard, Duke of York, Humphrey of Gloucester's political heir, thought of rescuing her in 1450. R.A. Griffiths, 'Richard, Duke of York and the Royal Household in Wales 1449–50', *Welsh History Review*, viii (1976), pp. 56–9.
3. For further particulars of Eleanor's case see Christina Hole, *Witchcraft in England* (1977), pp. 118–21, and H.A. Kelly, 'The Case Against Edward IV's Marriage and Offspring – Secrecy; Witchcraft; Secrecy; Precontract', *The Ricardian*, xi (1998), pp. 326–35. She died *c.* 1457.
4. Dauger said that he 'heard never no witchcraft of my lady of Bedford' and Jacquetta was granted an exemplification under the Great Seal.
5. Kelly, 'English Kings and the Fear of Sorcery', p. 236. It may be thought unusual that clergymen were not infrequently involved in these matters, but the perversion of sacred rites and ceremonies was, in Christina Hole's words, 'one of the blacker manifestations of medieval magic'. *Witchcraft in England*, p. 120.
6. *Three Books of Polydore Vergil's English History*, ed. Sir H. Ellis (Camden Society, 1844), p. 180. More, p. 47. These accounts may well be over-dramatised, but it is possible to allow that something of the sort occurred.
7. Quoted in P.W. Hammond and A.F. Sutton, *Richard III: The Road to Bosworth Field* (1985), pp. 155–6.
8. See W.E. Hampton, 'Witchcraft and the Sons of York', *The Ricardian*, v (1980), pp. 170–8.

Appendix 3

1. The portrait, now in the John Rylands Library of the University of Manchester, was discovered at Grafton in the early years of the twentieth century. It was thought to be the earliest representation of Shakespeare because the number '24' and the date '1588' appeared in the upper corners (the Bard celebrated his twenty-fourth birthday that year), but doubt has been cast on the identification in more recent times.
2. A. Strickland, *Lives of the Queens of England*, 8 vols. (revised edition, 1857), ii, pp. 319–20. MacGibbon, p. 18.
3. P.W. Hammond, 'The Journal of Elizabeth Woodville', *The Ricardian*, iv (1977), pp. 25–7.
4. *Ibid.*
5. J. Strutt, *The Sports and Pastimes of the People of England*, rev. J.C. Cox (1903), pp. 67–9.
6 H.L. Grey, 'Incomes from Land in England in 1436', *English Historical Review*, xxxxix (1934).
7. I am indebted to Susan Blake of Grafton Regis for this information and

also for a copy of the press cutting in the Northamptonshire Record Office.

8. See H.S. Bennett, *The Pastons and their England* (Cambridge,1922), pp. 29–33, 71–6.

Appendix 4

1. Presumably because he had come to doubt that 'Dame Elizabeth Wodehill' and his subject were one and the same person. H. Coore, *The Story of Elizabeth Woodville* (Halifax, 1845), p. 2.
2. He thought that Elizabeth and her daughters had gone into exile with Edward in 1470.
3. Coore, *Elizabeth Woodville*, pp. 10, 18, 26; MacGibbon, pp. 25–7.
4. Other sources name the Vernon youth as Roger, and refer to the location as Astwith Gorse.
5. Coore, *Elizabeth Woodville*, pp. 15–16.
6. The name derived from their crest, a bounding stag with a circlet of eglantine roses round the neck. They were distantly related to John Hardwick of Lindley (Leicestershire) who is said to have guided the Tudor forces on Bosworth Field.
7. Coore, *Elizabeth Woodville*, pp. 27, 29–30.
8. J.T. (Joseph Tilley), *The Old halls, Manors, and families of Derbyshire*, 4 vols. (1892–1902), iii, p. 26, n.
9. *Calendar of the Fine Rolls, Henry VII, 1485–1509* (1962), p. 390; Susan M. Wright, *The Derbyshire Gentry in the Fifteenth Century* (Derbyshire Record Society, 1983), p. 215.
10. Tilley, *Old Halls of Derbyshire*, p. 26.

Appendix 5

I am grateful to Dr David Marcombe for permission to include material which first appeared in the *East Midlands Historian*, vol. 4 (1994), pp. 16–19.

1. *Croyland Chronicle*, p. 483.
2. *Ibid.*, p. 469.
3. *Ibid.*, pp. 509, 467.
4. *Ibid.*, p. 510.
5. *Ibid.*, especially pp. 496–9. There are, of course, other possible, although arguably less helpful, criteria. Nicholas Pronay and John Cox advance reasons for supposing that the Continuator was particularly associated with Chancery (*The Crowland Chronicle Continuations 1459–1486* [1986], p. 80), but their evidence is described by Professor Kelly as 'meagre' (H.A. Kelly, 'The Croyland Chronicle Tragedies', *The Ricardian*, vii [1987], p. 505), and Dr Williams considers the connection 'remote' (D. Williams, 'The Crowland Chronicle Continuations 616–1500', *England in the Fifteenth Century*,

Proceedings of the 1986 Harlaxton Symposium, ed. D. Williams [Woodbridge, 1987], p. 386). Pronay and Cox also suggest that he (the continuator) had no 'interest in learning' (p. 82), an idea which seems rather whimsical given the high academic standards which all the candidates save Curtis had attained.

6. *Croyland Chronicle*, pp. 479–80, 496–7.
7. *Ibid.*, pp. 471–2.
8. *Edward IV's French Expedition of 1475*, ed. F.P. Barnard (1925, reprinted Gloucester, 1975). T. Rymer, *Foedera*, etc, v. iii. (1741), pp. 56–8. The surviving evidence is discussed more fully in J.R. Lander, *Crown and Nobility*, (1976), pp. 235–9.
9. Scofield, ii, p. 125.
10. R. Weiss, *Humanism in England during the Fifteenth Century* (Oxford, 1967), pp. 122–3. W.E. Hampton, *Memorials of the Wars of the Roses* (Upminster, 1979), pp. 25–6., 76, 162. *Croyland Chronicle*, p. 502.
11. A.B. Emden, *A Biographical Register of the University of Cambridge* (Cambridge, 1963), pp. 275–7. *The Dictionary of National Biography*, ed. L. Stephen and S. Lee, 63 vols. (1895–1900), xxiii, pp. 351–2. A.R. Myers, *The Household of Edward IV* (Manchester, 1959), p. 292. Weiss, *Humanism in England*, p. 124.
12. R. Horrox, Introduction to *British Library Harleian Manuscript 433*, 4 vols. (1979–83), i, pp. xviii–xix.
13. *Dictionary of National Biography*, xxiii, p. 351.
14. *Bartholomew Gazetteer of Places in Britain*, compiled by Oliver Mason (Edinburgh, 1986), p. 109.
15. *The Victoria County History of Northampton*, ed. R.M. Serjeantson and W.R.D. Adkins, ii (1906), pp. 514–5.
16. Emden, *Biographical Register*, p. 275. The designation 'master' is shared by (for example) Doctors Henry Sharp and William Hatclyffe (Edward IV's secretary). See *Calendar of the Patent Rolls, Edward IV – Edward V – Richard III, 1476–1485* (1901), pp. 163, 241, 410.
17. Quoted by P.W. Hammond and A.F. Sutton, *Richard III: The Road to Bosworth Field* (1985), p. 69.
18. His beautiful handwriting may be seen in his transcript of Seneca's *Tragedies*, now BL, Harl. MS 2485.
19. Pronay and Cox, *The Crowland Chronicle Continuations*, p. 155. I am indebted to Professor Tony Pollard for this reference.
20. *Croyland Chronicle*, p. 489.
21. The fullest studies are: A. Hanham, *Richard III and his early Historians* (Oxford, 1975), pp. 74–97; H.A. Kelly, 'The Last Chroniclers of Croyland', *The Ricardian*, vii (1985), pp. 142–77; Pronay and Cox, *The Crowland Chronicle Continuations*, pp. 78–98; and Williams, 'The Crowland Chronicle Continuations 616–1500', as above, pp. 371–90. See also Sir Goronwy Edwards's article 'The "Second" Continuation of the Croyland Chronicle: Was it Written "In Ten Days"?', *Bulletin of the Institute of Historical Research*, xxxix (1966), pp. 117–29, which long ago disposed of the belief (based on the 'dating colophon') that the continuator could be identified by his presence at Croyland at the end of April 1486.
22. Emden, *Biographical Register*, p. 276.

Appendix 6

1. BL, Harl. MS 433, ed. R. Horrox and P.W. Hammond, 4 vols. (1979–83), iii, p. 114; ii, p. 211.
2. A. Williamson, *The Mystery of the Princes* (Gloucester, 1978).
3. J. Leslau, 'Did the Sons of Edward IV Outlive Henry VII', *The Ricardian*, iv (1978), pp. 2–14, and *Ricardian Bulletin* (June 1981), pp. 11–18.
4. Francis Bacon, *The History of the Reign of King Henry the Seventh*, ed. R. Lockyer (1971), p. 160.
5. Mancini, p. 93.
6. *Croyland Chronicle*, p. 491.
7. *Rotuli Parliamentorum* (Rolls of Parliament), ed. J. Strachey *et al.*, 6 vols. (1767–77) , vi, p. 276.
8. *The Great Chronicle of London*, ed. A.H. Thomas and I.D. Thornley (1938, reprinted Gloucester 1983), p. 234.
9. *Ibid.*, pp. 236–7
10. More, pp. 83–4.
11. *Ibid.*, p. 81.
12. *Three Books of Polydore Vergil's English History*, ed. Sir H. Ellis (Camden Society, 1844), p. 188.
13. See Anne Crawford, 'John Howard, Duke of Norfolk: A Possible Murderer of the Princes?', *The Ricardian*, v (1980), pp. 230–4.
14. M. Lulofs, 'Richard III: Dutch Sources', *The Ricardian*, iii (1974), p. 13.
15. Bodleian Library, Ashmolean MS 1448, f. 287, quoted by P.M. Kendall, *Richard the Third* (1955), p. 411.
16. R.F. Green, 'Historical notes of a London citizen, 1483–1488', *English Historical Review*, lxxxxvi (1981), p. 488.
17. Richard described his erstwhile ally as 'the most untrue creature living' in an order instructing the Chancellor to bring or send him the great seal. Public Record Office C81/1392/6 quoted in P.W. Hammond and A.F. Sutton, *Richard III. The Road to Bosworth Field* (1985), p. 145.
18. Kendall, *Richard the Third*, p. 418.

Appendix 7

1. *Calendar of Letters and Papers, Foreign and Domestic, of the Reign of Henry VIII*, ed. J.S. Brewer *et al.*, 21 vols (1862–1932), iii, pp. 108–9.
2. *Ibid.*
3. The first Marquess of Dorset had helped the future cardinal after his resignation from Magdalen by presenting him to the living of Limington, in Somerset, and his sons (the present protagonists) had been Wolsey's pupils at Magdalen College School.
4. L. Fox and P. Russell, *Leicester Forest* (Leicester, 1948).
5. S.H. Skillington, 'Star Chamber Proceedings', *Transactions of the Leicestershire Archaeological Society*, xii (1921–2). The testimonies of Sir

William Skevington and Sir John Digby, pp. 141–6.

6. 'Heathley' cannot now be identified, but the name was often used to refer to the whole forest baliwick and may indicate that Dorset now dominated a significant part.

7. Skillington, *Star Chamber Proceedings*, Thomas Dunham's testimony, pp. 138–41.

8. *Ibid.*, John Gladwyn's testimony, pp. 133–6.

9. *Ibid.*

10. *Ibid.*

11. A.H. Thompson, *A Calendar of Charters and other Documents Belonging to the Hospital of William Wyggeston at Leicester* (Leicester, 1933), pp. 87–90.

12. It is likely that Lady Mary (whose father and grandfather had both died fighting for Lancaster) would have had a particular affection for an establishment which contained the tombs of the progenitor of the House, Earl Henry, his illustrious son Henry of Grosmont, Henry IV's first wife Mary de Bohun, and his stepmother Constanza of Castile.

13. Longland's visitation is described by A. Hamilton Thompson, *The History of the Hospital and the College of the Annunciation of St Mary in the Newarke, Leicester* (Leicester, 1937), pp. 143–96. The full evidences are transcribed in the third volume of the same author's *Visitations in the Diocese of Lincoln 1517–1531* (Lincoln Record Society, xxxvii, 1947).

14. Although the canons were by no means paragons of virtue. Brooksby 'kept arms in his house, and when he got drunk, which was often, his talk was all of war and fighting fields'. Thompson, *Newarke College and Hospital*, pp. 178–9.

15. *Ibid.*, pp. 156–7.

16. See, for example, the diverse opinions of how Chauncy came by his head-wound, *Ibid.*, p. 153.

17. He had taken possession of the money and carried it from the treasury into the vestry; but he was confronted there by a number of the canons and persuaded to restore it to the treasurer 'in a great fume'. *Ibid.*, pp. 176–7.

18. The full story is related by Thompson, *Ibid.*, pp. 151–3.

19. *Letters and Papers, Henry VIII*, iv, part 1, p. 978.

20. *Ibid.*, part 2, pp. 1664–5.

21. *Ibid.*, iii, part 1, pp. 238–46.

22. Skillington, *Star Chamber Proceedings*, Sir William Skevington's testimony, p. 143.

23. *Ibid.*, Thomas Dunham's testimony, p. 140.

Select Bibliography

This bibliography is limited to printed sources which best serve to illustrate Elizabeth Woodville's life and reign. The place of publication is London unless otherwise stated.

Acts of Court of the Mercers' Company 1453–1527, ed. L. Lyell and F.D. Watney (Cambridge, 1936).

(The) Anglica Historia of Polydore Vergil AD 1485–1537, ed. D. Hay (Camden Society, 1950).

Anstis, J., *Register of the Most Noble Order of the Garter*, 2 vols. (1724).

Ashdown-Hill, John, 'Edward IV's Uncrowned Queen: The Lady Eleanor Talbot, Lady Butler', *The Ricardian*, xi (1997).

Bacon, Sir Francis, *The History of the Reign of King Henry the Seventh*, ed. R. Lockyer (1971).

Baker, G., *History of Northamptonshire*, 2 vols. (1822–41).

Bennett, H.S., *The Pastons and their England* (Cambridge, 1922).

Bennett, M., *Lambert Simnel and the Battle of Stoke* (Gloucester, 1987).

British Library Harleian Manuscript 433, ed. R. Horrox & P.W. Hammond, 4 vols. (1979–83).

Buck, Sir George, *The History of King Richard the Third (1619)*, ed. A.N. Kincaid (Gloucester, 1979).

Calendar of Letters and Papers, Foreign and Domestic, of the Reign of Henry VIII, ed. J.S. Brewer *et al.*, 21 vols. (1862–1932).

Calendar of State Papers and Manuscripts Relating to English Affairs Existing in the Archives and Collections of Venice, and in other Libraries in Northern Italy, i, *1202–1509*, ed. R. Brown (1864).

Calendar of State Papers and Manuscripts existing in the Archives and Collections of Milan, i, *1385–1618*, ed. A.B. Hinds (1913).

Calendar of the Close Rolls, Edward IV – Edward V – Richard III, 1476–1485 (1954).

Calendar of the Patent Rolls, Edward IV, 1461–1467 (1898); 1467–1477 (1900); *Edward IV – Edward V – Richard III*, 1476–1485 (1901); *Henry VII*, 1485–1494 (1914).

Chamberlayne, J.L., *English Queenship 1445–1503*. Unpublished University of York D.Phil thesis (1999).

——, 'Crowns and Virgins: Queenmaking during the Wars of the Roses', in *Young Medieval Women*, ed. K.J. Lewis, N.J. Menuge, K.M. Phillips (Stroud, 1999).

Chapman, H.W., *The Sisters of Henry VIII* (1969, reprinted Bath 1974).

Chrimes, S.B., *Henry VII* (1972).

'Chronicle of the Rebellion in Lincolnshire in 1470', ed. J.G. Nichols, *The Camden Miscellany*, vol. 1 (Camden Society, 1847).

(The) Chronicles of the White Rose of York, ed J.A. Giles (1845).

Chroniques de Jean Molinet (1474–1506), ed. G. Doutrepont and O. Jodogne, 3 vols. (Brussels, 1935–7).

Colvin, H.M. *et al.*, *The History of the King's Works*, 6 vols. (1963–82).

Coore, H., *The Story of Elizabeth Woodville* (Halifax, 1845).

(The) Coventry Leet Book, ed. M.D. Harris, 4 parts (Early English Text Society, 1907–1913).

Crawford, A., 'John Howard, Duke of Norfolk: A Possible Murderer of the Princes?', *The Ricardian*, v (1980).

——, 'The King's Burden?: the consequences of Royal Marriage in Fifteenth-Century England', in *Patronage, the Crown and the Provinces in later Medieval England*, ed. R.A. Griffiths (Gloucester, 1981).

(The) Crowland Chronicle Continuations 1459–1486. ed. N. Pronay and J. Cox (1986).

Davies, R., 'Original Documents Relating to Lambert Symnell's Rebellion in the Second Year of King Henry VII', *Proceedings of the Archaeological Institute: 1846* (1848).

(The) Dictionary of National Biography, ed. L. Stephen and S. Lee, 63 vols. (1885–1900).

Edward IV's French Expedition of 1475, ed. F.P. Barnard (1925, reprinted Gloucester 1975).

Emden, A.B., *A Biographical Register of the University of Cambridge* (Cambridge, 1963).

Evans, H.T., *Wales and the Wars of the Roses* (Cambridge 1915, reprinted 1998).

Excerpta Historica, ed. S. Bentley (1833).

Fabyan, Robert, *The New Chronicles of England and France*, ed. Sir H. Ellis (1811).

Fahy, C., 'The Marriage of Edward IV and Elizabeth Woodville: a new Italian source', *English Historical Review*, lxxvi (1961).

Fitzroy, C., and Harry, K. (eds.), *Grafton Regis* (Whitchurch, 2000).

Fox, L., and Russell, P., *Leicester Forest* (Leicester, 1948).

Gairdner, J., *History of the Life and Reign of Richard III* (Cambridge, 1898).

G.E.C. *et al.*, *The Complete Peerage*, 12 vols. (1910–59).

Given-Wilson, C., and Curteis, A., *The Royal Bastards of Medieval England* (1984).

(The) Great Chronicle of London, ed. A.H. Thomas and I.D. Thornley (1938, reprinted Gloucester 1983).

Green, R.F., 'Historical Notes of a London Citizen, 1483–1488', *English Historical Review*, lxxxxvi. (1981).

Grey, H.L., 'Incomes from Land in England in 1436', *English Historical Review*, xxxxix (1934).

Griffiths, R.A., *The Reign of Henry VI* (1981).

——, 'Richard, Duke of York and the Royal Household in Wales 1449–50', *Welsh History Review*, viii (1976).

Halle, Edward, *The Union of the Two Noble Families of Lancaster and York*, 1550 (reprinted Menston, 1970).

Hammond, P.W., *Food and Feast in Medieval England* (Stroud, 1993).

____, 'The Journal of Elizabeth Woodville', *The Ricardian*, iv (1977).

Hammond, P.W., and Sutton, A.F., *Richard III. The Road to Bosworth Field* (1985).

Hammond, P.W., Sutton, A.F., and Visser-Fuchs, L., 'The Reburial of Richard, Duke of York, 21–30 July, 1476', *The Ricardian*, x (1994).

Hampton, W.E., *Memorials of the Wars of the Roses* (Gloucester, 1979).

____, 'Witchcraft and the Sons of York', *The Ricardian*, v (1980).

Hanham, A., *Richard III and his Early Historians* (Oxford, 1975).

____, 'Sir George Buck and Princess Elizabeth's Letter: A Problem in Detection', *The Ricardian*, vii (1987).

Harrod, H., 'Queen Elizabeth Woodville's visit to Norwich in 1469', *Norfolk Archaeology*, v (1859).

Helmholz, R.H., 'The Sons of Edward IV: A Canonical Assessment of the Claim that they were Illegitimate', in *Richard III: Loyalty, Lordship and Law*, ed. P.W. Hammond (1986).

Hepburn, F., *Portraits of the Later Plantagenets* (1986).

Hicks, M.A., 'The Changing Role of the Wydevilles in Yorkist Politics to 1483', in Ross, C. (ed.), *Patronage, Pedigree and Power in Later Medieval England* (Gloucester, 1979).

____, *False, Fleeting, Perjur'd Clarence* (Gloucester, 1980).

____, *Richard III: The Man Behind the Myth* (1991).

____, *Warwick the Kingmaker* (Oxford, 1998).

(The) Historical Collections of a London Citizen, ed. J. Gairdner (Camden Society, 1876).

Historical Manuscripts Commission. *12th Report, Rutland Manuscripts*, 4 vols. (1888–1905).

____, 78, *Report on the Manuscripts of R.R. Hastings*, 4 vols. (1928–47).

Historie of the Arrivall of Edward IV in England and the Finall Recouerye of his Kingdomes from Henry VI. A.D. M.CCCC. LXXI, ed. J. Bruce (Camden Society, 1838).

Hole, C., *Witchcraft in England* (1977).

Horrox, R., *Richard III: A Study in Service* (Cambridge, 1989).

(The) Household Books of John Howard, Duke of Norfolk, 1462–1471, 1481–1483, introduced by A. Crawford (Stroud, 1992).

Ingulph's Chronicle of the Abbey of Croyland, translated by H.T. Riley (1854).

Ives, E.W., 'Andrew Dymmock and the Papers of Antony, Earl Rivers 1482–3', *Bulletin of the Institute of Historical Research*, xli (1968).

____, 'Marrying for Love: The Experience of Edward IV and Henry VIII', *History Today*, l, (2000).

Jones, M.K., 'Collyweston – An Early Tudor Palace', in *England in the Fifteenth Century*, ed. D. Williams (Woodbridge, 1987).

Jones, M.K., and Underwood, M.G., *The King's Mother* (Cambridge, 1992).

Kelly, H.A., 'English Kings and the Fear of Sorcery', *Mediaeval Studies*, xxxix (1977).

____, 'The Case Against Edward IV's Marriage and Offspring: Secrecy; Witchcraft; Secrecy; Precontract', *The Ricardian*, xi (1998).

_____, 'The Croyland Chronicle Tragedies', *The Ricardian*, vii (1987).

_____, 'The Last Chroniclers of Croyland', *The Ricardian*, vii (1985).

Kendall, P.M., *Richard the Third* (1955).

_____, *The Yorkist Age* (1962).

Kingsford, C.L., *English Historical Literature in the Fifteenth Century* (Oxford, 1913).

Kincaid, A., 'Buck and the Elizabeth of York Letter: A Reply to Dr. Hanham', *The Ricardian*, viii (1988).

Lander, J.R., 'Marriage and Politics in the Fifteenth Century: the Nevills and the Wydevills', *Bulletin of the Institute of Historical Research*, xxxvi (1963).

_____, *Crown and Nobility 1450–1509* (1976).

_____, *Government and Community* (1980).

Laynesmith, J.L., 'Fertility Rite or Authority Ritual? The Queen's Coronation in England, 1445–1487', in *Social Attitudes and Political Structures*, ed. T. Thornton (Stroud, 2000).

Leland, J., *De Rebus Britannicis Collectanea*, ed. T. Hearne, 6 vols. (1770).

Leslau, J., 'Did the Sons of Edward IV Outlive Henry VII', *The Ricardian*, iv, (1978).

Letters and Papers Illustrative of the Reigns of Richard III and Henry VII, ed. J. Gairdner, 2 vols. (1861–3).

Letters of the Queens of England 1100–1547, ed. A. Crawford (Stroud, 1994).

(The) Lisle Letters, ed. M. Byrne, 6 vols. (1981).

Lowe, D.E., 'Patronage and Politics: Edward IV, the Wydevilles, and the Council of the Prince of Wales, 1471–83', *Bulletin of the Board of Celtic Studies*, xxix (1981).

Lulofs, M., 'Richard III: Dutch Sources', *The Ricardian*, iii (1974).

MacGibbon, D., *Elizabeth Woodville* (1938).

Mancini, Dominic, *The Usurpation of Richard III*, ed. and translated by C.A.J. Armstrong (2nd edn., Oxford 1969, reprinted Gloucester, 1984).

Maurer, H., 'The Amazing Elizabeth: A Possible Reconstruction of her Actions 1483–1487', *Ricardian Register*, xvi (1982).

Materials for a History of the Reign of Henry VII, ed. W. Campbell, 2 vols. (1873–77).

McFarlane, K.B., *The Nobility of Later Medieval England* (Oxford, 1973).

(The) Memoirs of Philip de Commines, ed. A.R. Scoble, 2 vols. (1855–6).

More's History of King Richard III, ed. J.R. Lumby (Cambridge, 1883).

More, St Thomas, *The History of King Richard III*, ed. R.S. Sylvester (1976).

Moreton, C.E., 'A Local Dispute and the Politics of 1483: Roger Townshend, Earl Rivers and the Duke of Gloucester', *The Ricardian*, viii (1989).

Myers, A.R., *The Household of Edward IV* (Manchester, 1959).

_____, 'The Household of Queen Elizabeth Woodville, 1466–7', *Bulletin of the John Rylands Library*, l (1967–8).

_____, 'The Household of Queen Margaret of Anjou, 1452–3', *Bulletin of the John Rylands Library*, xl (1957–8).

'Narrative of the Marriage of Richard Duke of York with Anne of Norfolk: the Matrimonial Feast and the Grand Jousting', *Illustrations of Ancient*

State and Chivalry from manuscripts preserved in the Ashmolean Museum, ed. W.H. Black (Roxburgh Club, 1840).

Nicolas, N.H., *Privy Purse Expenses of Elizabeth of York: Wardrobe Accounts of Edward IV* (1830, reprinted 1972).

Nichols, J., *The History and Antiquities of the County of Leicester*, 4 vols. (1795–1811).

Original Letters Illustrative of English History, ed. Sir H. Ellis, 1st series, i (1824).

(The) Paston Letters, ed. J. Gairdner, 6 vols. (1904).

Political Poems and Songs relating to English History, ed. T. Wright, 2 vols. (1859–61).

(The) Politics of Fifteenth Century England: John Vale's Book, ed. M.L. Kekewich *et al.* (Stroud, 1995).

Pollard, A.J., *Richard III and the Princes in the Tower* (Gloucester, 1991).

(The) Registers of Robert Stillington, Bishop of Bath and Wells, 1466–1491, and Richard Fox, Bishop of Bath and Wells 1492–1494, ed. Sir H.C. Maxwell-Lyte, Somerset Record Society, lii (1937).

Rotuli Parliamentorum (Rolls of Parliament), ed. J. Strachey *et al.*, 6 vols. (1767–77)

Ross, C., *Edward IV* (1974).

____, *Richard III* (1981).

Routh, P.S., 'Lady Scroop Daughter of K. Edward: an Enquiry', *The Ricardian*, ix (1993).

Scofield, C.L., 'Elizabeth Wydevile in the Sanctuary at Westminster, 1470', *English Historical Review*, xxiv (1909).

____, *The Life and Reign of Edward IV*, 2 vols. (1923, reprinted 1967).

Sharpe, R.R., *London and the Kingdom*, 3 vols. (1894–5).

Skillington, S.H., 'Star Chamber Proceedings', *Transactions of the Leicestershire Archaeological Society*, xii (1921–1922).

Smith, G., *The Coronation of Elizabeth Wydeville* (1935).

(The) Stonor Letters and Papers 1290–1483, ed. C.L Kingsford, 2 vols. (Camden Society, 1919).

Strickland, A., *Lives of the Queens of England*, 8 vols. (revised edition, 1857).

Sutton, A.F., 'Sir Thomas Cook and his "troubles": an investigation', *Guildhall Studies in London History*, iii (1978).

Sutton, A.F. and Visser-Fuchs, L., 'A "Most Benevolent Queen". Queen Elizabeth Woodville's Reputation, her Piety and her Books', *The Ricardian*, x (1995).

____, 'The Cult of Angels in Late Fifteenth-Century England: An Hours of the Guardian Angel presented to Queen Elizabeth Woodville', in *Women and the Book*, ed. L. Smith & J.H.M. Taylor (1996).

____, 'The "Retirement" of Elizabeth Woodville, and her Sons', *The Ricardian*, xi (1999).

____, 'The Device of Queen Elizabeth Woodville: A Gillyflower or Pink', *The Ricardian*, xi (1997).

____, 'The Royal Burials of the House of York at Windsor: II. Princess Mary, May 1482, and Queen Elizabeth Woodville, June 1492', *The Ricardian*, xi (1999).

Thompson, A.H., *A Calendar of Charters and other Documents Belonging to the Hospital of William Wyggeston at Leicester* (Leicester, 1933).

——, *The History of the Hospital and the College of the Annunciation of St Mary in the Newarke, Leicester* (Leicester, 1937).

Three Books of Polydore Vergil's English History, ed. Sir H. Ellis (Camden Society, 1844).

Thurley, S., *The Royal Palaces of Tudor England* (New Haven, 1993).

Tilley, Joseph ('J.T.'), *The Old halls, Manors, and families of Derbyshire*, 4 vols. (1892–1902).

(The) Travels of Leo of Rozmital, ed. and translated by M. Letts, Hakluyt Society, 2nd series, cviii: (Cambridge, 1957).

Tudor Royal Proclamations, ed. P.L. Hughes and J.F. Larkin, 3 vols. (New Haven, 1964).

Twigg, J., *A History of Queens' College, Cambridge, 1448–1986* (Woodbridge, 1987).

(The) Victoria County History of Northampton, ed. R.M. Serjeantson and W.R.D. Adkins, ii (1906).

Walpole, Horace, *Historic Doubts on the Life and Reign of King Richard III*, ed. P.M. Kendall (1965).

Ward, J.C., *English Noblewomen in the Later Middle Ages* (1992).

Warkworth, John, *A Chronicle of the First Thirteen Years of the Reign of King Edward the Fourth*, ed. J.O. Halliwell (Camden Society, 1839).

Weiss, R., *Humanism in England during the Fifteenth Century* (Oxford, 1967).

Westervelt, T., *The Woodvilles in the Second Reign of Edward IV 1471–83* (Unpublished University of Cambridge M.Phil thesis, 1997).

Williams, D., 'The Crowland Chronicle Continuations 616–1500', *England in the Fifteenth Century*, Proceedings of the 1986 Harlaxton Symposium, ed. D. Williams (Woodbridge, 1987).

Wood, A., *History of the University of Oxford*, ed. J. Gutch, 2 vols. (Oxford, 1792–6).

Index